P9-DWJ-855

THE ANGLICAN MORAL CHOICE

The Anglican Studies Series

The Anglican Moral Choice

Paul Elmen, editor

Morehouse-Barlow Co., Inc.
Wilton, Connecticut 06897

Morehouse-Barlow Co., Inc.
78 Danbury Road
Wilton, Connecticut 06897

ISBN 0-8192-1322-5

Library of Congress Catalog Card Number 82-62391

Printed in the United States of America

Table of Contents

Introduction

by Paul Elmen

It is a quaint ripple in the ecumenical currents of our time that each confessional body has a renewed impulse to define its own identity, often discovering something about itself which before then was unobserved. This book is a determined effort to investigate, for the first time in book form, the distinctive character of Anglican moral theology.

The task is undertaken with some apprehension. If one were to make valid generalizations about Anglican moralism, it would seem necessary to study how Anglicans actually behave, as distinct from comments about their behavior or suggestions about how they ought to behave. Living in the early years of the computer age, we have done what we could, which was to identify leading authorities in the field, ask them to report what Anglican theorists said in the past, and examine carefully actual decisions on three contemporary problems. Our apprehension is due to the obvious difference between an opinion publicly announced and a deed done. It is clear that a thief might well say he believed in private property.

Dean John E. Booty, of the School of Theology, University of the South, Sewanee, Tennessee, strikes a keynote. He describes the crucial moment in the English Reformation when the founding fathers turned uneasily from sacramental confession to what they called "a lively faith." The phrase is the theme of this book: Anglican morality has to do with the way a Christian actually lives in community, nourished by Word and sacrament. The Archbishop of Dublin, the Most Reverend H. R. McAdoo, in the second chapter observes the emphasis on concrete living rather than on conceptual forms in the seventeenth century, and says that this is also a characteristic of some important developments in contemporary theology. Next Dr. John R. Orens, sometime lecturer at Boston University, demonstrates the contribution of the Anglican Left, stressing its discovery that concern for one's fellow human beings is an inevitable consequence of a serious sacramental life, with its prayer, theology, and public worship. With the permission of the editor, W. Taylor Stevenson, we present a revised form of Orens' article, which originally appeared in *The Anglican Theological Review* in January,

1981. In the last chapter of the historical section, Dr. Peter Toon, Director of Post-Ordination Training in the dioceses of St. Edmundsbury and Ipswich, England, writes of the early evangelicals, dispelling a current notion that the evangelicals have only recently discovered a social relevance and become concerned with problems of secular living.

We turn then to some statements of contemporary Anglican moral theory, beginning with T. S. Eliot's memorable account of Lambeth, 1930, in the main a conference reflecting the ideas of William Temple. Eliot warns about what he considers a peculiarly Anglican threat to orthodoxy: deciding what any decent person would say about a problem, and then turning to some form of justifying theology. Reprinted by permission from the publisher, Harcourt Brace Jovanovich, Inc. Professor Timothy F. Sedgwick of Seabury-Western Theological Seminary argues that Anglicans have a far richer tradition of moral theology than that supplied by the Tractarians. With the permission of the editor, we present Sedgwick's article, which appeared originally in *The Anglican Theological Review* in January, 1981. The Reverend Theodore A. McConnell of New York, traces the background of what has always been one of Anglicanism's most cherished guidelines to moral action, the classical *via media*. We are a people, he shows, devoted to *measure*, to balance by restraint, to judgment by moderation. The Reverend Edwin G. Wappler, Rector of St. Wilfrid's Church, Marion, Alabama, points to the leading role played by Anglicans in the recent wave of so-called "New Morality." We have long been accustomed to turn to the data of experience rather than to formal codes of behavior.

What emerges from these discussions of Anglical moral history is general agreement that we have from the sixteenth century taken seriously the notion that a lively faith cannot be arrested by theological propositions, by mystical ecstacy, or by ecclesiastical pronouncement. We have pinned our moral faith on the words of the post-communion thanksgiving: "to continue in that holy fellowship, and do all such good works as God has prepared for us to walk in." Though one may not be a saint, the good Christian lives a sober, righteous, and godly life. What is steadily urged is that virtue must shape itself as deed, life being a continual fellowship with God. Our contribution to the plenitude of faith is the reminder that faith in Christ does not call us away from the everyday realities of existence, isolating us from our wordly neighbors by exotic cultic acts which are only vaguely related to secular existence. A mainline Anglican does not think that belief is an affirmation of theological principle, but rather a disposition to act as though those propositions are true. We kneel at the altar, following the directions of the cherished Prayer Book, but when the Eucharist is over, we simply continue in a holy fellowship. Shaking the rector's hand at the door is a kind of commitment.

As a consequence, the doctrines to which Anglicans are most devoted are such life-affirming ones as the Incarnation and the Creation, rather than to the Fall and the Atonement. We began by affirming that the Scripture should be available to the people in the street, and not simply to the learned religious. Living has always seemed to us more important than logic, *praxis* better than *theoria*, the aim being to express the Gospel by a lived concreteness rather than by doctrinal orthodoxy. The intention is not to devalue theological truth, but on the contrary to affirm that here is an inseparability between the moral life and the truth, a convergence between *veritas* and *utilitas*. We think that theological reflection and liturgical correctness and a faithful polity are all enriched by what Joseph Sittler called "the engendering deed." A quintessential Anglican, George Herbert, wrote

"Who sweeps a room, as for thy laws,
Makes that and th' action fine."

It will occur to our readers that Anglicans did not introduce this motif. It has been prominent whenever someone has read thoughtfully John 7:17 ("If any man will do his will, he shall know of the doctrine, whether it be of God,") and Matthew 7:21 ("Not every one that shall say to me Lord, Lord, shall enter the kingdom of heaven, but he that doeth the will of my Father which is in heaven.") This kind of sacramental morality inspired the medieval Catholic theories of the Just War and the Just Price, as it was the heart of the teaching of the English Reformers, Colet and More. Jeremy Taylor's *Holy Living* struck the central note, but he had simply carried on an insight of the Florentine humanists of the quattrocento. It is the reason Paul Elmer More hit on an unexpected term when he set out to define Anglicanism: "I do not see that we can do better than adopt a title which offers itself as peculiarly descriptive, despite the unsavoury repute it may have acquired from its usurpation by certain sects of philosophy; I refer to the title 'pragmatism.' " There are of course elements of the mode related to American pragmatism, but also to Cicero's *ars vivendi*, as well as to the tradition of English empiricism. What is denied is the distinction between the secular and the sacred. "The English priest," says Martin Thornton, "plays cricket on the Green not in spite of his priesthood, but because of it."[1]

The engendering deed is not of course an Anglican invention, nor do all Anglicans at all times follow its teaching. In the third section of our book, Anglican decisions on three current problems are brought under scrutiny. Professor Harmon L. Smith of Duke University looks at a trouble record of our search for the morality of contraception, and Professor William Muehl of Yale University Divinity School studies the Anglican ambiguities of the church-state relationship. Finally the Reverend William W. Rankin, Rector of St. Stephen's Church, Belvedere, California, reviews our ways of reacting to the threat of war. The three chapters are proof enough, if more is needed, that the fertile tradition of the engendering deed has not been allowed a brilliant development, and that distinctive Anglican morality has made only a modest contribution to the holy secularity which the seventeenth-century Carolines dreamed about.

The contribution may finally be that Anglicans were early aware of a theme which is achieving widespread popularity in contemporary methodological studies. Karl Barth, for instance, has agreed that "there is a form of knowledge which arises directly from the event of life."[2] In an inaugural lecture at Frankfort in 1965, Jürgen Habermas spoke approvingly of what he called "a self-respecting style of thought" which had as a motivating power a form of action, in this case the emancipation of humankind from hypostacized powers.[3] H. G. Gadamer speaks for a whole generation of exegetes who say that the meaning of a text can only be discovered when it is brought to bear on some problem of contemporary living.[4] So others have perhaps made better use of a biblical theme long treasured by Anglicans.

That there has not been a more aggressive development of the theme by Anglicans may be due to the fact that there are certain dangers involved in believing that conduct not only validates but in a certain sense creates truth. Vaihinger has shown that false notions may on occasion have fruitful results, so that practicality can never be an adequate test of truth. Concentrating on *praxis* at the expense of *theoria* can obscure the fact that a whole human being is involved when anyone thinks or acts. Forgetting this could lead to a diminished Christian lifestyle, for instance, when the Episcopal senior warden is indistinguishable from the president of the local golf club. If holiness is identified with respectability, which in turn is reduced to good manners, an important dimension of actual life is lost, and there is no sense either of radical evil or saintly virtue. Its reductionist power is visible in the comment of an Anglican bishop that "Orthodoxy is reticence."

Christianity cannot be diminished to a passion for order, especially if in that order injustice is enshrined. When Christian living is simply habit and decorum, there will be astonishment and even hostility before ecstatic forms of piety such as mystical prayer or talking with tongues. Some Anglicans are uneasy before the baroque Christianity of southern Europe, and few are likely to experience at the family service the fits of passion Wordsworth knew:

> "The holy time is quiet as a Nun,
> Breathless with adoration."

Fortunately there are other Wordsworths in this roomy church, and the sense of unfathonable mystery is kept alive by brighter broad churchmen, by devout Anglo-Catholics at the Eucharist, by evangelical charismatics at a healing service. Without this presence, and the *measure* that comes from it, the Anglican morality might be simply clumsy, like the "muscular Christianity" of Charles Kingsley, and be identified by other churchmen as the weak wordliness practiced by the parsons of the hunting shires. Such unfriendliness led James Joyce to identify the Anglican ordinal with *The Sporting Times*.

So our egotism about Anglican morality is easily subdued, though perhaps we present the subject with secret pride and love. Anglican morality as a trait complex must wait for the approval of those who understand and are sympathetic with what T. S. Eliot wrote in *Little Gidding:*

> "Here, the intersection of the timeless moment
> Is England and nowhere. Never and always."

It is the style of the seventeenth-century Sir Thomas Browne, who wrote this to his son, traveling in France: "Je vous recommend à dieu. If you find any pretty insects of any kind, keep them in a box." It is the style of our contemporary Rose Macaulay, writing in *The Towers of Trebizon:*

> " 'Take my camel, dear,' said my Aunt Dot,
> as she climbed down from this animal
> on her way from High Mass."

I. The Early Years

1

The English Reformation: A Lively Faith and Sacramental Confession

by John E. Booty

The Rejection of Sacramental Confession

The English Reformation involved a moral revolution, a radical change effecting the future development of Anglican moral theology. As is true of revolutions in general, this one began with an attack on an established institution, that of sacramental confession. John Jewel identified this instituion, also known as the Sacrament of Penance, as "private confession, which many have used as a rack of men's consciences to the maintenance of their tyranny."[1] By means of this specialized form of confession the Western Church provided both discipline and consolation, discipline to curb the all too prevalent tendencies to sin among the faithful and consolation to ease troubled consciences. While enforcing moral, legal norms the priest interrogated the parishioner. Sins were noted, analyzed, and classified. Penances were prescribed. Confession could be routine with the recitation of some such form as that provided in the Salisbury Primer, where the penitent begins, saying:

> Fyrst, I knowlege my selfe gylty unto Almyghty God, unto our lady saynt Mary: and to all the company of heven: and to you my goostly father: that syth the tyme of my laste confessyon, I have offended by lord God grevously, and specially in the seven deedly synnes.
>   Pryde.
> I have synned in pryde of herte, not lowly thankynge God of gyftes and connynge whiche he hath lent me. Also I have synned in pryde of clotynge: in strength: in eloquence: in beaute: in proude wordes. Whereof I cry God mercy.[2]

The process could be harsh, the priest probing roughly; excommunication was always a possible outcome. But the true aim was expressed in absolution, the curing of that sense of guilt that so beset

Western Christians. The priest possessed the power of the keys, "the power of the keys to raise imperfect to perfect sorrow," the power of indicative absolution: "ordained priests truly forgive and effectively console."[3]

Revolutionary criticism does not provide for a balanced view of that which is brought under attack. The Reformers claimed that sacramental confession was legalistic, Pelagian, laxist, and magical. Thomas Tentler, in a recent careful examination of medieval confession, does not altogether deny the validity of the criticism. It could be all that the Reformers claimed it to be, but it was also evangelical, Augustinian, rigorist, and rationalistic. It was, in brief, paradoxical.[4] It was a matter of judgment for the Reformers to say, and to support their convictions, that sacramental confession was so faulted that it must be abolished. Their convictions were based not on the sin, greed, or paucity of confessors, but rather on its fundamental nature: it was designed to console the sinner and it did not.

The Reformers were compelled to reject sacramental confession on account of their convictions concerning the Gospel. They centered their attentions not on the imposition of moral and legal norms, but on "the true, lively, and Christian Faith." The evidence is abundant, but nowhere more eloquent and clear than in the *First Book of Homilies* (1547). Thomas Cranmer there contrasted "dead faith" with "lively faith." The latter, he wrote in the second homily,

> is not onely the common beleefe of the Articles of our faith, but it is also a true trust and confidence of the mercy of God through our Lord Jesus Christ, and a stedfast hope of all good things to be received at Gods hand: and that although wee, through infirmitie or temptation of our ghostly enimie, doe fall from him by sin, yet if we returne againe unto him by true repentance, that he will forgive, and forget our offences for his Sonnes sake our Saviour Jesus Christ . . . This is the true, lively, and unfeigned Christian faith, and is not in the mouth and outward profession onely: but it liveth, and stirreth inwardly, in the heart. And this faith is not without hope and trust in God, nor without the love of God and of our neighbours, nor without the feare of God, nor without the desire to heare Gods word, and to follow the same in eschewing evill, and doing gladly all good workes.[5]

The lively faith has no need of sacramental confession and, indeed, stands in danger of being corrupted if not destroyed by the legalistical Pelagianism of the Sacrament of Penance. Correct moral behavior is not bred of the imposition of moral and legal norms, but rather of faith in God. As William Tyndale said, "Deeds are the fruits of love; and love is the fruit of faith."[6] Thomas Becon asserted the primacy of faith (salvation "only by grace through faith, and that not of ourselves") and the inevitability of good works: "For if your repentence, faith, and love be Christian and unfeigned, then shall good works ensue and follow agreeable to the same."[7]

The Prayer Book Catechism makes clear the proper order: first, the recitation of our faith in the Apostles' Creed and then the Decalogue, followed by the Lord's Prayer.[8] As Richard Hooker put it, the Apostles' Creed gives us "the substance of Christian beliefe," while "the Decalogue of Moses declareth summarilie those things we ought to doe; the prayer of our Lord whatsoever we should request or desire."[9] The critical thrust, where moral behavior is concerned, is centered on the two tables of the Mosaic law, love of God and love of neighbor, and is thus on love or charity. Another homily by Cranmer, "On Christian Love or Charity," argues firmly that there is nothing more necessary to the Christian life than charity. Where charity is cultivated, there is righteousness, where it is neglected, there "is the ruine or fall of the world, the banishment of vertue, and the cause of all vice." What is charity? It "is to love God with all our heart . . . That is to say, that our heart, minde, and study be set to beleeve his word, to trust in him . . ." The Christian's entire affection is first of all directed toward God and God's honor.

> This is the first and principall part of charity, but it is not the whole: for charity is also to love every man, good and evill, friend and foe, and whatsoever cause be given to the contrary, yet nevertheless to beare good will and heart unto every man, to use our selves well unto them, as well in wordes and countenances, as in all our outward actes and deedes: for so Christ himselfe taught, and so also hee performed indeed.[10]

The message is simple, as Cranmer put it in his homily "Of Good Works Annexed unto Faith." First of all, we must have faith in God, giving ourselves "wholly unto him," loving him in all circumstances, "in prosperitie and adversitie." And then, for God's sake, in whom we live, we must love all people, "friends and foes, because they be his creation and image, and redeemed by Christ," as we are.[11] This general exhortation is followed by the author's own, contemporized version of the Ten Commandments. As the Creed is the rule of faith so is the Decalogue the rule of conduct "wherein standeth the pure, principall, and right honour of God, and which wrought in faith, God hath ordeined to bee the right trade and path way unto heaven."[12] But the chief emphasis is on the love of God from which proceeds truly and inevitably love of all that God has made and most especially charity toward our neighbors.

That love of God and love of neighbor should be the focal point for the development of a "reformed" moral theology is not surprising. It is expected of someone like Cranmer, who put such great emphasis on "communion" with God and with one another. The sacraments of baptism and Holy Communion were understood by this liturgical genius to be the means, the principal means, of participation, "he in us and we in him," and the Lord's Supper as the means not of changing bread and wine, but of changing us, cleansing us from our sins and empowering us to live as becomes those whom Christ indwells.[13] The personal and social implications of communion with/participation in God in Christ through the Holy Spirit are nowhere more forcefully put by Cranmer than when he says:

> more cruel and unreasonable be they than brute beasts, that cannot be persuaded to be good to their Christian brethren and neighbours, for whom Christ suffered death, when in this sacrament they be put in remembrance that the Son of God bestowed his life for his enemies. For we see by daily experience, that eating and drinking together maketh friends and continueth friendship: much more ought the table of Christ to move us so to do.

To charity, Cranmer wrote, "we be stirred and moved, as well by bread and wine in this holy supper, as by the words of scripture recited in the same."[14]

Word and Sacraments

The confessional, with priest and penitent alone together, was displaced in the English Reformation by the people of God, the congregation gathered for worship as directed by *The Book of Common Prayer*, by Word and Sacraments reminded of God's love and mercy, the sacrifice of His only Son for us, arousing in us holy fear for the consequences awaiting those who persist in their selfish ways, arousing responsive love, love inspired by the constant awareness of God's steadfast love in spite of all selfishness and sin. God in Word and Sacraments brings us to contrition, a state of being defined by Hooker as that "pensive and corrosive desire that we had done other than we have done."[15] Thus made contrite, Christians repent of their sins in each other's presence, in communion acknowledging and bewailing "our manifold sins and wickedness," begging God's mercy that we may be forgiven and "may ever hereafter serve and please thee, in newness of life, to the honor and glory of thy name."[16] What the contrite and penitent faithful ought to do in specific cases as a result of this penitence is not dictated in any detail. For most it is enough that they persist in communion with God, whose grace shall guide them in their various ways and in the midst of ever changing circumstances. In the Thanksgiving at Communion this prayer is made: "We now most humbly beseech thee, O heavenly Father, so to assist us with thy grace, that we may continue in that holy fellowship [the Church], and do all such good works as thou hast prepared for us to walk in."[17] No priest gives specific instructions, so penance is meted out, no satisfaction is prescribed, although quite clearly what shall be done under the guidance of God's Spirit shall witness to God's glory and be in obedience to the holy law directing us to love God and neighbor.

Not that there were no concrete directions available for guidance. As we have noted, the Creed is accompanied by the Ten Commandments and the Lord's Prayer, both endlessly expounded in catechism and in sermons, and, one could reasonably imagine, in private instruction in schools and in families. Furthermore, the Creed, Ten Commandments, and Lord's Prayer were prominently displayed on the walls of parish churches, displacing statues and relics as objects for contemplation and meditation by the more literate parishioners.[18] Then too, there was the rigorous supervision of the morals of parishioners for which church officials were largely responsible. The records of civil and ecclesiastical courts in the sixteenth century provide abundant proof that this was so. Quarter Sessions dealt with various and sundry crimes ranging from sedition to cozening, from homicide to poaching—all crimes against the commonweal. Church courts were much occupied with sexual offences and thus came to be known as "bawdy courts," but they also dealt with church attendance, church and churchyard disturbances, recusancy and conventicles, and much more.[19] The accused being convicted was assigned penance, purgation, or excommunication. For instance,

Peter Geffrye and Thomas Geffrye are common swearers and blasphemers ... Thomas acknowledged the fault. He is to declare this before the parishioners and give 12d for the poor.

Penance certified.
Christopher Singleton is a drunkard. . . . He promised to reform. Monished to desist and pay 12d to the poor box. Henry Judson for fornication with his maid Faith Hancocke. . . . He confessed and is to do three penances in public places in Cranbrook, Maidstone and Ashford and in his church next Sunday.[20]

Such records provide evidence that the ordinary Christian's conscience was provided with much guidance. The spectacle of public penance in market square and in parish church was as edifying as any word read or preached and perhaps infinitely more impressive. The stringent and at times coercive application of the law to personal and social cases was necessitated by sin, by pride, covetousness, and unfaith. But it is important to realize that the work of the courts was not regarded by the English Reformers as the best means of effecting righteousness in the land. They looked to the preaching of God's Word as the chief, most powerful, most Christian means for the raising up and guiding of the people of God, the citizenry of the English nation.

It would be impossible to exaggerate the importance of preaching in the sixteenth century Church of England. Hugh Latimer, preaching in Edward the VI's presence in 1549, loudly proclaimed that there is no salvation without the honoring of God's Word and no hearing without a preacher. "There must be preachers if we look to be saved."[21] Furthermore, the power of the keys, the power to bind and to loose, which had been located in the priestly power related to the Sacrament of Penance, was now regarded as residing in the preaching of God's Word. John Jewel was not reluctant to say

that Christ hath given to his ministers power to bind, to loose, to open, to shut; and that the office of loosing consisteth in this point, that the minister ... by the preaching of the Gospel offers the merits of Christ and full pardon to such as have lowly and contrite hearts ...

These keys "we with Chrysostom say they be 'the knowledge of the Scriptures': with Tertullian we say they be 'the interpretation of the Law'; and with Eusebius we call them 'the word of God.' "[22] The preacher is the mouthpiece of the Lord conveying God's Word in such ways that dull minds are awakened and the Word finds access to the minds and hearts of the auditors—so effectively that their lives are changed, they repent, are turned around (*metanoia*), and witness in their lives to the righteousness of God. Thus in preaching are found the keys. The preacher is, in John Donne's words, "*Carmen musicum*, a musical and harmonious charmer, to settle and compose the soul again in a reposed confidence, and in a delight in God."[23]

Thus, the preacher working out of his text, making application of it, deliberately seeking to move the affections of his congregation, might suggest in most concrete terms what a person ought to do in a given case. Chief among the sins identified by preachers in sixteenth century sermons was covetousness. This sin was strongly denounced in John Colet's *Oratio habita ad Clerum in Convocatione* (1511), in Hugh Latimer's sermons wherein the covetousness of nobility, landlords, and others was decried, in the teachings of the commonwealth men, and in the preaching of John Jewel.[24] And it was identified specifically with the avaricious lusting for wealth and power displayed by nobility and gentry who enclosed lands to the destruction of England's yeomanry and the increase of the multitudes of wandering poor.[25] But the denunciation of covetousness was not an end in itself. The end in view of the preacher was the inculcation of godliness, the clearing away of all that obstructs that which the *Discourse of the Commonweal* regards as the natural virtues "whose effects be to do good to others, wherein shows forth the image of God in man whose property is ever to do good to others and to distribute his goodness abroad."[26] Communion was the end in view, communion with God and with neighbors, mutual caring such as builds the commonweal, the *communio Christiana*.

However, the power of the keys was expressed most strongly where the preacher placed the Word before the believers, leaving the ultimate and specific application to them as they are enabled by grace, empowered by God's Spirit. Jewel, preaching on the sacraments in his Cathedral Church at Salisbury, provides an example of effective preaching, preaching which is not concerned to make concrete application, which echoes the style of late medieval meditation, and yet places the Word before the believers so vividly that it cannot be ignored and specific ramifications overlooked. Citing Jerome on Psalm 147, Jewel affirms, "When we heare the word of God, the flesh of Christ, and his blood is powred into our eares."[27] Jewel meant that as we receive the sacrament of Christ's body and blood we must "behold his death upon the cross, and the shedding of his blood for our sins." And thus he proceeds to say: "Let us set before our eyes that dreadfull tragedie, and the causes and effectes of his death: that so our heartes may be the rather mooved to yeelde that allegeance, obedience, and reverence, which is due."[28] Jewel then reviews the story, the process of salvation, and speaks of humility "shut up under sin," God sending his Son that "whosoever believeth in him should not perish, but have life everlasting. That Son perished on the cross, "obedient unto death," for our sakes, to save us from sin and guilt. This Jesus was then highly exalted, and we were exalted with him. "Thus he made us an acceptable people, and hath renewed the face of the earth."[29] All of this is laid before us on the table. What shall we do in response?

Let us die with Christ, let us bee crucified unto the worlde. Let us say, praise the Lord, O my soule, and al that is within me, praise his holy name. Let us purpose, and promise amendement of our life: let us goe out with *Peter* and weepe: ley us fall at Christes feete with *Marie Magdalene,* and with our teares washe his feete: Let us say, with David, I have sinned to the Lorde . . . Let us say, have mercie on mee O God, according to they great mercie: thou art my God, I am thy servant, O save me for thy mercies sake. Let us offer up our bodies, a living, pure, holy, and acceptable sacrifice to God. So shall we be partakers of the death of Christ, and of his resurrection.[30]

Moral theology in the sixteenth century Church of England thus involved the whole of life, proceeding from faith and issuing in newness of life, enabled by God's Word in preaching and in the visible words of the sacraments. It involved such participation in Christ that moral choices were made, as it were, spontaneously, in keeping with such holy participation. It was not limited to the confessional and while it necessarily involved repentance (*metanoia*) such turning from selfishness to charity was not limited to penance.

The Place of "Sacramental Confession"

It is true to say that the English Reformers, having rejected sacramental confession as practiced in the medieval church, did not reject everything associated with it, nor did they altogether reject private confession to a priest. Most importantly, in the formative period of Anglicanism, the Church of England recognized how fragile humanity was, how prone to err, and how crippled humans could be by conscientious scruples and unresolved guilt. Thus the sixteenth century Prayer Book provided specific acts of penitence in which the faithful could be consoled and their lives reformed. Most prominent were the General Confession in Morning Prayer and Holy Communion, the Great Litany, and the service of Commination which ends with an admission of sin, a prayer for pardon, and the recitation "after the minister" of the traditional:

> Turn thou us, O good Lord, and so shall we be turned. Be favorable (O Lord) be favorable to thy people, which turn to thee in weeping, fasting, and praying; for thou art a merciful God, full of compassion, long-suffering, and of great piety [pity]. Thou sparest when we deserve punishment, and in thy wrath thinkest upon mercy. Spare thy people, good Lord, spare them and let not thy heritage be brought to confusion. Hear us (O Lord) for thy mercy is great, and after the multitude of thy mercies, look upon us.[31]

Such corporate exercise, repeated time and time again, played a most important role in reforming and consoling the faithful and in the formation of character to the benefit of individuals and of the commonweal.

Furthermore *The Book of Common Prayer* required the clergy to exercise their pastoral responsibilities, as in the Visitation of the Sick and in the rubric at the beginning of Holy Communion where the minister is ordered to confront those who have offended God and neighbors, requiring repentance. More than this, pastoral care of the most intense and serious kind is enjoined for those whose consciences are especially troubled, as in the Visitation of the Sick where a rubric reads, "Here shall the sick person make a special confession if he feel his conscience troubled with any weighty matter,"[32] and in the third exhortation of Holy Communion which provides that if a person is unable to quiet his or her conscience "then let him come to me, or some other discreet and learned Minister of God's word, and open his grief, that he may receive such ghostly counsel, advice, and comfort, as his conscience may be relieved."[33] The sixteenth century would have in mind here the over-scrupulous as well as the hardened sinner. Over scrupulosity, involving such immersion in one's guilt as to weaken and perhaps destroy lively faith, was considered a serious sin. Richard Hooker, in Book VI of his *Lawes*, stated that to help the over scrupulous God in his mercy has ordained

> consecrated persons, which by sentence of power and authority given from above, may as it were out of his verie mouth

ascertaine timorous and doubtfull minds in their owne particular, ease them of all their scrupulosites, leave them settled in
peace and satisfyed touching the mercie of God towards
them.[34]

The Puritan/Anglican theologian of Cambridge, William Perkins,
expressed his concern for the pastoral problems faced by ordinary
people by solving cases of conscience and providing a manual,
published posthumously, for the use of the faithful in the church.
His *Cases of Conscience* was not as exhaustive as Jeremy Taylor's
Ductor Dubitantium or Richard Baxter's *Christian Directory*. It is
true that Perkins tended toward that legalism which Hooker denounced, especially in his legalistic use of the Bible, yet this legalistic tendency "must be balanced," as Breward says, "with his
insistence that where the service of God and need of man appeared
to clash, the service of man took precedence, because God was best
served in the service of our fellow men."[35]

For those committed to Reformation doctrine, the danger was
ever present that a new legalism would intrude which, in the use of
prideful clerics, would become just as tyrannical as the old legalism
of the confessional and the sacerdotal priesthood. Hooker was particularly sensitive to this possibility. The church of necessity had
constantly to be on guard, protecting the proper balance between
"lawful authority and just liberty" and thus striving to protect the
duty of Christians, informed by the Word in the church, and in the
midst of the particulars of a given situation making responsible
decisions: faith finding expression in deeds of love toward God and
neighbor. We turn now to Hooker, who belongs to the main stream
of thought in the sixteenth century Church of England, but who in
his irenicism seems to broaden the range and scope of that thought,
thus providing a landmark in the development of Anglicanism and
of Anglicanism's teaching concerning moral choice.

Hooker and Salvation

Richard Hooker (1554–1600), Master of the Temple in London
and Rector of Bishopsbourne in Kent, summarized and refined the
teachings of the English Reformers and formularies concerning the
lively faith and morals. In his dispute with the Puritan Walter
Travers at the Temple in London, Hooker located the foundation of
Christian faith in "the writings of the Evangelists and Prophets."
This foundation is "salvation by Christ alone."[36] Such salvation
consists of justification and sanctification. Synthesizing the best in

Reformation and Roman Catholic teaching,[37] Hooker insisted that salvation is an act of pure grace whereby Christ's merits are imputed to us for righteousness: justification is not dependent upon any inherent quality or merit of our own.[38] And yet Hooker also insisted that at the very moment of justification, through the indwelling of the Holy Spirit, the *habitual* righteousness of sanctification is ingrafted or infused in us. That is, faith, hope and love (the moral virtue of charity) are ingrafted on the outset, as must be the case if justification is to be realized. Santification begins at the beginning of life in Christ and grows with the increase of *actual* righteousness in the maturing Christian.[39] Salvation, therefore, is the work of God externally imputing Christ's merits to us for our righteousness while at the same time, through the internal workings of the Holy Spirit, those virtues are infused whereby the Christian grows in grace. Thus Hooker says to the Protestants that there is an infusion of grace at the time of justification, and to the Roman Catholics he says that we are justified by imputation and without any merit of ours. He agrees with the Protestants and their relational view of salvation, but he also agrees, although guardedly, with the Roman Catholics and their quantitative view of grace.[40] That the emphasis falls upon relational rather than quantitative understanding is not surprising, given the further development of his theological insights in Book V in *Of the Lawes of Ecclesiastical Polity* (1597).

In Book V Hooker emphasizes the concept of participation.[41] The word *participation* is biblical, with a long history in philosophy and theology, from Gregory of Nyssa, to Thomas Aquinas, to Calvin and Cranmer. Hooker understood its meaning in relation to 1 Cor. 10:16 and John 6. In the former it is *koinonia,* or fellowship (a two-sided relationship) and in the latter it is *menō (menein),* meaning to dwell in or be in union with another, as in John 6:56: "He who eats my flesh and drinks my blood abides (*menei*) in me, and I in him." For Hooker, salvation involves participation: "that mutuall inward hold which Christ hath of us and wee of him, in such sort that ech possesseth other by waie of speciall interest propertie and inherent copulation."[42] The concept further emphasizes the relational view of salvation.

In Chapter 56 of Book V, Hooker begins with a discussion of mutual participation within the Godhead, and then of the human and divine in Christ, and finally comes to the mutual participation that exists between the Christian and Christ. Through participation we are in God and being in God we are in the Church, Christ's body, through the power of the Holy Spirit: the one follows the other as inevitably as day follows night. We are all in Christ and thus in Christ's body the Church. "And his Church he frameth out of the very flesh, the verie wounded and bleedinge side of the Sonne of man. His body crucified and his blood shed for the life of the world, are the true elements of that heavenlie beinge, which maketh us such as him selfe is of whome wee com."[43]

Hooker affirms that this participation is for all (God's first will is that we all should be saved) but he observes that it is not the same in all persons. There are various kinds and degrees of holiness among the faithful. Reverting to the theology developed in the *Discourse of Justification*, Hooker wrote:

> we participate Christ partelie by imputation, as when those thinges which he did and suffered for us are imputed unto us for righteousness; partelie by habituall and reall infusion, as when grace is inwardlie bestowed while wee are on earth and afterwardes more fullie both our soules and bodies made like unto his in glorie. The first thing so infused into our heartes in this life in the Spirit of Christ, whereupon because the rest of what kinde so ever doe all both necessarilie depende and infalliblie also ensue, therefore the apostles terme it sometyme the seede of God.[44]

Hooker further clarified his meaning in a statement that emphasizes the equality of all Christians where the imputation of Christ's merits is concerned and the inequality of the same where sanctification is concerned. Participation in Christ is the fruit of *imputed* grace, but this participation is further advanced in some than it is in others. It is imputation that matters most. Degrees of development apply only to *infused* grace:

> although even in this kinde also the first fruites of Christes Spirit be without latitude. For wee have hereby onlie the beinge of the Sonnes of God, in which number how farre soever one may seeme to excell an other, yeat touchinge this that all are sonnes they are all equales, some happelie better sonnes then the rest are, but none any more a sonne then another.[45]

For Hooker sacraments are means of grace, signifying God's "favour and undeserved mercie towards us," bestowing God's "holy spiritt which inwardlie worketh," and especially, "saving vertues, such as are, *faith, charitie,* and *hope,* lastly the free and full remission of all our sinnes."[46]

This is the grace which *Sacraments* yeeld, and whereby wee are all justifyed. To be justifyed, is to be made righteous. Because therefore, righteousness doth imply first remission of sinnes, and secondlie a sanctifyed life, the name is sometyme applyed severally to the former, sometymes joyntlie it comprehendeth both. The generall cause which hath procured our remission of sinnes is the blood of *Christ*, therefore in his blood wee are justifyed, that is to say cleered and acquitted from all sinne.[47]

To obtain this justification, initially, faith alone is required. But for remission of sin after baptism, faith must be accompanied by penitence. Furthermore, Hooker understood that the faith which justifies is conjoined to hope and love and thus has a moral dimension—it is a lively faith. Saying that we are saved by faith alone does not exclude the necessity of hope and love: the saying simply means that we are not saved by any merit of our own. Hooker was most anxious to emphasize that faith is a saving virtue, a work of divine grace, an effect of the Holy Spirit working in and through the sacraments, and elsewhere, *and* that it is not a bare faith, but one that is active in good works. Turning his back on scholastic distinctions, he wrote:

Lett it . . . suffise us, to receive *Sacraments* as sure pledges of Gods favour, signes infallible, that the hand of his saving mercie doth thereby reach forth itselfe towards us, sending the influence of his Spiritt into mens hearts, which maketh them like to a rich soyle, fertile with all kind of heavenly vertues, purgeth, justifieth, restoreth the verie dead unto life, yea raiseth even from the bottomles pitt to place in thrones of everlasting joye.[48]

On the basis of such an understanding, Hooker defined baptism as "a sacrament which God hath instituted in his Church to the ende that they which receave the same might thereby be incorporated into Christ and so through his most pretious merit obteine as well that savinge grace of imputation which taketh away all former guiltiness, as also that infused divine virtue of the holy Ghost which giveth to the powers of the soule theire first disposition towards future newnes of life."[49] Hooker defined the Eucharist in relation to his understanding of baptism: "Whereas . . . in our infancie we ar incorporated into Christ, and by baptisme receyve the grace of his sprite [spirit] without any sense of feelinge of the guifte which God bestowethe, in the Eucharist, we so receyve the guifte of God, that wee knowe by grace what the grace is which God giveth us, the degrees of oure owne increase in holiness and vertue wee see and can judge of them, wee understande that the strengthe of our life begun in Christe is Christe, that his fleshe is meate, and his blood drinke, not by surmised imagination but trulye, even so trulie that throughe faith wee preceive in the bodie and bloode sacramentallye presented the verye taste of eternall life, the grace of the sacramente is here as the foode which wee eate and drinke."[50]

Hooker's theology is consistent: doctrine, ecclesiology, ethics, liturgy coinhere in such a way that you cannot rightly discuss one without discussing all. The faith of Christians is a lively faith, grounded in relational participation in Christ, expressed intellectually in terms of justification, santification, and righteousness, habitual and actual, realized in the Church by the power of the Holy Spirit working through Word and sacraments in the context of an ordered and affective structure of worship, and issuing in holiness, such behavior as accords with the example of Christ in whom the faithful participate. That holiness consists of the humility of repentance, "the aversion of the will from sin," "submission to God by supplication and prayer," and "the purpose of a new life, testified with present works of amendment," or contrition, confession, and satisfaction.[51] Within certain limits prescribed by law, the Christian is held responsible for making wise moral choices and is given the freedom and the support to do so.

Hooker and Moral Choice

It is against this theological/ecclesiological/liturgical background that Hooker's philosophical ethics, and more specifically his discussions of moral choice in Book I of the *Lawes* must be considered, for the discussion of "choice" in Hooker presupposes a strong conviction that there is no right choice without precedent grace. It is equally true to say that for an adequate understanding of Hooker's view of the lively faith, one must take seriously his philosophical consideration of moral choice.

Hooker teaches that God reveals to humans the laws necessary to their perfect happiness. Such laws are moral laws, the laws of well doing discerned by the power of human reason. Because we are not perfect in ourselves, and our wills are deterred from obeying reason and pursuing the good by those sensible appetites that are so strong in us, God has made known his laws (supernatural and natural) to us through Scripture and has provided means of grace in Word and sacraments. Such means of grace assist us in willing that Good which we desire by nature. In Book I Hooker put it this way, in a summary statement:

> We see ... that our sovereign good is desired naturally; that God the author of that naturall desire had appointed naturall meanes whereby to fulfill it; that man having utterly disabled his nature unto those meanes hath other revealed from God, and hath receaved from heaven a lawe to teach him how that which is desired naturally must now supernaturally be attained; finallie we see that because those later exclude not the former quite and cleane as unnecessarie, therefore together with such supernaturall duties as could not possiblie have beene otherwise knowne to the worlde, the same laws that teacheth them, teacheth us also with them such naturall duties as could not by light of nature easilie have bene knowne.[52]

It is essential to realize that this construction of things requires that humans possess some degree of freedom to choose or to refuse the good revealed by God through nature and through Scripture. Choice is therefore of critical importance to Hooker, and

> Choice there is not unlesse the thing which we take be so in our power that we might have refused and left it. If fire consume the stubble, it chooseth not so to doe, because the nature thereof is such that it can do no other. To choose is to will one thing before another. And to will is to bend our soules to the having or doing of that which they see to be good. Goodnesse is seen with the eye of the understandinge. And the light of that eye, is reason. So that two principall fountaines there are of humaine action, *Knowledge* and *Will*, which will in things tending towards any end is termed *Choice*.[53]

Hooker acknowledged the difficulty encountered by the will in striving after the Good, the ways in which the inferior natural desire we call appetite solicits the will to follow the affections rather than to obey the supernatural laws, the nagging question as to whether that which is good is humanly possible, and the difficulties or unpleasantness attendent upon some good that causes the will "to shrinke and decline from it." Nevertheless, he insists that in spite of appearances to the contrary we possess a certain freedom in relation to the Good, being made in the likeness of God we resemble our maker in the manner of his operation,[54] and thus: "There is in the will of man naturally that freedome, whereby it is apt to take or refuse any particular object whatsoever presented unto it."[55]

The Puritan tract, A Christian Letter (1599), attacked Hooker at this point and for his presumption in having said, "There is not that good which concerneth us, but it hath evidence enough for it selfe. if reason were diligent to search it out."[56] Hooker made clear his conviction, in response, that while the human will possessed aptness to choose the Good, on account of sin it had lost the ability to pursue the Good. On the basis of his distinction between aptness and ability, Hooker emphasized the absolute necessity for supernatural grace to the proper operation of that which we possess by nature. Deny aptness to human beings and you deny their very humanity (because man's distinctive nature is his capacity to reason and to choose, however fallen and faulty he may be) and reduce humanity to the level of "brute creatures."[57] Hooker argued that belief in the natural or created aptness of the human will to choose or not to choose the Good can be "taught without contradiction to any syllable in the confession of the Church, or in those sentences of holy Scripture by you [the Christian Letter] alleadged."[58] Hooker ended his rebuttal of the Puritan accusation with a Pauline statement of his own position:

In summe the grace of God hath aboundantlie sufficient for all. Wee are by it that we are, and att the length by it wee shall bee that wee would. What wee have, and what wee shall have, is the fruite of his goodnes, and not a thing which wee can claime by right or title of our owne worth. All that wee can doe to him commeth farre behind the summe of that we owe, all wee have from him is meere bounty. And seing all that wee of ourselves can doe, is not only nothing, butt naught, lett him alone have the glorie by whose only grace, wee have our whole abilitie and power of doing well.[59]

What is the Good, the highest virtue and most complete happiness we can choose? In one place Hooker speaks of that infinite Good which is God: "therefore he our felicitie and blisse. Moreover desire tendeth unto union with that it desireth. If then in him we be blessed, it is by force of participation and conjunction with him."[60] We return, then, to that participation which looms so large in Hooker's theological exposition in Chapter 56 of Book V. In another place Hooker speaks of the supernatural virtues of faith, hope, and charity or love, God's way, "the worke of God," a lively, clothed faith. Faith is first and consists of belief in God through Christ, its principle object being "that eternall veritie which hath discovered the treasures of hidden wisdome in Christ," hope has as its principle object "that everlasting goodnes which in Christ doth quicken the dead," and charity is directed toward "the incomprehensible beautie which shineth in the countenance of Christ."[61] Such virtues are all directed Godward and all shape and form the Christian in the exercise of moral choice and moral goodness in this world, in the Christian's daily life. Participation in Christ is the root virtue out of which all flows, toward which all tends.

Conclusion

Richard Hooker's concept of moral choice owes much to Aristotle and to Thomas Aquinas. In particular he reflects the influence of Aristotle's *Nichomachean Ethics* (1112^a–1113^b), but he is not a slavish imitator of Aristotle. His concept of communion or participation involves something of the Platonic mode of thought. Where Aquinas tended to think of participation in terms of cause and effect, Hooker was thinking of participation in "perfect form." And, concerning moral choice, where Aristotle's understanding focuses more on *deliberation* than the action of the will, Hooker emphasizes the voluntary *action* of the will. But Hooker was no simple voluntarist. The will to which he referred is *rational* will. Well doing consists in moral choice through the activity of the will as it is informed by the eye of reason and thus discerns the Good. We are free to choose but we cannot choose the Good without divine assistance. Thus I would prefer to say that for Hooker the will, perceiving the Good as empowered to do so by reason, participates in what well doing for which it has been prepared, acquiescing to the divine will for humankind.[62] Nevertheless, it is still true to say that for Hooker the emphasis falls on action rather than on deliberation or contemplation. The law of reason is the *moral* law, encompassing both "Knowledge and Will." Participation in Christ involves the realization of true *koinonia* in relationship to the people around us, our families, the commonwealth, at the workplace and among the nations of the world.

Hooker was an eloquent spokesman for nascent Anglicanism and contributed towards its development. As it matured Anglicanism affirmed the rightness of that tension which Hooker tried so desperately to explain to his Puritan adversaries, the tension involved in the insistence on the necessity of human freedom alongside the necessity of grace to enable humanity in the exercise of that freedom in turning from evil, in choosing the Good. Sacramental confession as practiced at the end of the Middle Ages was rejected and emphasis placed upon the Christian, living in the community of the faithful, assisted by Word and sacraments, making moral judgments, personal and social. This was the lively faith to which Cranmer referred, the lively faith that also involves humility, repentance, and the enactment of laws to curb humanity's tendencies to harm others for the sake of satisfying base appetites. Provision was made for confession to a priest for the consoling of troubled consciences and for overcoming the sin of over-scrupulosity, for removing all that inhibits effective action, the lively faith. Authoritative discipline thus had its rightful place in the cultivation of the lively faith and was itself a means of grace. But most important to the English Reformers were Word and sacraments (visible words), inspiring the faithful to repentance, nurturing Christians, strengthening their participation in Christ, helping them to grow in righteousness. By various means people were assisted to discern all that is true and good and thus informed by reason to so act as to attain some measure of goodness in this life. This understanding requires, as Hooker suggests, some measure of tolerance in the Christian community, recognition of human worth as well as human sin, recognition that all are sons and daughters of God although to varying degrees. Of primary importance was the recognition that all are equal before, all justified, all participate in Christ, all are inheritors of everlasting life, however different they may be, however imperfect, however good. What matters is faith in God through Christ by the Spirit, with the recognition that this faith is lively, fruitful, issuing in good works.

Anglicans are engaged in a lively faith, participants in Christ and thus in the church with its Word and sacraments, its holy community. This faith, as Cranmer said, is "a true trust and confidence of the mercy of God through our Lord Jesus Christ, and a stedfast hope of all things to be received at Gods hand ... And this faith it not ... without love of God and of our neighbours, nor without feare of God, nor without desire to heare Gods word, and to follow the same in eschewing evill, and doing gladly all good workes."[63]

Where would you place anglican moral theology in the debate between Luther + Aquinas?

Anglican Moral Theology in the Seventeenth Century: An Anticipation

The pt of this essay is that current RC theology was anticipated by the 17th C anglicans
1) Hierarchical but scriptural + could call folks to lives of moral devotion duty

by H. R. McAdoo

It would be a grave error of judgment to imagine that the study of Anglican moral theology in the seventeenth century is merely an exercise in filial piety or in antiquarian research. The real significance of the Anglican restructuring of moral theology during that period becomes fully apparent when that structure is set over against the effects of the quiet revolution taking place in contemporary moral theology over the past couple of decades. Such a comparison reveals a striking anticipation on the part of the Anglicans of most of the major elements in that revolution the fruits of which may be seen in the works of contemporary Roman Catholic moralists such as Bernard Häring, Gerard Gilleman, Josef Fuchs, Enda McDonagh and many others.[1] It is no exaggeration to say that what has come about is [no less than a total transformation of Roman Catholic moral theology,] its nature, method and objective, which has resulted in a remarkable convergence with traditional Anglican moral theology. The Second Vatican Council insisted that "special attention needs to be given to the development of moral theology" and underlined the need for a fresh emphasis on scriptural teaching, on vocation and on charity.[2] But the process of transformation had begun before the Council and moral theology was being rescued from what Cardinal Suenens has called "the dominance of canonists" and was being relocated within the totality of the Gospel.[3] The roots of change go back to people like John Michael Sailer in the last century whose language was that of the Kingdom and not of jurisprudence,[4] but the fruit matured only in our own time. It is therefore not simply interesting but practically important to signalize the parallels between the restructuring of Anglican moral theology in the seventeenth century and that which has been taking place under our eyes in the second half of this century.

An inventory of the elements in the restructuring of moral theology today is therefore very illuminating and will serve to make the point by way of introduction to the salient features of Anglican moral theology in the seventeenth century. What during that period evolved left an indelible imprint on how Anglicans in later times face moral choice in a world infinitely more complex than that in which their forebears attempted to explain to their fellows the purpose and implications of membership in the household of faith.

That there is a new moral theology in the making will be clear from the following headings, and specialists will be able to add to and expand them.[5]

The Features of Modern Moral Theology

(1) First among the elements which have given a new face to moral theology in our time is the rethinking of *the nature of moral theology itself*. The fundamental change here is the re-siting of moral theology within the kerygmatic totality of the Gospel. As long ago as 1948, Archbishop Donald Coggan published *The New Testament Basis of Moral Theology*.[6] Anticipating what subsequently and independently came to be the main-line direction, particularly for Roman Catholic writers, he maintained that moral theology is rooted in the New Testament concept of faith and in the New Testament concept of love. "Christian ethics are responsible ethics," he wrote, and this is so because "the insistence that *kerygma* precedes *didache*, indeed that *didache* is the outcrop of *kerygma*."[7]

Two sets of ideas formative for the new approach to moral theology emerge here and are faithfully mirrored in the restructuring that has gone on ever since. These are the relating of moral theology to the *kerygma* in a living relationship, and the viewing of Christian ethics in terms of response. The roots of this go deep, as already indicated, and Bernard Häring traces them back to Sailer and Hirsch who pioneered the changes: "the basis of their moral theology is the Gospel . . . we may, in fact, use the present day term 'kerygmatic theology' of their writings." Emphasizing their rejection of the procedure and technique of jurisprudence, he adds that they sought to shape "a moral theology where primary concern should be to restate the perfect ideal of the whole Christian life and to underline the means of attaining it."[8]

Häring himself sees the subject in terms of "response, responsibility, dialogue," asserting that "we come to the heart of religion only at the point of encounter between the word of God and the response of man."[9] His moral theology is Christocentric: "The principle, the norm, the centre and the goal of Christian moral theology is Christ. The law of the Christian is Christ Himself in Person. He alone is our Lord, our Saviour. In Him we have life and therefore also the law of our live."[10] Moral theology is then all about the response of discipleship within the household of faith: "We understand moral theology as the doctrine of the imitation of Christ, as the life in, with, and through Christ. Therefore its starting point cannot be man, as might be tenable in the science of natural ethics. The point of departure in Catholic moral theology is Christ, who bestows on man a participation in His life and calls on him to follow the Master."[11]

Similarly, Josef Fuchs sees moral theology "as un unfolding, a revelation and explanation of the joyful message, the good news, of Christ's call to us, of the vocation of believers in Christ."[12] All this, together with the implications of the following headings, surfaces for example in the work of Enda McDonagh, the title of whose book *Invitation and Response* sufficiently indicates his direction. Indeed, speaking of the recent developments, McDonagh goes so far as to say that these "are at least so far-reaching as to make manuals in near-universal use even ten years ago almost entirely irrelevant now."[13] Let a modern Anglican, Herbert Waddams, sum it up: "It can hardly be stated too strongly that moral theology is basically dealing with our life as it is lived in union with Christ."[14] There is the radical difference and the direct consequence, equally far-reaching, is that moral and ascetic theology are no longer understood as separate areas and concerns.

(2) It is now *a moral-ascetical theology.*

(3) Connected with the foregoing, it thinks in terms of the *imitation of Christ* and of *incorporation in him* through membership in his body, by means of the Word and Sacrament and faith's response.

(4) It is *Christ-centered,* for Christ is the norm of moral theology and the law for Christians. This new law gives a different orientation to all decision-making.

(5) It is *charity-based* and sees love as the fulfilling of the law. Law is not disregarded and has a necessary function and place as love's protection, but it is no longer the *point de départ*. Seen from within the common life in the body of Christ (the *koinonia*), law becomes a word of God to his people, evoking love's reponse: "If you love me, you will obey my commands," (John 14:15); "love means following the commands of God" (2 John 6).

(6) Its subject is the *Christian-in-the-Church*, not just "the penitent." Arising directly from this,

(7) It thinks in terms of discipleship, of *metanoia* and of *conversion*.

(8) It is contextualized, less by a rigid framework of rules and regulations, than by the living experience of the Church in grace and faith.

(9) It deals with the whole life of the member of the Church as *a vocation* fulfilled through response and responsibility.

(10) It regards the virtues not as abstracts but as the characteristics of this life-style, finding their full expression in love.

(11) By stressing the role of *obedient love*, it links the themes of vocation, of the primacy of charity and of Christ-centeredness (Compare No. 5 above).

Obedient love is both the form and the content of the life-style in the new community of reconciliation. Inwardly and outwardly, through grace, it expresses membership. It actualizes the relationship between Christ, the Head, and the members and at the time provides both the motivation and the standard for the Christian's decision-making.[15] "The central motive of Christian morality is love, love in so far as it is obedient."[16] This is not the love-monism of the agapists. Law and commandment have their place in the vocation of discipleship within the grace-endowed *koinonia*—"they are living words of Christ addressed to us,"[17] and thus love is obedient love, responsive and responsible.

(12) It evinces a growing awareness of *the difference between "case" and "situation."* There has appeared an increased interest in compensationism, or "the way of prudence." Theologians like Josef Pieper see prudence as the situation conscience and Kevin Kelly

praises the preference of the seventeenth-century Anglicans and Aquinas for right reason in the direction of the moral life, as against systems. Something similar appears in the contemporary Anglican, Trueman Dicken, when he writes "morality must be rational and must pay heed to the facts and to the rules which prudence derives from them."[18]

(13) *The pre-occupation of moral theology* is less with the confessor seen as judge in the tribunal and more with the Christian endeavoring to achieve through grace a spiritual and personal maturity. Fuchs is typical when he holds that "the renewal of moral theology ought to put an end to the one-sided idea ... that the main object of the discipline is the training of future confessors."[19] Moral theology must be aplied to nourishing the new life—"become what in reality you are." "The genuine scope of Christian morality" writes Häring, "is the formation of Christ in us."[20]

(14) It is becoming more *historically conscious* or, as Häring put it in his *Medical Ethics*, "it is more open to a dynamic view of man's development and his call to maturity."[21] There is involved here new thinking on natural law and on contemporary man's self-understanding, both of which themes are discussed for Anglican moral theology by John Macquarrie in *Three Issues in Ethics* (1970).

Enough has been noted in this inventory to indicate that Josef Fuchs in his valuable restructuring of the science was not being extravagant, when he spoke of the need for "an intensified Christianizing of moral theology."[22] Such a bird's eye view of what has been happening in our own times will enable us to obtain a truer perspective of what took place in Anglican moral theology three centuries ago. At times we are likely to experience a sensation of *déjà vu* which may well deepen our appreciation of the value of the Anglican inheritance in this branch of theology.

The Restructuring of Moral Theology in Seventeenth-Century Anglicanism

The Structure of Caroline Moral Theology was the first endeavor to assemble and to evaluate the work of the Anglican moralists and writers on spirituality and on the implications of membership.[23] The object of the exercise was to establish that Anglicanism had a distinctive moral theology with a markedly positive approach to the discipline. The shape of this became apparent as analysis of the

Summary

material revealed three interwoven strands, traditionalist in respect of law and human acts, reforming in respect of mortal and venial sin, repentance and the concept of membership, and what may be described loosely as a mixed assessment of conscience and casuistry. Deeply involved with all this were the kind of practice and the ideal for Christian living which informed the many catechetical and devotional works of the seventeenth-century Church of England.

In a work devoted to the Anglican moral theology of the seventeenth century, Father Kevin Kelly repeatedly emphasized what he saw as the positive aspect of its approach and the radical revision of the concept of moral theology which the Anglicans upheld.[24] Much of the *Structure of Caroline Moral Theology* revealed the dependence of the Anglicans on Aquinas and their stress on right reason, and Kelly regarded their work as challenging Roman Catholic moralists to retrace their steps—something which we now see to have been in progress before and after 1967 when his valuable study was published. He did not hesitate to say at the time that the Anglican moralists "were worthy of attention by their present-day Catholic counterparts" and that in some areas "their doctrine seems much closer to the stream of traditional Christian thought on this question than that of many of their Roman Catholic contemporaries and even, it must be admitted, than that of many present-day Roman Catholic moralists."[25] This is very significant if one casts one's mind back to our inventory of the features of contemporary moral theology. Kelly regarded the Anglican treatment of such matters as that of an uncertain conscience as "highly scientific and very satisfactory."[26] All this bears directly on the point made at the beginning of this essay, namely, that Anglican moral theology in the seventeenth century was in many respects far ahead of its time and anticipated many of the developments in that discipline with which we are now familiar. In the light of these developments, what picture emerges from a fresh assessment of Anglican moral theology in the seventeenth century?

A *Positive Approach*

One may note, then, certain general characteristics of this structure. There is a determination to restate the goal and to redefine the nature of moral theology. One encounters a readiness to revise and at the same time to retain. There is an emphasis on the rôle of reason and an awareness of a creative tension between authority and freedom—"lawful authority" and "just liberty" are recurring

phrases. Involved with this is a developing idea of law understood
not solely in terms of promulgation and restriction but also in terms
of an implanted pattern of characteristic behavior. Hooker is a
major example of this and it was one of the objectives of *The
Structure of Caroline Moral Theology* to demonstrate the extent of
the debt owed to Aquinas by the Caroline divines in respect of law,
human acts and conscience, a thesis since confirmed by Kelly and
J.K. Ryan.[27] Robert Sanderson's favorite reading was the *Secunda
Secundae.*

Equally necessary however to the evaluation of the work of the
Anglican moralists is the realization that they were always ready to
reform wherever they considered that a New Testament norm was
being displaced. This is notably true in the case of repentance, for
they held that the Roman Catholic moral theology of the day had
substituted the idea of penance for the concept of *metanoia*. This
linked up intimately with their conviction that moral theology was
about the whole of the Christian's life as a member of the Body of
Christ and was therefore a moral-ascetical theology and a "practical divinity," their favorite term to describe the discipline. Consequently, moral theology could not be tied almost exclusively to the
confessional although they were far from depreciating the value of,
and sometimes the necessity of, having a spiritual director as indeed
The Book of Common Prayer directs.[28] Moral theology was for the
educating and strengthening of the individual conscience as the
member of the Family faced decision-making and choice in an often
perplexing world. In that world, the Christian-in-the-Church lived
through a Life not his own transmitted to him by the Spirit through
the means of grace, the Book and the Bread, within the eucharistic
fellowship of the baptized who shared in the apostolic faith.[29]
Already today's student of moral theology will be experiencing the
feeling of having been here before. This happens as one looks more
closely at the base on which so much else of this seventeenth-
century structure stands.

The Scope and Definition of the Subject

Robert Sanderson is arguably the clearest and most profound of
the Anglican moral theologians,[30] and Kevin Kelly's comment is:
"For him moral theology is the science of Christian living."[31] Sanderson's definition of the scope of moral theology is therefore something of a trend-setter; "But when all is done, positive and
practique Divinity is it must bring us to Heaven: that is, it must

poise our judgements, settle our consciences, direct our lives, mortify our corruptions, increase our graces, strengthen our comforts, save our souls. . . . There is no study to this, none so well worth the labour as this, none that can bring so much profit to others, nor therefore so much glory to God, nor therefore so much comfort to our own hearts, as this."[32]

The view, content and function of moral theology here set forth is explicit and implicit in seventeenth-century Anglicanism. The definition was later on borrowed without acknowledgement by Wilkins—a natural compliment from one whose preaching and teaching concentrated on the practical impact of religion on life.[33]

Jeremy Taylor's work covers so much of the field of moral—ascetical theology and his writings on the spiritual life were so widely read that his approach to practical divinity was inevitably influential in the life of Anglicanism.[34] In fact, he calls it "the life of Christianity" and "the life of religion."[35] As he develops his picture of moral theology, Taylor reveals certain positive characteristics which are common to all Anglican writings of the period. For example, there is the stress on growth into personal maturity—every man his own casuist. Caroline thinking has at its center the education of the individual conscience. As Kevin Kelly noted of Sanderson "he sees that every human action is a personal action. It has to be performed by the person himself, not by his adviser. Hence, he lays great stress on the personal judgment involved. If advice is needed, it must take the form of spiritual guidance, not spiritual dictatorship."[36] Häring has underlined the same point and it has been developed at some length for our contemporary situation by John Macquarrie, who observed that the complex world of today demands a new moral theology in which "each one has to become his own moral theologian."[37] This particular emphasis in the Anglican writings is the form taken by them as the equivalent of the modern stress on responsibility. In fact, not only Sanderson but Taylor, Baxter and Sharp recommend seeking guidance on occasion. What they are opposing is any exercise of authority which limits the individual's true freedom by inculcating spiritual follow-my-leaderism instead of counsel leading on to mature initiative. In their view, the current tieing of moral theology to the confessional almost exclusively made for a situation in which authoritarianism and legalism reinforced each other and debased the concept of what moral theology was all about.

Something of this appears in Jeremy Taylor's view of the subject: "For I intend to offer to the world a general instrument of moral theology, by the rules and measures of which, the guides of souls may determine the particulars that shall be brought before them; and those who love to inquire, may also find their duty so described, that unless their duty be complicated with laws, and civil customs and secular interests, *men that are wise may guide themselves in all their proportions of conscience*: but if their case be indeed involved, they need the conduct of a spiritual guide, to untie the intrigue, and state the question, and apply the respective rules to the several parts of it." As he develops this Taylor, like others among his peers, anticipates the reorientation in moral theology first associated with Gilleman[38] but now common coin today, when he insists that preaching the way of love is the best way to fit men for decision-making: "preach and exhort to simplicity and love; for the want of these is the great multiplyer of cases." When this simplicity and charity, this attitude of responding responsibly to the divine initiative (for "God is love; he who dwells in love is dwelling in God"), are missing or debilitated, an entry is created into moral theology for legalism and minimalism: "men do not serve God with honesty and heartiness, and they do not love him greatly; but stand upon terms with him and study how much is lawful, being afraid to do more for God and for their souls than is simply and indispensably necessary ... but the good man understands the things of God; not only because God's Spirit, by secret immisions of light, does properly instruct him; but because he hath a way of determining his cases of conscience which will never fail him."[39]

Martin Thornton recognizes the extent and depth of the Anglican reappraisal: "This Caroline method produced the integrated science of moral-ascetical theology, the art of full co-operation with grace, in a total Christian life. It emphasized progress towards perfection rather than keeping on the right side of the law."[40] In a penetrating comment he confirms our assessment of the range and impact of the Anglican re-structuring in the seventeenth century: "Over-emphasis on conscience can become just as unhealthy as over-emphasis on the confessional: we can be too subjective or too objective. The need is for a completely trinitarian system of habitual recollection with a moral content: the Caroline teaching on divine law based on reason, interpreted by conscience trained and guided by the Holy Spirit, but with the whole coloured and inspired by affective devotion to Christ, who is both God and man, lawgiver and Redeemer."[41] Perhaps enough has been said by way of illustration to justify Thomas Wood's general comment on the English theologians of the period: "To the latter, casuistical divinity meant the practical application or interpretation of Christian moral principles in all the conditions of men's lives, in order that they might be led on to the Christian ideal of holiness: it included not only the resolution of hard cases of doubt and perplexity and all the juristic side of moral theology, but also the entire range of ascetic theology, the whole being regarded as one comprehensive science ... their ideal was not to remove from men the exacting duty of probing and resolving their own moral difficulties, but rather to train them in self-reliance as the *responsible* and consecrated servants of God in Christ."[42]

Let one of the Carolines conclude this section. Archbishop John Sharp was one of the most acute and perceptive of the Anglican moralists, and in a sermon he outlined with his customary lucidity the Anglican view of the instrumental rôle of moral theology in the life of Christianity: "The design of Christianity is not to adjust the precise bounds of virtue and vice, lawful and unlawful ... for the best that could have come from such a design had been only this, that men by this means might have been fairly instructed how they might have avoided the being bad, though they never became very good. But the design of Christianity is to make men as good as they possibly can be; as devout, as humble, as charitable, as temperate, as contented, as heavenly-minded, as their natures will allow of in this world."[43]

Passing in review the Anglican picture of what practical divinity was in itself and what its objective was, one may say that written large across it are the words *kaine ktisis*, for its concern is with the re-creation of the human person.[44]

Changes and Emphases in the Structure

The nature of the changes and the reasons for them are bound up with this enlarged view of moral theology and its scope. There are in the Anglican moral theology of the seventeenth century three specific revisions of current thinking all of which have their counterparts in the modern restructuring. Linked with these and with their new view of what moral theology is all about is the Caroline emphasis on sincerity as an essential element in Christian life and practice. "Sincere in their obedience" was Beveridge's way of putting it and this sense of the reality of membership runs through the writings of the period. "Sincere obedience" is Jeremy Taylor's description of what is involved in Christian belonging.[45]

The three areas in which seventeenth-century Anglicanism held that change was necessary were:

I. The question of the relationship of "the perfection of wayfaring men" to the aims and practices of religion.

II. The question of the meaning of repentance and its relationship to the obedience of membership.

III. The question of the current distinction between mortal and venial sin and its bearing on the obedience of the Christian.

The areas are inter-connected and the Carolines, like their modern counter-parts, regarded themselves as restoring a New Testament norm in each case. Whether in some limited respects, notably their casuistry, they went too far is debatable, but the objective is clear, namely, a positive restructuring.

"The Perfection of Wayfaring Men"

The New Testament injunction "Be ye perfect" is repeated by more than one Caroline theologian and finds an echo in most of them. The same note is struck by Häring.[46] It sounds daunting and unrealistic in an age when absolutes are at a discount and all is reckoned as relative. It is important therefore to understand that the seventeenth century was not thinking in terms of an unreal perfectionism. William Nicholson's treatment is typical in the way in which he marries the traditional thinking of Aquinas with the new view of moral theology. He writes, "There is one perfection of this life, another of the life to come. Now the law of God expects from us in this life, not absolute perfection, but such a perfection as is to be had in this life, which the School calls *perfectio viatorum*, the perfection of wayfaring men, and defines it thus; when the will of men habitually entertains nothing that is contrary to the love of God" (S.T. 2.2. 44 art. 4. *ad secundam*). Nature needs grace to attain this, he continues, and even then it does not raise man to "an unsinning obedience, but it makes him 'a new creature,' creates in him a sincere obedience to the whole Gospel."[47] Here, the *kaine ktisis*, sincerity and obedience, merge with the whole concept of the new life and the new law which is at the heart of a revised and renewed moral theology. It might be an extract from *The Law of Christ* and whatever may be said about Caroline rigorism in some areas, it is not here that this appears for what is at issue here is a seriousness and a sincerity which belong to the New Law.

Jeremy Taylor demonstrates the same approach: "The state of regeneration is perfection all the way, even when it is imperfect in its degrees. The whole state of a Christian's life is a state of perfection. Sincerity is the formality or the soul of it: a hearty, constant endeavour is the body or material part of it; and the mercies of God accepting it in Christ, and assisting and promoting it by his Spirit of Grace, is the third part of its constitution, it is the spirit."[48] This is no ill-conceived doctrine of assurance that perfection is already realized. Rather is it their way of asserting that response and responsibility are pivotal as sincere endeavor is backed by the reality of grace and the concept of duty, and yet "it is imperfect in its degrees."

The new law, the new life and the new person are never far from the center of this moral-ascetical theology. William Payne is representative when he comments, "Repentance is the same thing in Scripture with conversion, regeneration, the new birth, the new creature, the new man, and the like."[49] However some of his peers may disagree in detail about this way of putting it, Payne is stating a top priority for the Anglican moralists and the further questions of repentance and distinction of sins are closely linked with this picture of the nature, aim and style of membership in the New Community. They were reacting against any suggestion of a two-tier level of practice, a double standard. That attitude to life which they variously called "obedience" and "conformity" flows from a response of sincerity and endeavor cooperating with the assistance of the Spirit, as Taylor put it, to produce that habitual disposition which Nicholson saw as being at the heart of *perfectio viatorum*.

One is conscious of a marked quality of seriousness in their outlook. The very word itself is in the title of a bestseller which was the last example of its kind: William Law's *A Serious Call to a Devout and Holy Life* (1728), the whole theme of which is to promote earnestness about Christian practice in daily living. It bears directly on our subject to recall that Law used in this book a good deal of material from his earlier work entitled *Christian Perfection* (1726), which influenced both the Wesleys. We can see what Thornton meant by his comment that the Caroline integrated science of moral-ascetical theology "emphasised progress towards perfection rather than keeping on the right side of the law."

Taylor's claim that just as moral theology needs to be clear as to the meaning of repentance, so the latter concept requires to understand what is implied by the distinction of sins, and this leads to a consideration of the second and third areas of revision.

The Meaning and Place of Repentance

The object of the exercise was the re-instatement of the New Testament concept of *metanoia.* Thus, in turning to the Scriptural meaning of the term, the Anglicans took the emphasis off sacramental penance and placed it firmly on repentance as a virtue and as a major element in the new life of obedience in love. Always bearing in mind what they believed about individual counsel and absolution, they desired to ensure that neither the doctrine of forgiveness nor the practice of confession could be used as a way of evading the response and responsibility which lie at the heart of *metanoia.* We find both Stillingfleet and Roger Boyle making this point, and John Donne notes that to confuse penance with repentance is to take the part for the whole.[50] Taylor too deals with it: "It is usual to discourse of sorrow and contrition, of confession of sins, of making amends, of self-affliction, and some other particulars but because they are not parts but actions, fruits, and significations of repentance, I have reserved them for their proper place."[51] Repentance itself is "a whole state of the new life, an entire change." Elsewhere, Taylor calls it "sincere obedience" and this is the authentic revisionist note echoed by others like Wake who saw it as "a real conversion . . . a change of life."[52]

Some of the Anglicans, like South, maintain that "repentance is not itself this course of new obedience, but it does infer and produce it, and that is its inseparable effect or consequent."[53] Sharp is as usual clear and interesting in that he sees repentance as consisting of two parts, the inward part "which is what we properly call repentance (metanoia)" and the outward part, the life of obedience.[54] Others among them hold by the old term "contrition" in this connection but contemporary ideas on "attrition" come under criticism, particularly the view that attrition is sufficient, as Stillingfleet put it, to "dispose a man to receive grace in that sacrament (penance)."[55]

In short, there is a range of emphasis but the positive line taken is unmistakable. Finally, following the short invitation at Holy Communion, the Church catechism and the Homilies, they saw repentance and faith as being so close as to be interdependent. Indeed, the Homily *Of Repentance* goes so far as to say that repentance has four parts, contrition, confession, amendment of life—and faith. Sanderson insists that repentance and faith cannot exist apart from one another and Taylor says "the Gospel is nothing else but faith and repentance."[56] Similarly, Payne asserts that "repentance is the whole practical condition of Christianity, and together with faith, makes up the entire duty of the Christian." This is from one angle, a setting out in practice of what the Anglican definitions of moral-ascetical theology are all about and one can see why Jeremy Taylor insisted that moral theology depended to a large extent on the notions of repentance which it taught and put into practice.

Distinction of Sins

Much the same motivation and basic considerations underlie the Caroline attitude to the current distinction between moral and venial sin. Straight away, however, it must be said that they accepted the existence of a distinction and the obvious fact of a difference in degree. Francis White explained that "all the Protestants in substance of matter, acknowledge a difference of venial and moral sin . . . and many of them admit the terms and form of speech." The difference of viewpoint is "in the sense and exposition of this distinction . . . by denying that any sins are venial by nature, or by the moral law . . . though there be a difference of offences, yet there is not such a difference, as for any of their sins to be by nature venial."[57] What they were concerned to demonstrate was that all sin has a common nature and therefore to suggest that a certain class of sin had by its nature an inherent right to pardon was to set up the wrong type of question. What bearing, for example, would such thinking have on the concepts of sincerity and *metanoia*? The grounds of their objection to the distinction as they understood it to be used in their times were that it could help to lower standards in practice and tended to shunt moral-ascetical theology into the legalist siding by introducing the nicely-calculated less or more. Taylor made the point, "To distinguish a whole kind of sins is a certain way to make repentance and amendment of life imperfect and false" and he added, "It is rather a dispensation or leave to commit one sort of them." Moreover, it introduces uncertainty so that "Men call what they please venial."[58] In fact a modern Anglican, H. M. Waddams, makes both points[59] and one recalls Kenneth Kirk's comment that the distinction was theologically unreal and dangerous for the individual but real and valuable for the director.[60]

Obviously it is against all common sense to suggest that there are not minimal sins, and while it is possible to detect a superficial ambivalence in this regard, a hint of rigorism, this was more by way of over-reacting on the part of the seventeenth-century Anglicans, than by design or principle. Taylor is representative when he asserts that "sins differ in degree." "Sins are greater or less in their principle as well as in their event," he writes, and "the greatness of sins is in most instances by extension and accumulation." If the Anglican moralists show a tendency rather than a trend here this is ultimately traceable to a view of moral theology which concentrates on discipleship rather than on spiritual bookkeeping. Moreover, in practice, they distinguish between "sins of presumption" and "sins of infirmity." If a criticism is to be made it must be that if they regarded a profit-and-loss account morality as unreal, their insistence that all sin shares a common disorder could on occasion be twisted into producing unreality of another kind. What is more valuable and more modern in their treatment of this question is the emphasis laid on the will. Sanderson notes that "How much measure you abate in the wilfulness, so much weight you take off from the sin."[61] He distinguishes between sins of ignorance, infirmity and presumption, a distinction stemming from the faculties of understanding, emotions and will. The measure of gravity lies in the degree in which the will dominates the act: "every sin is simply and absolutely by so much greater or lesser, by how much it is more or less voluntary."[62] The title of the pamphlet ascribed by some to Henry Hammond, *Sins of Weakness and Wilfulness*, underlines the point. Indeed, the Carolines are in line with Darwell Stone's definition of mortal and venial sin: "the essential distinction of 'mortal sin' from 'venial sin' lies in the former being a real act of the will while the latter falls short of this."[63]

The more psychological approach is evident too in Taylor's contention that "no sin is absolutely venial but in comparison with others: neither is any sin at all times and to all persons alike venial." Also, "If any man about to do an action of sin, enquires whether it be a venial sin or no,—to that man, at that time, that sin cannot be venial."[64] South concurs that "by such antecedent thought and design beforehand, (it) is changed from a sin of infirmity into a sin of presumption."[65] On the other hand, says Taylor, something which is grave in matter may have its offense diminished by reason of imperfection in the agent or in the act itself. He is, of course, referring to serious matter (in the thing itself or because of attendant circumstances), full advertence and full consent. Thus, in the writings of the period, the results may fairly be said to balance out in practice, a view confirmed by Martin Thornton's summing up: "The Caroline moralists did not uphold the parity of sins; there is still the distinction between those of malice and infirmity, neither, within these categories, are all sins equal. The objection was against the mathematical exactness with which scholastic and contemporary Roman theology tried to classify sin, and the objection was sustained not simply because of the resultant laxity but because law had replaced teleology. Caroline thought was interested not so much in rigorous moral ife as in the glory of God whose service is perfect freedom."[66]

Getting Down to Cases

Casuistry means getting down to cases and here again the Anglican moralists believed that change was required. The change in method would inevitably reflect their attitude to the major question of the nature of moral-ascetical theology and to the other questions which have been under review. Since casuistry is the application point at which "practical divinity" becomes most practical, it is the point at which definition and method must be all of one piece. The overall picture of the Christian life as depicted by these Anglican writers is then the ultimate determinant for casuistic method just as it creates the form, content and scope of practical divinity as they understood it. To grasp this is to grasp the rationale of seventeenth-century Anglican moral theology. Once again, Martin Thornton's assessment is just: "This objection (i.e. to probabilism as a casuistic method) was not simply against laxism but against the legal or static concept of morals. With Aquinas, the Carolines stood firm on the teleological principle: the human end is not moral goodness but glory; morals and ascetics are inseparable."[67]

Given then that the overall view of moral theology is a formative element in Caroline casuistic method, how then has this worked out in practice and what characteristics has it produced?

Three features suggest themselves as distinctive in Caroline casuistry. Firstly, there is the authority accorded to the individual conscience with its accompanying emphasis on personal responsibility. Secondly, there is the stress laid on the rôle of reason in moral acts. A third feature, connected with the second, is a preference for some form of tutiorism, although this statement requires certain important qualifications. Also noteworthy is the explicit insistence that casuistry must be based on Scripture and reason and not upon "authorities" and canon law. Furthermore, the concept of law with which the Anglican theologians work is not that of jurisprudence (in which promulgation counts for so much) but that of law seen as an implanted directive.[68] Both factors are not without bearing on a general aim of simplifying the whole subject, for, as Taylor complained, "In moral theology what God hath made plain, men have intricated."[69]

The Authority of the Individual Conscience

"We do believe," wrote Sharp, "that in matters where a man's conscience is concerned, everyone is to be a judge for himself, and must account for himself." This is indicative of the whole tenor of seventeenth-century Anglican moral theology, but Sharp is being equally representative when he goes on to emphasize that this does not exclude taking the advice of competent authorities or seeking spiritual counsel when necessary—quite the contrary.[70]

The end product of sound casuistry, says Taylor, is true peace of conscience, but if the Carolines advocate their customary attention to detail here as elsewhere, there can be no question of scrupulosity. No man is bound to do better than his best, is Taylor's comment. Conscience is the norm for human actions, says Sanderson, and the immediate norm of conscience is right reason. Kevin Kelly's study of the Anglican moralists concurs in this estimate of what are the formative features in this casuistry. The big questions of authority and freedom, of authoritarianism and legalism were always present for the Anglicans who saw very clearly that a juristic moral theology was defective in itself and in its objective and that it also inevitably produces a legalistic casuistry. Kelly too has perceived this necessary linking and he writes, "It has been noted by recent Anglican writers that the English moralists of the seventeenth century saw conscience and its role in the moral life in the wide context of the problem of the fusion of liberty and authority in the sphere of moral action. The contemporary scene in which their moral thought developed made this a most pressing problem. Their solution lay in a most insistent emphasis on the personal responsibility of the individual in moral action. ... This emphasis on the personal responsibility of the individual was naturally expressed in the formula that his moral action must be guided by his own reason. As has been noted throughout the exposé of their teaching, this did not imply, at least among the more prudent writers ... any neglect of authority or wise counsel. It merely insisted that where such authority or counsel entered in, the action still remained a personal action of the individual and hence his own reason had still to put its seal on it so that it might fully deserve the title of a 'human' action.

It was remarked in the preceding section that the judgement of the individual conscience was upheld by these writers as the safeguard of this personal liberty. It was the conscience of each man that made his action really personal. It put the imprint of right reason on his moral action."[71]

This is to the point and in accord with the evidence and it is worth stressing here that the Anglican casuists saw casuistry not so much as a way of obtaining liberty but as the means for establishing valid principles of action when a doubt had arisen. This was not only due to their turning away from an over-juristic moral theology but to the concept of law already outlined. It is therefore particularly interesting to see how Kelly proceeds from here in close parallelism with the Caroline writers. For him, moral law is the framework of right direction within which human liberty finds its most perfect exercise and fulfilment ("whose service is perfect freedom"). He sees the distinction between law and liberty as valid for human law but not for law in the moral order. This law flows from man's nature and "it is nothing other than the demands of this nature tending to its own natural fulfilment," a phrase that might have come from *The Ecclesiastical Polity*. "Hence," writes Kelly, "it is quite clear that moral science must aim at directing man's life according to these demands of his nature. In other words, it must make the object of its pursuit man's complete fulfilment, the perfection of man. Therefore, any distinction between 'law' and 'liberty' in this sphere is in utter contradiction to this notion. Man arrives at complete liberty only by discovering the full implications of this 'law' and directing his life in accordance with them, since this law is synonymous with man's rational pursuit of his own perfection."[72]

Here, the notes of a remarkable symphony strike upon the ear in which Hooker and Häring, Aquinas and Nicholson, and all whose work in the seventeenth and in the twentieth centuries evinces convergence, are participants. It is enough for the purposes of this essay simply to remind ourselves of the sort of things said in this connection by Hooker, whose writings on law were magisterial for subsequent Anglican theologians. Law is "a directive rule unto goodness of operation." It is a pattern of characteristic behavior through which all things "incline to something which they may be." Law is that which "directeth them in the means whereby they tend to their own perfection." The function of right reason is paramount for man's understanding of and participation in this law: "The nature of goodness being thus ample a law is properly that which reason in such sort defineth to be good that it must be done. And the law of reason or human nature is that which men by discourse of natural reason have rightly found out themselves to be all for ever bound unto in their actions." Hooker goes on to say that although "our sovereign good is desired naturally," yet human nature has been marred so that this desire cannot be fulfilled naturally. A New Law has therefore been given in Christ "to rectify nature's obliquity" and "to teach him how that which is desired naturally must now supernaturally be attained." This new law does not abolish natural law nor does revelation make reason unncessary.[73]

It is in this setting of a living concept of law that the Anglican writers see the individual conscience and its authority and the vital place and function of reason in moral action. To this second feature in Caroline casuistry we may now turn.

The Role of Reason

"For them the part of conscience in the moral life and the part of reason in that life are co-extensive. They insist so vehemently on the power of conscience precisely because they realize so fully the importance of reason in moral actions. It is this latter element which must be seen as the more fundamental."[74] This is easily demonstrable from the works of the Anglican moralists in which "right reason" plays a major role in the responsible exercise of liberty within a dynamic concept of law which itself evokes that responsibility.

Speaking of his casuistic method Jeremy Taylor says, "I affirm nothing but upon grounds of Scripture, or universal tradition, or right reason," thus bringing to moral theology the same general theological method which has come to be an Anglican hallmark. Later in the same account of his method, he adds, "In probabilities, I prefer that which is the more reasonable, never allowing to anyone a leave of choosing that which is confessedly the less reasonable in the whole conjunction of circumstances and relative considerations."[75] South asserts the only rules of conscience to be the "two grand rules of right reason and Scripture."[76] The able casuist Joseph Hall chooses "those decisions, which I hold most conformable to enlightened reason and religion."[77] Sharp's whole approach to the subject turns, as we shall see, on reason and what is reasonable. The position that overemphasis on conscience leads to an intellectualization of the human act, leaving little room for love since everything centers on an act of judgment, is the position of those who picture the moral life as based on the virtues, first among which is charity.

This view gives to prudence as the practical wisdom a very important role. In spite of their stress on conscience, there can be little doubt that their heavy emphasis on "right reason" and on personal freedom in responsibility makes much of this to be implicit in seventeenth-century Anglican moral theology.[78] It is worth nothing that John Wilkins, whose major interest after the new science was moral theology, had something to say about the role of prudence in the totality of human actions. This is not surprising since he uses Aquinas freely and without acknowledgement just as he borrows Sanderson's definition of moral theology without comment on its origin. Wilkins merges the *Summa Theologica's* view of prudence as practical wisdom with the main ideas of the Wisdom books. The chief function of "wisdom or prudence" is to direct, and "this it doth both as to the end and the means." Prudence or wisdom he holds to be at the center of the exercise of the virtues and it "consists in a solid judgement to discern the tempers and interests of men, the state of business, the probabilities of events and consequences, together with a presentness of mind to obviate sudden accidents." It is of interest that although most of Wilkins's surviving sermons deal with practical divinity, he has comparatively little to say in any comprehensive way about conscience.[79]

Methods and Systems

The third and final feature to be noted is their casuistic method itself. The Anglicans of the seventeenth century found themselves in reaction from the probabilism then current, and this explains, but only in part, the position which they took. For the probabilist of their day, the existence of one respectably authoritative opinion in favor of disregarding the law was sufficient to authenticate an action morally, even if more probable opinions supported the law. Anglican moralists held that this put too much at risk and encouraged a casuistry of circumventing law. At that time there certainly was contemporary evidence of abuse. Yet it is only fair to add that today's probabilist would defend the system on the grounds that it has the practical advantage of resolving the agent's indecision. He would maintain moreover that the less probable opinion may conceivably be the true one, and also that probabilism insists in a realistic way that a doubtful obligation does not bind.

A critical reply would be that, even though the outworking of probabilism is frequently similar in effect to the requirements of "right reason," a fundamental difference is at issue. This hinges on the whole idea of what moral theology is about and on the concept of law premised. Should moral theology (given the existence of doubt in a set of circumstances) be concerned with seeking the most reasonable course of action, or should it be seeking a way of turning the doubt into a practical certitude? The latter approach stems from the axioms of jurisprudence and transfers these to the law of the moral order. This is where theologians like Kevin Kelly with his emphasis on the central directive function of prudence find themselves endorsing the Caroline restoration of "right reason" as the norm and guarantor of the full dignity of the responsible human act. This, rather than a system for the solution of doubts, is what he proposes and he holds that this "is in complete accord with the teaching of St. Thomas and these Anglican writers."[80] In fact, Sharp, for example, advises the man who is a prey to equal doubts "on both sides" to consider "what prudential inducements he has to do the action or forbear it."[81]

Caroline reaction against what South termed "that new invented engine of probability"[82] was a unanimous reaction which must be judged in the light of the probabilism they knew. They contended that this system undermined the responsibility and obedience by which their concept of moral theology set such store, and that it adversely affected simplicity and sincerity in making moral choices. Consequently, and in reaction from this situation, they all tended to be probabiliorists of a sort while some leaned to tutiorism, though here much depended on the meaning and use of the term. Kelly commends their "reasonable tutiorism," the adjective being justified by the Caroline refusal to depose the norm of "right reason" in favor of a system.[83]

In differentiating between these two systems, the way in which the Anglicans handled the difference brings out a distinctive quality in their casuistry. Probabiliorism takes the view that where an obligation is involved, it is right to give one's self the benefit of the doubt *only* when freedom from the obligation is more probable than the obligation. The central tenet of tutiorism being that, in a doubt, the safer way must be chosen, it is easy to see how the one can shade into the other. A criticism by modern probabilists is that probabiliorism inevitably leads to tutiorism, and the real practical problem of doubt is to find something, some principle, which makes choice possible. As Taylor put it, "In a doubting conscience the immediate cure is not to choose right but to choose at all."[84]

As ordinarily understood it is fair to say that tutiorism is hardly a working principle for day-to-day use. So why does Kelly speak approvingly of the reasonable tutiorism of the Anglican moralists? The clue is surely in the word "reasonable," and there is additional clarification in the way in which they qualify the term "safest." For them, more probable is generally the equivalent of more reasonable, as when Talor says "In probabilities, I choose that which is more reasonable."[85] When he adds: "In doubts, I choose what is safest" or when Robert Sanderson writes: "In doubtful cases wisdom would that the safer part should be chosen,"[86] does this categorize them as tutiorists *pur sang*? Hardly, because qualifications are at once apparent. For example, Taylor says that tutiorism is "good advice, but not necessarily in all cases" since on occasion it could be simply "a prudent compliance either with a timorous or with an ignorant conscience."[87] On the whole, his view is that "the degrees of safety are left to follow the degrees of probability. For when the safety does not depend upon the matter, it must depend upon the reasons of the inducement: and because the safety must increase consequently to the probability, it is against charity to omit that which is safer, and to choose that which is less safe."[88] Clearly Taylor's tutiorism is qualified by probabiliorism and by what is reasonable. In other words, safer may mean more probable.

One of the few who attempted to clear up this confusion of terms and meanings is John Sharp. His casuistry aims at simplicity and it centralizes the role of reason. Sharp's axiom is "that in all doubtful cases, the side which, all things duly considered, doth appear more reasonable, that is to be chosen."[89] The word "reasonable" has replaced the term "safe": "I do purposely avoid the expressing of it so, because of the uncertain meaning of the *safer side*. For according as that word is expounded . . . so is the rule, so worded, true or false." The analysis is a penetrating one: if safety be taken to mean a course opposed to any danger, this is an inadequate and even an inadvisable rule to follow. If it means taking a course on the safety-first grounds that otherwise some law would be transgressed then a person would be better to opt out of normal society. Sharp asks further if it is always a primary obligation to keep out of danger and suggests that there may be honest and compelling reasons for forsaking the safer course. Accordingly, for Sharp, the safer side means the more reasonable course of action and his definition has something in common with Kelly's view of the directive function of prudence.[90] While Sharp does not use the word here, it is of interest that he does specify prudence as having this function in the case of indifferent actions (i.e., those which are neither commanded nor forbidden): ". . . we are to look upon it as an action in which our conscience is not so much concerned as our prudence." He sums up his own position: "The truth is, when all is said, every man in doubtful cases is left to his own discretion, and if he acts according to the best reason he hath, he is not culpable, though he be mistaken in his measures." Häring's preference is for equi-probabilism: "Equiprobabilism is the sound mean between rigorism and laxism" and it is noteworthy that, in his view, the upholders of this principle "prefer that which is favoured by the better reasons."[91]

Sharp and Sanderson are on the whole very alike in their general approach but in this particular question Sanderson is more tutiorist in the restricted sense of the term. When it is a matter of doubt concerning the lawfulness of the thing itself, he holds that "in such a case the person (if he be *sui juris*) is certainly bound to forbear the doing of that thing of the lawfulness whereof he so doubteth, and if he forbear not, he sinneth . . . and the reason why he ought rather to forbear than to adventure the doing of that whereof he doubteth is, because in doubtful cases wisdom would that the safer part should be chosen." In effect, he is saying that it is better to obey doubtingly than to disobey doubtingly and his definition reads: "that part is safer, which if we choose we are sure we shall do well; than that which if we choose, we know not but we may do ill."[92]

So, seventeenth-century Anglican casuistry takes a shape which with its credits and debits is a distinctly positive shape.

Anglican Moral-Ascetic Theology in Aim and Practice

As we ask ourselves what was the immediate aim of this revised moral theology and how these writers communicated it to the Church in their own day, we are in fact seeking to understand the meaning of membership as they taught it.

If one attempts an analysis of the devotional and catechetical literature of the period one obtains a picture of what membership implied for the seventeenth-century Anglican, both lay and clerical. For the former, what comes through is a practical yet devotional religion in which the details of daily duty were linked with and energized by worship and the sacramental means of grace. It is a picture in which Devotion, Detail and Duty are combined. But at the center of the picture is its true subject which imparts perspective to all the other elements of the composition—what Reynolds called "a branch of the life of Christ in us," the concept of "incorporation," the idea of "life."[93] This is central and this is where the new moral-ascetical theology of seventeenth-century Anglicanism bears directly on the meaning of membership. The parallel with the twentieth-century developments needs no underlining.

As to the clergy in their work, the pastoral pattern as it relates to membership which they set before themselves may also be seen in these books and in other sources as well. It is a pattern in which preaching, catechising and counseling feature prominently. The evidence that this was in fact what was done, often combined with group-meetings such as Baxter's Thursday evenings, is considerable. Taylor, in an episcopal Charge, set out the pattern clearly: "Let every minister teach his people the use, practice, methods and benefits of meditation or mental prayer. ... Let every minister exhort his people to a frequent confession of their sins, and a declaration of the state of their souls; to a conversation with their minister in spiritual things, to an enquiry concerning all parts of their duty: for by preaching, and catechising, and private inter-course, all the needs of souls can best be served; but by preaching alone they cannot."[94]

These handbooks, often used as companions to the Bible and the Prayer Book, constitute a contemporary mirror for membership.[95] They also help us to see how the Caroline view of moral-ascetical theology worked out in pastoral and parochial terms. As to content, one appears to be justified in dividing them roughly into three types. There are books which are purely devotional and there are those in which devotion and practical direction are combined. Then there were the catechetical books which influenced the end-product of Caroline "practical divinity," namely the attitude pro-duced to religion and life. For if character-building for citizenship in the new community was the objective, no detail of how this was to be achieved was neglected. These books, working with the catechism-structure of creed, commandments, prayer and sacra-ments, drew an outline of Christian life in the contemporary world. Taken together, these three types of books give a picture of the kind of membership in the Church at which people were expected to aim. In describing the form and content of that picture, there are certain key-words: duty, devotion, detail, edification, reason, life. Running through the whole is the theme of obedience. It has been said of Isaac Barrow that "his rôle as a preacher was to be an expounder of moral theology."[96] His two favorite terms were obedience and practice, but firmly linked with grace and devotion: "to maintain in us a constant and steady disposition to obedience ... we do need continual supplies of grace from God." It is in this,

Barrow affirms, that "the life of practice" consists for without devotion "darkness" and "a deadening coldness" will result.[97]

As to the books themselves, examples of the first type which is almost entirely devotional are Andrewes's *Preces Privatae* and Cosin's *Collection of Private Devotions*. The second class is the largest and combines devotion and direction. A classic example would be Taylor's *Holy Living* and one can see the type emerging clearly in Richard Sherlock's *The Practical Christian*—a revealing title— which the author describes as "a summary of Christian practice." The third group is represented, as already indicated, by the catechetical books of which there are numerous examples such as those by Andrewes, Sherlock, Nicholson, Beveridge, Hammond and Ken. Partly summaries of doctrine, they contain also a strong directional element. The way in which their use in the parishes was fitted into the general picture of membership has been mentioned and George Herbert makes a contemporary allusion: "The country parson values catechizing highly: "For there being three points of his duty; the one, to infuse a competent knowledge of salvation in every one of his flock; the other, to multiply and build up this knowledge to a spiritual temple; the third, to influence this knowledge, to press and drive it to practice, turning it to reformation of life, by pithy and lively exhortations; catechizing is the first point and but by catechizing, the other cannot be attained."[98] The great importance of this pastoral technique in an age when not everyone was literate is obvious. It is therefore worth attempting to cut a cross-section through this literature for what it reveals about the working out in practice of the principles of Caroline moral-ascetical theology. By and large, the manual on the Christian life tended to be more widely used than the purely devotional books and thus combined with the catechetical handbooks to produce a pattern of membership which has decided characteristics. Both the pattern and the characteristics are the outcome of the view of moral-ascetical theology as practical, positive and concerned with the individual in the whole range of his Christian membership and human experience.

The Idea of Duty

The cross-section will reveal certain layers which run through the material as a whole and one of these is the concept of duty. It is certainly a sinewy concept but by no means a forbidding one. It gave muscle to the practice of membership but the term carried with it nothing of the Pelagian overtones of cold self-reliance. For duty was seen as integrated with devotion and both were means to an end, a new quality of life which Reynolds describes as "the life of Christ fashioned in our nature and conversation."[99] Barrow explicitly includes the whole idea of duty within that charity which is the fulfilling of the law: "Scripture . . . often expresses charity to be the fulfilling of God's law, as the best expression of all our duty toward God, of faith in Him, love and reverence of Him; and as either formally containing or naturally producing all our duty toward our neighbour."[100] It is true that *The Whole Duty of Man*, one of the most influential of this second class of books, lowers the temperature somewhat and becomes pedestrian at times. Yet it spoke to the needs of the day and it firmly fixed a goal of practical duty for the ordinary member of the Church. Thus, the clear-cut position occupied in the picture by the idea of duty owes a lot to this bestselling manual. But more still is owed to the Church Catechism with its two Duties memorized by everyone in his youth. Nor does it escape us that the two Duties are duties to love, followed in the Catechism by "the Desire" and by the catechist's insistence that these duties cannot be performed without "special grace" and "diligent prayer."

Furthermore, popular books such as *The Whole Duty of Man*, Taylor's *Holy Living* and Andrewes's *Pattern*, are built around the verse "live soberly, righteously and godly in this present world." This theme was reinforced daily for the worshipper by the words of the General Confession, "a godly, righteous and sober life," for here is crystallized men's threefold duty, to God, the neighbor and themselves. So, by the liturgy, by the catechism and by popular manuals of membership, the idea of duty became a central one absorbed into the whole approach of men to life, living and Christian practice. It goes a long way to explaining the term "practical divinity," for with these writers the idea of duty is inseparable from the idea of grace, and both are means to an end. More and Scougal describe that end as the Divine Life which is rooted in obediential faith and which branches out into charity and humility. In a book, significantly entitled *The Divine Life*, Baxer summed up: "It is an infinite value that is put upon the blood of Christ, the promises of God, the ordinances and means of grace, and grace itself, and the poorest duties of the poorest saints, because they are for an infinite, eternal glory . . . no action is low that aims at heaven."[101] The whole purpose of Jeremy Taylor's *Holy Living* is to explain the Christian's duty and to relate to this the help of grace through prayer and sacrament as men face the external and internal obstacles to that duty. He wrote that "It is infallibly certain that there is a heaven for all the godly and for me amongst them, if I do my duty."[102]

It is the way in which this idea of duty is related to devotional practice as the means and to the Christian life-pattern as the end which imparts sweetness as well as strength to the Anglican piety of the period. These books are strongly sacramental and lay firm emphasis on prayer and meditation, but the objective is always present. The heart of this matter, writes Scougal, is not just in orthodoxy or in keeping the rules, but is only understood in terms of "union," "participation in the divine nature . . . or in the Apostle's phrase, it is Christ formed in us."[103] Significantly, his book is called *The Life of God in the Soul of Man*. In the works of Henry More the same theme appears and is developed with greater depth of treatment, just as it appears in the writings of his fellow Cambridge Platonist John Smith.

Devotional Practice, Detail and Edification

The cross-section further reveals other strata which are equally characteristic, in their several proportions, of this thoroughly integrated approach to membership, its meaning and implications. The emphasis on duty is integrated with the stress on grace and the goal of moral-ascetical theology is seen to be part and parcel of a sacramental religion in which the practices and ordinances of religion are closely related to the living of our lives as members of the new community of faith. As it reminds men of individual duties and of social justice, this approach to religion is at the same time constantly reminding them that this life of day-to-day membership and the divine life which activates it are all of one piece here and now and in the future: "It is the same moral and spiritual life which shall have no end, but endure to eternity" wrote Richard Baxter in *The Divine Life*, "It is a living to God in love; but only initial, and very imperfect here."[104]

This pervading sense of the goal and the objective is what underlies the concern with detail and with the building up in membership ("edification" as they phrase it) evident in these handbooks. Duty is there in the setting of sacrament, prayer and grace, so that the solid and substantial type of religion inculcated by these books, with their reasonableness and sturdiness, is lightened and warmed by a fervor, a sweetness and sureness of touch and an awareness of human grandeur and failure. The earnest realism of *The Whole Duty of Man* is balanced by a devotion of the Sacred Humanity in Anthony Horneck and Jeremy Taylor and even in Isaac Barrow. This is the direct consequence of their view of moral-ascetical theology as one discipline concerned with one total area, the life of the Christian in the Church seen in terms of union, incorporation and imitation. What constitutes then this concept of edification is not only duty and devotion but detail. This is where application enters men's Monday mornings—hence "practical divinity." Yet it is the elements of devotion and duty which rescue Jeremy Taylor's "Live by rule" from asphyxiation by legalistic fussiness.

These books link carefulness to prayerfulness with a view to character-building in membership (edification) and the ultimate objective is never lost sight of in the process. It is a building up in "obediential faith" since the response to the New Law is that of faith. This is the real context of their concern with detail. William Law could use Taylor's phrase "live by rule" and he could write of the need for "religious exactness" but the main theme runs through all: "For till goodness comes from a life within us, we have in truth none at all."[105] This is the continual reference back for Law's "religious use of everything we have." It is seen with equal clarity in Lewis Bayly's *The Practice of Piety* which achieved at least fifty printings and translation into four languages in its day. It was part of Mrs. Bunyan's modest dowry and it influenced her husband. It is the stress on becoming "a new creature" which motivates the book's detailed devotion, with its prayers for different situations as a man endeavors to bring life's varied aspects into a daily program. Scougal sees the necessity of such a rule but warns against "fettering ourselves by some devices of our own to Rules and Forms which we will always adhere to" for these are only means to an end, the new life in the new community: it is "a union of the soul with God, a real participation of the Divine nature ... or in the apostle's phrase, it is Christ formed in us."[106]

The same due proportion as between the objective and the helps to achieving it is observed by the lay-theologian Robert Nelson in his *The Practice of True Devotion, in Relation to the End, as well as the Means of Religion* (1698). The book recommends "the exact performance of duties" by a full program of private prayer, daily Church attendance where possible, of rules for rising and going to bed, for business and recreation, for means and fasting. Prayer and discipline, self-examination and Communion are the foundations of what Nelson calls "solid and substantial piety," and all is set within a deep awareness of the Catholicity of the living Church. Yet these are but the means to the end, "that we should become new creatures."[107] As we remarked earlier, the *kaine ktisis* is an ever-present reality for the Anglican theory and practice of moral-ascetical theology. This relating of means to end in a time perspective is what Nelson's book is all about, and he insists too, as does Thomas

Comber (who wrote another of these books)[108] on the relationship of private to public worship. Indeed, the liturgy in a constitutive element in the piety promoted by all three divisions of these manuals. The context of seventeenth-century Anglican spirituality is as ecclesial and liturgical as it is personal. Books of the first type such as John Cosin's *Collection of Private Devotions* (1627) display both a depth of liturgical devotion and the same attention to detail. Prayers are provided for every occasion, even for waking or going out or when the clock strikes. Yet even here it is moral-ascetical theology which forms the practice of piety. Examination by the decalogue points on to the emerging type of book like that of Robert Sherlock in which this was a feature. Indeed such books lead straight in to the catechetical handbooks already mentioned which had such an influence in presenting to the ordinary Christian that picture of membership which is the end-product of Caroline moral-ascetical theology. These books cover a wide range—prayer, sacraments, worship, faith, hope and love and a variety of problems such as duels, divorce, usury, suicide, sabbatarianism, commercial ethics, the duties of different callings—in short, the real world of the seventeenth-century Anglican. In that world, the Christian pattern unfolds for each life as the Life transforms life: "Only remember what the love of God requires of us is an operative, material and communicative love; 'If ye love me, keep my commandments,' so that still a good life is the effect of the sublimest meditation." So wrote Jeremy Taylor in *The Great Exemplar*[109] and there is little more to be said. All the key words are there in those "sums of divinity" as the Carolines called the catethetical books, for they summed up instruction in doctrine, devotion and practical teaching for living. The aim of the whole operation, says the author of one of them, was to produce a generation "steadfast in the Faith and sincere in their obedience."[110] The context of that obedience and indeed its content also was love's response to love incarnate, "If ye love me, keep my commandments." That love to which men respond within the household of faith is incarnate in the person of the Son, so that in a moment of simplicity Edward Reynolds could write "Christ and the Christian are but one."[111] So we come full circle through the centuries back to the sort of thing Bernard Häring has been saying to this generation: "Christian morality is life flowing from the victory of Christ ... all men are called to share in this union with Christ through imitation of Him. To be mystically identified with Christ, to live in Christ, means to be a member of His Body, to be made a subject of His Kingdom."[112]

Postscript

In compiling this assessment of Anglican moral theology in the seventeenth century I have made use of two sources of my own. Clearly the first is *The Structure of Caroline Moral Theology* (1949) but the reader will have noted that there is much additional material in the present analysis as compared with the earlier publication. There is furthermore a fresh evaluation of the whole subject in the light of developments in moral theology generally since 1949. The other source used here is the part-content of a section from my Scott Holland lectures. These lectures, given at the invitation of the trustees of the Holland Trust, were delivered in 1973 but not subsequently published. They covered a wider field (in which the Anglican moralists of the seventeenth century were only a part of the whole) but I have made a full use of that section in the foregoing chapter. The publication of the present volume has afforded a welcome opportunity to assess the Carolines anew in relation to the radical changes in the perspective, content and method of modern moral theology, so much of which the Anglicans strikingly anticipated in their own remarkably prophetic handling of "practical divinity."

Politics and the Kingdom: The Legacy of the Anglican Left

by John Richard Orens

Mention of Christian Socialism no longer provokes, as it once did, the complaint that noun and adjective have rarely been so mismatched.[1] But although the term itself has become familiar, the idea behind it remains alien to many Anglicans. There is a dim awareness of the work of F. D. Maurice, Charles Kingsley, and other nineteenth-century clerics who adopted the name Christian Socialist, but more often than not their labors are seen as an example of Victorian philanthropy, worthy enough at the time but of little interest in the age of the welfare state. Conservative Anglicans, therefore, have found it easy to argue that the social activism which swept the Church during the 1960s was an aberration with no roots in the Anglican past. Radicals in the Church, taking these self-appointed guardians of the faith at their word, have been quick to embrace political and theological nostrums from every conceivable tradition except their own.[2] Yet there is an embarrassment of riches in the history of Anglican social protest. To be sure, Christian Socialism has always been the faith of a small minority. But these gallant men and women have had an influence far greater than their number would suggest because they thought deeply, felt passionately, and based their efforts not upon any secular ideology, but upon Scripture and the creeds, remaining faithful throughout to the incarnationalism which has become the hallmark of Anglican theology.[3] Thus, to study their labors is to enter into a godly heritage which can help and sustain our own attempts to bring God's justice to the world.

Much has been made of the fact that the man whom Anglican radicals have revered as their spiritual father was himself fearful of radicalism. And it cannot be disputed that Frederick Denison Maurice (1805–1872), around whom the first group of Christian Socialists gathered in 1848, was an unlikely candidate for the role he was to play. Respectful of tradition and committed to the *via media* in an era of bitter ecclesiastical and secular controversy, Maurice spent much of his time seeking to reconcile the seemingly irreconcilable. His conception of the Church as at once Catholic and Protestant, liberal and orthodox, free and established was matched by his vision of the ideal State as at once monarchical, aristocratic and democratic. But Maurice was neither an ecclesiastical statesman nor a politician. He was a prophet whose vision, however imperfectly expressed, retains its compelling power.[4]

"The great body of Englishmen is becoming utterly indifferent to us all," Maurice lamented in 1850, "smile grimly and contemptuously at our controversies and believe that no help is to come to their suffering from any of us."[5] The Evangelicals had awakened the Church to the need for holiness; the Tractarians had sounded the clarion of apostolic authority; liberals had kept the Church mindful of the demands of reason. Yet the people were starving for lack of the bread of life. More clearly than most of his contemporaries, Maurice understood the sickness that was sapping the strength of the English Church. Taking the Fall as their starting point, Evangelicals had tried to frighten people into repentance, warning that the gaping jaws of hell would surely swallow up the unconverted. The Tractarians brought a renewed emphasis on the Incarnation, and with it a greater respect for human nature and the created world. But they too believed that there can be only enmity between God and the great mass of unconverted humanity. Even those made regenerate by baptism can be easily plunged into eternal death by post-baptismal sin. This bleak view of the prospects of enjoying the world to come was more than matched by the gloom with which Anglicans of all parties regarded the prospects of joy in this world. For the overwhelming majority of men and women, they believed, God has ordained a life of poverty and pain. The duty of the poor was to patiently endure their suffering, remembering the catechism exhortation to order themselves "lowly and reverently before (their) betters." The well-to-do had a responsibility to be charitable; some Evangelicals had gone further and pressed for laws to abolish slavery and to protect workers from the worst ravages of the Industrial Revolution. But poverty and inequality themselves could never be eliminated.

> The rich man in his castle,
> The poor man at his gate:
> God made them high and lowly,
> And ordered their estate.

This was the good news the Church of England preached to the poor.

The tragedy, Maurice was quick to point out, is that the Church has good news for the poor. Made in the image of God, the destiny of every man and woman is to sit at the right hand of the Most High. We do not need to live in fear of our maker because no sin, not even the Fall itself, can alter the fact that God is our loving Father. It is this truth which was revealed in the person of Jesus Christ. The Incarnation was not the temporary sojourn among us of the second Abraham, but the presence in our midst of the second Adam, the head of humanity and the ground of our being.[6] Had Maurice preached only this he would have been embroiled in controversy. Indeed, it was because he doubted that anyone could so resist the love of God as to be doomed to endless torment that he lost his lectureship in theology at King's College, London in 1854. But Maurice taught more than that we would all go to Heaven when we died. He insisted that the Kingdom of God has been established on earth. This world is no mere antechamber to a ghostly world to come, for it is on earth that God's loving purpose is to be accomplished. Human society, he argued, like human nature itself has been hallowed by the Incarnation. It was this belief that humanity, created in the image of the social God, is bound together in Christ, and the conviction that divine justice demanded justice on earth that led Maurice and his friends—Charles Kingsley, John Malcolm Ludlow, Thomas Hughes, and others—to call themselves Christian Socialists, much to the dismay of High and Low Churchmen alike.

To be sure, Maurice never explained precisely what he meant by Christian Socialism. Indeed, apart from supporting trade unions and cooperative workshops, he had no program for the reformation of society. The abolition of private property he dismissed as unthinkable. Moreover, so suspicious was he of anything savoring of party in Church or State that it was with considerable relief that he watched his little Christian Socialist group disband in the mid-1880s. But although his practical accomplishments were few, Maurice bequeathed a valuable theological legacy. He was one of the first prominent churchmen to insist that suffering and injustice be abolished rather than endured; that competition be replaced by cooperation; and that it is God's will that all men and women, not merely the well-to-do, be graced with life, joy and hope. By emphasizing Christ's redemption of our social life, by teaching that God's Kingdom is to be realized on earth, and by forcefully calling upon

Anglicans to return to "the churchmanship of the love of God," Maurice was able to bear powerful witness against the fashionable heresy that Christian morality must bow down before the laws of political economy.[7] It was these principles which were to nourish the second—and more radical—generation of Christian Socialists, the most courageous of whom was Stewart Headlam (1847–1924).[8]

As a young man, Headlam had been dismayed by the religious controversies which threatened to tear the Victorian Church apart. His father's Evangelical faith was too gloomy to appeal to the high-spirited lad. But Headlam, like Maurice, found the Tractarians little better. Although attracted by their worship, he was offended by their emphasis on human sinfulness and their insistence upon the doctrine of everlasting damnation. While a student at Cambridge he went to hear the celebrated Dr. Pusey preach, only to leave the church depressed. All Pusey had spoken about, Headlam later complained, was death and the imminence of death, at a time when what concerned Headlam was "life and the living of it more abundantly."[9] As for the Broad Church party, although he had no quarrel with their biblical criticism, Headlam found their theology pale and unattractive.

It is hardly surprising, then, that when Maurice arrived at Cambridge in 1866 to take up his post as Professor of Moral Theology, Headlam quickly became one of his most fervent disciples. Here at last was a theologian whose views were both orthodox and humane. To follow Maurice was no easy thing in those days. Headlam offended his Evangelical bishop—John Jackson of London—and lost his first curacy because of his outspoken belief in universal salvation. But despite his unpopular ideas, once ordained to the priesthood Headlam seemed destined to secure for himself a safe, if not exalted, position in the Church of England. Appointed in 1875 to a curacy at St. Matthew's, Bethnal Green—one of the largest parishes in the poverty-stricken East End of London—Headlam proved himself to be a tireless worker whose labors won the love and respect of his working-class congregation. His rector, Septimus Hansard, himself a friend of Maurice and Kingsley, could not have been more delighted with his new assistant. But soon Headlam's principles would bring the young man to blows with both Hansard and Bishop Jackson.

Like most of Maurice's disciples, Hansard had advanced little beyond well-meaning calls for cooperative workshops and the establishment of responsible trade unions. But faced with the appalling poverty of the East End, and with the indifference of the upper classes to its inhabitants, Headlam abandoned Maurice's faith in the beneficence of the well-to-do and the strange notion that socialism need not touch the privileges of the well-born and the well-heeled. The time has come, he thundered from the pulpit, to abolish the class system itself. He exhorted the poor to be filled with righteous indignation so that they could accomplish this revolutionary purpose themselves, rather than waiting in vain for the help of middle-class clerics and philanthropists.[10] Distressed though Hansard was by this radical rhetoric, he was more appalled still by Headlam's surprising adoption of the trappings of Anglo-Catholic ritualism; a step so remarkable and so prophetic of the direction the Christian Socialist movement would take that it demands special attention.

Like Maurice, the Tractarians had denounced the Church's subservience to the upper classes. But Tory in their politics, fearful of change in Church and State, and isolated from the harsh reality of life in the growing industrial slums, the Oxford Apostolicals could do little more than wring their hands at the suffering around them.[11] The character of Anglo-Catholicism began to change when the movement left the confines of Oxford in the 1850s and 1860s. Although most Anglo-Catholic clergy found comfortable livings, others, led by their sense of priestly vocation, ventured into the neglected and poverty-stricken districts of the nation's cities. Left behind were the academic concerns of Oxford in the Tractarian reverence for ecclesiastical authority. In their place the "slum ritualists" brought a rough and simple faith expressed in beautiful, although often eccentric, ceremonial, and a pastoral zeal which compelled them to champion the cause of their parishioners against slum lords, sweatshop owners, and even bishops. The ritualists were not theologians, and were hard pressed to explain just why they had decided to meddle in wordly matters. But neither their lack of theological sophistication, nor the puzzlement of their fellow churchmen, kept them from doing God's work among the poor.

It was the example of these selfless priests, many of whom he met in East London, that led Headlam to take the side of the Anglo-Catholic party. The Catholic faith—in particular its sacramentalism, its organic conception of the Church, and its profound reverence for the Incarnation—he came to regard as the only possible foundation of Maurice's humane theology. In the Mass, Headlam now saw the liturgical embodiment of Maurice's vision. The beauty of ritualistic worship, he contended, was itself a powerful witness against the Manichean God of gloom whose frightful visage Maurice had tried to banish from the English Church. "[W]e worship not to bribe an angry God," Headlam explained, "but to give thanks to a loving one; not to wring something out of Him, but to give something to Him. Our worship, our adoration must be Eucharistic; all joy, mirth, beauty are sanctified by it."[12] But if all joy, mirth, and beauty are sanctified by the Mass, what does this mean for the multitudes denied those gifts by poverty? Headlam's answer was uncompromising. The God of beauty is also the God of justice; the incarnate Lord present in the Mass is none other than the revolutionary carpenter of Nazareth. Thus, the Eucharistic feast is the universal Passover, the foretaste of the messianic banquet. The holy communion, he wrote with startling directness, pledges all who partake to be holy communists.[13] In this way did Headlam join the sacramentalism of the Tractarians with the social gospel of Maurice.

The poor people of Bethnal Green heard Headlam gladly; their rector did not. Septimus Hansard had no stomach for truly revolutionary politics. As for Headlam's newfound Catholicism, Hansard feared that if left unchecked it would lead to civil war at St. Matthew's and the descent of Catholic zealots and Protestant extremists upon the parish. A way had to be found to rid himself of his meddlesome assistant. He did not have to wait for long. In October 1877 Headlam gave a talk at a local workingmen's club on the virtues of theatres and music halls. There was nothing in his lecture which would be found shocking or even controversial today. His purpose was simply to vindicate the right of his overworked parishioners to enjoy the "bright and pretty" entertainment of the popular stage. But at a time when a bishop was forced to attend *Hamlet* incognito lest his presence cause a scandal, Headlam's argument was bound to raise a storm, particularly because, among other things, he urged young women to emulate the example of their spirited sisters in the chorus line.[14] Bishop Jackson was furious, and the Evangelical prelate's anger was further provoked when Headlam replied to his criticism by insisting that music-hall entertainment—scanty costumes, beer drinking, and the rest—was justified by the doctrine of the Real Presence. This was not, as it might first appear, mere verbal fencing. Headlam took his faith with the utmost seriousness. He was convinced that a truly incarnational theology must have a place for the simple pleasures of this life. But Jackson had neither the patience nor the sympathy to understand Headlam's point of view. The Bishop continued to hurl invectives, and Hansard, taking advantage of the dispute, quickly sacked his curate.

Headlam now entered the ecclesiastical wilderness. Every cure he was to hold he soon lost; after 1883 he never again held a church appointment. For many years he was even denied a license in the diocese of London, first by Bishop Jackson and then by his successor, Frederick Temple. Yet Headlam would not submit. On the contrary, he became even more outspoken. He defended the right of atheists to sit in Parliament; he won election to the London School Board on a platform of free secular education and the abolition of Church schools; he went bail for Oscar Wilde; and he never stopped preaching the revolutionary gospel of the Kingdom of God. Neither did he once consider resigning his orders or leaving the Church. What others took to be the idiosyncratic enthusiasms of an unorthodox cleric were, instead, the passions of a man deeply committed to the Gospel and determined to vindicate God in the eyes of the poor and the powerless. Fortunately, Headlam did not have to battle alone. In his struggles he had the support of the Guild of St. Matthew, a society of determined Christian Socialists which grew out of the communicants' guild he had founded in Bethnal Green. Although small—it never had more than four hundred members—the guild numbered among its adherents many of the most talented priests in the Church of England.[15] The story of the guild and of its irrepressible Warden is one of the most entertaining chapters in modern Church history. But it is the theology upon which Headlam's varied crusades were based which concerns us here. This theology played an important part in determining the course of Anglican social protest. It stands, moreover, as a challenge to our current enchantments with other-worldly spirituality and shallow activism.[16]

Like Maurice, Headlam forcefully insisted that Christian faith is trust in a divine person, not belief in a set of metaphysical postulates. The first question of theology, therefore, is: "Who is God?" The obvious answer, enshrined in the creeds but overlooked in practice, is that God is our loving Father. Surely Headlam argued, this can only mean that God wants to save us all, that he wants us to be happy, that he wants us to live together as brothers and sisters in Christ. If Christians will but take these simple truths seriously, they will quickly find themselves in the vanguard of the struggle for social justice. The same is true of anyone who understands the Incarnation. Headlam never tired of contending that the doctrine of the Incarnation is not a philosophical exercise. To say that God became Man is to assert the high estate to which the whole human race is called. The fact that God became incarnate in the person of

Jesus Christ reveals how different He is from the gloomy portraits painted by misguided pietists. God is no aloof tyrant or ghostly abstraction. In his earthly life he had healed the sick, driven the money changers from the temple, and preached good news to the poor. Uncomfortable though it must be for conventional Christians, Headlam argued, the poor can take heart in the knowledge that the fullness of God's love was made manifest in a revolutionary carpenter from Nazareth.

These great truths, Headlam believed, are set forth in the sacraments, particularly baptism and the Eucharist. By admitting infants to baptism, the Church is clearly proclaiming the equality of all human beings in the sight of God. Rich and poor, noble and commoner, are washed in the same water, raised to the same life, made brothers and sisters in Christ. Throughout their lives, moreover, Christians are fed with the same food: the body and blood of their risen and revolutionary Lord. Far from being essentially an opportunity for personal communion, the Eucharist is the feast of the Kingdom which sanctifies the longings of oppressed humanity. It is important to note here that underlying Headlam's treatment of the sacraments is a refusal to make a sharp distinction between natural and supernatural grace. Creation itself, he argued, is a sacrament: an outward and visible sign of inward and spiritual grace. Baptism and the Eucharist, therefore, are more than effective signs of the Kingdom; they point to God's abiding presence in his world. To be a sacramentalist, Headlam insisted, is to cherish earthly love, beauty, and fellowship, and to reject puritanical otherworldliness. It is no coincidence, he observed shrewdly, that modern puritans have no use for any pleasure except the pleasure of making money.[17]

Headlam was not an academic theologian and his ideas, developed in the heat of battle and expressed in fragmentary form in sermons and pamphlets, sometimes seemed crude and idiosyncratic. But contrary to appearances, he was a remarkably perceptive thinker whose work laid the foundation for nearly all subsequent radical Anglican theology. It was Headlam who first clearly pointed out the relation between the Incarnation and the sacraments on the one hand, and the struggle for justice on the other. Almost alone among his contemporaries, Headlam saw the Mass as a feast of liberation. Instead of jettisoning Scripture, creeds, and the Prayer Book, he clung to them as charters of the coming Kingdom of God far more revolutionary than the manifestos of the secular Left. Indeed, it was his conviction that clergy eager for social reform would do well to first tend to their priestcraft before plunging into social work. There is nothing wrong with trying to meet the needs of poor parishioners, he observed, but far more important is witnessing to the Gospel so effectively that the poor themselves are stirred to do God's work.[18] In short, Headlam taught those Anglican socialists who came after him that Christianity is never more radical than when it is orthodox.

To be sure, not everyone on the Anglican Left was willing to accept Headlam's leadership. For all the respect and affection in which they held him, many Christians who shared his concerns found Headlam too strident and his politics too revolutionary. Others were distressed by his defense of the music hall and scandalized by the compassion he showed sexual offenders: adulterers, homosexuals, and prostitutes.[19] Thus, by the end of the 1880s, other groups proclaiming the social gospel began to appear. The largest and most important of these was the Christian Social Union which grew out of the same liberal Catholic circle led by Charles Gore (1855–1932) which produced the controversial *Lux Mundi* essays. On the surface, the contrast between the new organization and the Guild of St. Matthew was striking. In its desire to attract as broad a membership as possible, the Union deliberately avoided taking a stand on controversial issues whether political or theological. Bishops and academics flocked to the Union precisely because it gave them an opportunity to show their concern for the poor without requiring that they do very much about it. The Union's first president, Bishop Westcott of Durham, had not advanced much beyond Maurice's vague political views. Understandably, Headlam and his friends were impatient with their respectable rival's timidity. "Here's a glaring social evil," they would announce mockingly, "let's read a paper about it."[20] Gazing at the prelates who entered the Union, members of the Guild could console themselves with the fact that only one of their company had become a bishop.[21]

But such criticism was not entirely fair. The research and papers which the Guild looked down upon played an important part in awakening the Church to its social responsibilities, and in strengthening the efforts of sympathetic members of Parliament to pass valuable reform legislation.[22] Moreover, despite the caution of some of its members, the Union did much to spread the ideals to which Headlam had borne such faithful witness. The Union's statement of principles was almost indistinguishable from that of the Guild. In particular, like the Guild, the Union insisted that the Gospel, not the dicta of political economists, was the standard of economic and political morality. "Christian Law," it proclaimed, "[is] the ultimate authority to rule social practice."[23] Charles Gore and Henry Scott Holland (1847–1918), the two men most responsible for founding the Union, shared Headlam's conviction that a right understanding of the Incarnation would compel Christians to take the needs of the world seriously and, therefore, to struggle against social injustice. Even more important, they were sophisticated theologians capable of presenting these ideas systematically, a task which was beyond Headlam's grasp. Indeed, *Lux Mundi* itself, although remembered primarily as a landmark in the reconciliation of Anglo-Catholicism and biblical criticism, was devoted in large part to presenting an incarnational understanding of nature and society very much like that of Maurice and Headlam.[24] Undoubtedly the donnishness of the Union's leaders was a disadvantage. Unlike Headlam, Gore and Holland were never altogether comfortable with workingmen or Bohemians. But their academic respectability won them a hearing in circles deaf to the pleas of the Guild of St. Matthew.[25]

Whatever the differences between the Guild and the Union, together they pushed the Anglican Left down a path which would have startled Maurice. From a vague call for understanding between classes and voluntary cooperation, Christian Socialism had been transformed into a clarion call against class privilege. Legislative redress, which the early Christian Socialists had regarded with suspicion save in exceptional cases—sanitary reform and the protection of trade unions, for example—was not being actively sought. From a cause with a humane but ill-defined piety, it had become militantly sacramental. Significantly, the same changes were transforming the face of Christian Socialism in the American Episcopal Church. Bishop Frederick Dan Huntington (1819–1904), the first president of the Church Association for the Advancement of the Interests of Labor (CAIL), edged away from his former confidence in class cooperation and asked angrily how long the rich could expect to escape the fires of judgment.[26] His son James (1854–1935), a charter member of CAIL and the founder of the Order of the Holy Cross, was even more outspoken, denouncing the condescending philanthropy of the rich as strongly as did Stewart Headlam.[27] As in England, moreover, the leadership of the Christian Socialist movement tended to come from the ranks of the High Church party. To be sure, Anglo-Catholics did not dominate the Anglican Left in the United States to the same extent as they did in Britain. William Dwight Porter Bliss (1856–1926), for example, a member of CAIL and the head of the American branch of the Christian

Social Union, was both an unabashed socialist and a liberal Evangelical. But like their High Church friends, Bliss and others like him insisted on the indissolubility of right doctrine and social justice.[28] Indeed, to the dismay of many a conservative, Christian Socialism, at least the vague sort represented by the Christian Social Union, was well on the way to becoming the conventional wisdom not only of the Church of England, but of the Anglican communion.[29] Yet despite these accomplishments, by the turn of the century it was obvious that they were not enough to enable Christian Socialists to face the challenge of a new age.

The issue which brought the Anglican Left to a crisis was political, or so it seemed. Headlam and most of his contemporaries, while eager to work with radicals of all sorts, had held themselves aloof from the new Labour party, suspicious of its habit of identifying socialism with trade unionism, and fearful of identifying the Kingdom of God with the demands of any secular movement, however noble. Young Christian Socialists, on the other hand, were appalled by what they perceived to be their elders' middle-class prejudice. The failure of either the Guild of St. Mathew or the Christian Social Union to win substantial numbers of workers to the Christian Socialist cause they regarded as evidence of the urgent need to draw closer to the secular Left. In 1906 they founded the Church Socialist League—an American branch was organized in 1911—with the avowed goal of breaking once and for all with ecclesiastical paternalism. One young radical captured the new mood tersely. The Church faced a simple choice, William Temple (1881–1944) declared: socialism or heresy.[30]

But no sooner had the League been organized than its creators discovered that the debate over political strategy had concealed the real questions dividing Christian Socialists. Was their goal to win the nation to socialism, the Church to socialism, or socialists to the Church? If Christian Socialism and secular socialism shared the same goals, did this mean that the Kingdom of Heaven could be ushered in by act of Parliament? Was Christianity nothing more than "the religion of which socialism is the practice?" Was the League to hold fast to the Catholic principles of the Guild of St. Matthew, adopt the looser theology of the Christian Social Union, or open its doors to Christians regardless of creed or denomination? By 1914, unable to reach a decision on these thorny questions, the Church Socialist League was in disarray. The First World War, which did so much to shatter the liberal idealism of Christians and secularists alike, all but killed it as it did the League in the United States. For a time, indeed, it appeared as if the Christian Socialist movement itself had reached a dead end. This is not to say that there was a wave of conservative sentiment among Anglicans. On the contrary, the belief that the Gospel demanded social reform had all but become the official position of the Church of England and, indeed, of the American Episcopal Church.[31] Socialist priests were no longer the rarity they had been only a few years earlier. Instead it was the old-fashioned apostles of individualism and condescending mission work who now felt out of place.[32] But with the general acceptance of Christian social responsibility there was a loss of prophetic fire. The vision of the Kingdom of God which had animated the work of Maurice, Headlam, Gore, and Holland was in danger of being replaced by the politics of the Welfare State. William Temple expressed the new mood well when he abandoned his fiery call for socialism, advocating instead "steady, gradual, yet perceptible conservative reform."[33] Fortunately, this excessive caution did not go unchallenged. Two figures emerged who, in very different ways, reasserted and developed the revolutionary insights of pre-war Christian Socialism.

A veteran of the Guild of St. Matthew, Percy Widdrington (1873–1959) had been one of the Young Turks who had helped organize the Church Socialist League.[34] During his years as Vicar of St. Peter's, Coventry there was no parish priest as stalwart a champion of the Mass and the Labour party than he. But Widdrington was never altogether comfortable with either the Church Socialist League or the Labour party. Like Headlam, he feared that the secular Left had abandoned socialism for the more attainable goal of bureaucratic collectivism. Even more distressing, Christian Socialists, in their eagerness to draw closer to the working class, were either unable or unwilling to criticize this change in direction. If the soul of the Left were to be saved, Widdrington argues, there would have to be a return to first principles. In particular, it was the duty of Anglican radicals to develop a Christian sociology which could then serve to guide the Church in making economic and political decisions. Although too academic to appeal to impatient activists, Widdrington's plea did not fall upon deaf ears. Indeed, in the years just before the First World War there had been widespread dissatisfaction among radical intellectuals, both Christian and secular, with the direction the socialist movement was taking.[35] But it was not until 1921 that Widdrington and some friends produced their manifesto: a volume of essays significantly entitled *The Return of Christendom*.[36]

In many ways, the book hearkened back to the days of Headlam, Gore, and Holland, particularly in its insistence on the necessity of

Catholic dogmas as the basis of social reform.[37] But whereas the earlier Christian Socialists had devoted most of their attention to the problem of poverty, Widdrington and his circle were concerned with the spiritual sickness of industrial society. Capitalism, they agreed, encourages a false and exaggerated individualism: an ideology of production for the sake of production, and profit for the sake of profit. Self-expression and pride in one's craft are being crushed by this Mammon-worshiping civilization. Unfortunately, neither collectivism nor communism offers any hope of challenge. Both seem interested in little more than determining who should profit from the industrial machine. The only cure for our diseased society, the essayists argued, is a return to the principles of Christian society, to the reestablishment of the medieval idea of Christendom.[38]

All the contributors to *The Return of Christendom* were aware that their argument could be interpreted as a call for retreat from radical politics and even from the modern world itself. They went to great lengths, therefore, to insist that although they were no longer prepared to identify themselves with the rest of the socialist movement, they had no intention of giving up the struggle against capitalism. "In the light of the Incarnation," Lionel Thornton declared, "the present social order is an open denial of Christ; for it condemns the majority of mankind to be economic slaves ministering to the selfishness of the minority. To acquiesce in it is to crucify Christ afresh."[39] For Widdrington, Christian sociology was anything but an intellectual diversion. The Church Quiescent and "capitalist plutocracy" were still the enemy, he believed, but before they could be fought effectively the gospel of the Kingdom of God would have to be restored to its proper place as the "regulative principle of theology." Once "aflame with the faith of the Kingdom," he wrote excitedly, the Church "will be compelled to adopt towards our industrial system the same attitude which our missionaries take toward the social order of heathendom. It will then challenge the Industrial World as it challenged the forces of Roman Imperialism in the days of persecution." Lest anyone underestimate how revolutionary a task it was that he had in mind, Widdrington declared that making the Kingdom of God the foundation of theology would effect a "Reformation in comparison to which the Reformation of the sixteenth century will seem a small thing."[40]

It was with such a Reformation in mind that in 1923 Widdrington launched the League for the Kingdom of God to which many former members of the Church Socialist League flocked. Living as we do in an age in which doctrine is not taken seriously, it may seem strange that so much hope could be placed in something so arcane as the regulative principle of theology. Were we to recognize that Christian belief is more than mere intellectual assent, nothing would seem more appropriate than beginning the awesome task of challenging the Church and the world with study and theological renewal. Indeed, a whole generation of Anglicans could trace their commitment to social change to the Anglo-Catholic Summer School of Sociology which Widdrington and the League for the Kingdom of God helped establish in 1924. But although Widdrington helped shape the thinking of many concerned Anglicans, the great Reformation he sought did not come to pass. As his interest turned increasingly away from day-to-day politics, the League found that it had less and less to do. Within a decade it had virtually disappeared. What survived was the Christendom Group, an intellectual fellowship that had grown out of the circle responsible for *The Return to Christendom*. Here the work of developing a Christian sociology continued. Unfortunately, despite the undeniable talent of its members and the respect in which its work was held, the Christendom Group had a direct influence only on a relatively small number of Anglo-Catholics.[41]

With hindsight, it is easy to understand why Widdrington and his friends failed to accomplish as much as they might have. For all their high hopes and often stirring rhetoric, they never seemed sure of what it was they wanted to do. Theirs was not merely an academic venture, yet so determined were they to develop a proper theological perspective on economics and politics that their work took on an unrealistic or even utopian character in the eyes of many concerned clergy and laypeople. Nor was this assessment wide of the mark. In part because of their neo-Thomist understanding of natural law, the members of the Christendom group had an exaggerated confidence in the ability of theology to determine social practice. Thus, instead of studying contemporary economics or political theory, they looked back to the Middle Ages for inspiration. Suspicious of such modern social thought, they were prey to dubious schemes of all sorts, particularly the "social credit" theories of Major C. H. Douglas which held that most of the world's ills could be cured by a direct assault on "finance capital." Like the Guild of St. Matthew, moreover, both the League for the Kingdom of God and the Christendom Group were decidedly anti-Protestant, thereby excluding many otherwise sympathetic Anglicans.

The fact remains that there is much that is of enduring value in Widdrington's bold attempt to develop a Christian sociology. In marked contrast to the enthusiasm among socialists, both secular and Christian, for State control of most of the economy, Widdrington and his friends warned of the dangers to true common life from bureaucratic tyranny. The widespread confidence in democratic controls, they noted perceptively, will be ill-placed as long as government is remote from the people and the people themselves hae been reduced to little more than social atoms.[42] This is one of the reasons that the Christendom Group was so interested in the Middle Ages, regarding that era as one in which a more humane social order had been envisioned even though it was not fully realized. To be sure, this was an idealized view of medieval society. But the ability to use the past to criticize the present should not be dismissed lightly; the trivialization of history is one of the most serious handicaps to social criticism in our own day.[43] Similarly, there was more to the Christendom Group's advocacy of social credit than economic illiteracy. Money, members of the Group were convinced, has become an idol. "[T]hings matter more than money," explained Eric Mascall. "You may say that it is not touching a very high spiritual level to tell people that potatoes are more important than money. But it is *theology*, it is *good* theology, it is good Catholic doctrine, Christian faith, to say that potatoes matter more than money."[44] Above all, Widdrington and other proponents of Christian sociology reminded the Left that the transformation of the world is essentially a moral and spiritual task, rather than simply a matter of rearranging the economy. Economics are important. But only the doctrine and the vision of the Kingdom of God can give direction and hope to those rightly eager to do battle with injustice and oppression.

Interestingly, one problem to which neither the Christendom Group nor the League for the Kindgom of God devoted much attention was how the vision can transform parish life, and how the parish, in turn, can transform the life of the surrounding community.[45] Indeed, this oversight had been characteristic of the Anglican Left as a whole. Christian Socialists had, of course, been devoted pastors. They had revived failing city parishes, provided needed social services, and had preached the good news of God's kingdom. But for a number of reasons—their liturgical conservatism, their determination to keep their attention fixed on broad political questions, and the indifference of their working-class neighbors—most radical priests had not departed from the usual forms of Anglo-Catholic worship, nor had they made the parish the center of their political activities, preferring instead to work through national organizations. It was left to Conrad Noel (1869–1942) and the Catholic Crusade to attempt the arduous task of so altering the life and worship of the local Church that it became a veritable outpost of the Kingdom.[46]

Like Widdrington, Noel had been a member of the Guild of St. Matthew and the Church Socialist League. But his Bohemian temperament and ardent spirit were far closer to Headlam's than they were to those of his more scholarly friend. His path to ordination was certainly no easier than Headlam's had been. At one point, the Evangelical Bishop of Exeter refused to admit him to holy orders, complaining that Noel was both a Papist and a pantheist, the latter charge based upon Noel's Maurician emphasis on God's immanence in creation. Once ordained, moreover, Noel followed Headlam's rebellious example, turning down the opportunity for preferment if he would only trim his radical sails. But whereas Headlam was forced from the parish ministry, Noel was fortunate in finding a loyal and unusual patron, the socialist Countess of Warwick, who presented him with the living of Thaxted in 1910.

When Noel arrived in the small Essex farming village, the beautiful and spacious church was full of ugly Victorian furnishings which accurately betrayed the low state of its religious life. Significantly, Noel began his ministry by clearing the church of its clutter and beautifying its worship. Aided by his gifted wife, Miriam, he tore down the chancel screen, threw out the moldy Bible boxes with which wealthy parishioners had reserved their seats, moved the choir to the back of the church and took away their surplices. The chancel was hung with bright banners, flowerpots were placed throughout the church, and new vestments were purchased of the sort Percy Dearmer, whose curate he had once been, did so much to popularize: vestments patterned after graceful medieval English models rather than the stiff and cumbersome monstrosities then in use in Roman Catholic churches. Soon the Mass replaced Sunday Mattins, and processions of people and clergy became the rule on holy days. To what must have been Headlam's delight, pub parties followed the Sunday service. Nowhere was joy in the common feast of the people of God more apparent than in Thaxted church.

Noel's labors, it is important to point out, were not those of a clerical aesthete or a liturgical antiquarian. He was distressed by the hordes of tourists who descended on the church to admire the ceremony, indifferent to the faith which it embodied.[47] Just how subversive Noel's understanding of the liturgy was is best illustrated by his decision to reintroduce the Corpus Christi procession in

Thaxted. Although sometimes tolerated, Benediction and other sacramental devotions had been forbidden since the Reformation. But when Bishop Watts-Ditchfield of Chelmsford forbade the proposed procession, Noel was unyielding. What is at issue, he argued, is not the future of a quaint ceremony, but the showing forth of Jesus Christ. "The Catholic Crusade welcomes all who wish to join the Procession of the Divine Outlaw and to receive His blessing to encourage them in battle," he announced boldly. "Mere onlookers are not welcomed." Benediction was a call to arms, "uplifting the Son of Man as God of justice in our midst."[48] This was not empty bravado. Exasperated though he was by Noel's audacity, Widdrington grasped the seriousness of his friend's purpose and sought to explain it to the Bishop. "You do not understand Noel's position," he wrote in words worth pondering by anyone tempted to underestimate the Vicar of Thaxted, "unless you realize that his passionate belief in the establishment of the Kingdom on earth is the master idea of all his teaching. It is this which separates him from the pietists and those who confuse the Catholic Faith with the religion of the sanctuary boy."[49]

It was around struggles such as this that the Catholic Crusade grew up. Founded in 1912 as a result of Noel's dissatisfaction with what he regarded as the vague theology and cautious politics of the Church Socialist League, the Catholic Crusade emerged in the postwar years as the most revolutionary of Christian Socialist groups. It was not the largest, nor did it attempt to be. On the contrary, every effort was made to insure that joining the Crusade would be no easy matter. Determined that the parish be the heart of the new fellowship, Noel insisted that branches could only be organized at churches conducted by Crusade priests. Probationary members were sternly warned that only those willing to lose their jobs and their friends, and give, if necessary, their money and their lives were welcome. This was not surprising, for the Crusade's goal was nothing less than "to shatter the British Empire and all Empires to bits, . . . to break up the present world and make a new, in the power of the outlaw of Galilee."[50] Noel was not foolish enough to believe that he and his followers would accomplish this in their lifetime. But he was convinced that it was only by boldly challenging the principalities and powers of this world that the Christian could be faithful to his baptismal vows.

Noel's mastery of the grand gesture and the noble phrase—much of his rhetoric seems to have come straight from the sagas of William Morris—should not blind us to the deep faith upon which his socialism was based. An amateur biblical scholar of no mean ability who was also widely read in patristic and medieval social thought, Noel was careful to remain true to the great teachings of the Church. Indeed, although he was sympathetic toward the efforts of Roman Catholic modernists to free their Church from biblical literalism, Noel was anything but a conventional liberal.[51] To be sure, like Maurice, Headlam, and the early Greek Fathers, he stressed God's immanence. "God is *perpetually* 'intruding' himself into this world," he explained, "and is himself its very Substance. Every wayside flower is a sacrament of his Body and Blood. . . ." Noel went further still, contending that God is "manifest in splendid men and women," and that "every human heroism [is] a Revelation." But this was not meant to deny God's transcendence or Christ's divinity. God is fully incarnate in "Jesus, the Christ, His Only Son, Our Lord, wholly God and wholly Man, conceived by the Holy Ghost, born of the Virgin Mary . . . , who rejoices that her son is casting down the mighty from their thrones and exalting them of low degree. . . ."[52]

It was only because he believed these things with all his heart that Noel could boldly draw the political consequences he did from Scripture and the creeds. The Kingdom of God, he insisted, is no ethereal place, but "the whole world of men and women become conscious of commonwealth and living for the common good; the world, that is, according to God's original plan." Noel admitted that the realization of this earthly paradise lay beyond history. But having rejected the usual distinction between the natural and the supernatural, he could hardly rest content with passive adventism. "The Divine Outlaw," he was convinced, had "founded a Red Army composed chiefly of the rank and file, to turn the world upside down and prepare for the coming in glory of the International Commonwealth of God. . . ." It is, moreover, an army of both the quick and the dead. "[T]hose who by the Power of Christ have overcome sin," Noel asserted, "will one day rise with glorious bodies to enjoy and help in the ordering of the Good Life to come, the overmastering Life of the Golden Age."[53] Needless to say, this conception of the Church was as incomprehensible to liberals, for whom the communion of saints and the Second Coming were pious metaphors, as it was to conservatives, for whom those doctrines referred to wholly other-worldly realities.

Noel was more radical than most Christian Socialists, and his zeal for revolution sometimes led him astray. Thus, although he was as contemptuous of the bureaucratic State as were Headlam and

Widdrington, Noel was a staunch admirer of Lenin and the Soviet Union. But his political eccentricities, which had catastrophic consequences for the Catholic Crusade, cannot obscure the bright vision which animated his labors. In the glorious Easter Mass at Thaxted there was made manifest the holy dream to which Maurice, Headlam, Gore, Holland, Widdrington, and countless others had borne witness. Unfortunately, vision does not guarantee success. Quite apart from its ardent but confused politics, the Catholic Crusade suffered from a number of handicaps which severely limited its influence. As we have seen, Noel's theology was by no means careless or heterodox. But it was idiosyncratic, and the dramatic nature of his call for Catholic radicalism probably confused more Catholics and radicals than it attracted. Moreover, by insisting that only Anglo-Catholics could join the Crusade, Noel excluded many Anglicans who might otherwise have supported him. Equally important, the Crusade was so dominated by Noel that differences of opinion could not be tolerated, nor was it possible for other leaders to emerge. Thus, when factional squabbles did break out in the late 1930s over the question of Stalinism, the Crusade fell apart. Not surprisingly, the Order of the Church Militant, which Noel organized to take its place, disappeared soon after his death.

With the collapse of the Catholic Crusade, the great stream of radical Anglicanism began to dwindle. Christian Socialist societies continued to exist, but these largely interdenominational groups lacked the theological acuity and vision of the earlier movement. This decline was not limited to Britain. The Church League for Industrial Democracy, the successor to the American Church Socialist League which numbered among its leaders Vida Scudder (1861–1954) and William B. Spofford, Sr. (1892–1972), all but vanished after 1945. At fist glance, this sudden collapse is puzzling, even when the advent of the Cold War and the widespread disillusionment with the Soviet Union are taken into account. It raises the question of why a movement so faithful to the gospel of the Kingdom of God led such a stormy life and achieved so little. But as it is phrased, the question is misleading. In some ways, the Anglican Left was the victim of its own remarkable success. The things for which it fought—the abolition of condescending mission work and the related notion of the priest as gentleman, the criticism of privilege based on birth and wealth, and the frank avowal of the Church's responsibility to defend the poor and oppressed—have become so widely accepted that it is sometimes hard to understand how they could ever have been resisted. The fact that two friends of the Christian Socialist movement, William Temple and Michael Ramsay, were elevated to the primacy of All England, is itself a stunning accomplishment for a cause whose leaders at one time had to struggle simply to be ordained. But remarkable though these achievements are, they did not herald a renewal of prophetic witness. Rather, they were the prelude to an accommodation between the Church and the welfare State. Indeed, the primacy of William Temple went a long way toward consecrating that relationship. On the one hand, Temple's social theology was rooted in the broad but orthodox incarnationalism of the Anglican Left. His criticism of capitalist society, drawn from sources as diverse as John Ruskin and the Christendom Group, was perceptive and at times impassioned. But Temple drew back from advocating radical reforms. Thus, although he shared Christian Socialist misgivings about both the Labour party and the centralized State, his own proposals seemed to give the archepiscopal imprimatur to what became the program of the Atlee government.[54]

Success alone, it is clear, does not explain the disintegration of the Christian Socialist movement. The fate of the Anglican Left was, in part, the result of its own serious mistakes. Rightly convinced of the importance of sound theology and Eucharistic worship, Anglican radicals were quick to erect barriers between themselves and other Christians, be they Protestant or Roman Catholic. Those of their fellow Anglicans whose Evangelicalism or liberalism they found offensive were also subjected to harsh and not always justified criticism. Maurice had cautioned against this sort of dogmatism and, as he feared, it led to sectarianism within the Christian Socialist camp itself. Moreover, for all their insistence on Catholic doctrine, many Christian Socialists were so involved in the day-to-day struggle to rouse the Church from its torpor that they sometimes confused orthodoxy with revolutionary rhetoric. Headlam and Noel in particular, impatient with pietistic other-worldliness, tended to minimize the value of asceticism and personal spirituality except when harnessed to political ends. This lack of balance, in turn, made it all the more difficult for the Anglican Left to secure a hearing in the Church and in the universities and theological colleges where its ideas could have been developed and passed on to succeeding generations. At the same time, the conviction that ultimately the Church alone holds the keys to the Kingdom of God, encouraged Anglican radicals to leap from theology to action without first carefully studying economics or political theory. Not surprisingly, they often made exaggerated claims for their programs for changing society. Maurice refused to venture beyond advocating cooperative workshops and class cooperation. Headlam was obsessed with Henry George's Single Tax theory of land reform which, although not without merit, could hardly accomplish the things which Headlam expected of it. Similarly, the medievalism of Widdrington and his friends, useful though it was in criticizing industrial society, offered little guidance for the future. And Conrad Noel took up the cause of Bolshevism, an action born of impatience for the Kingdom of God but which sorely hindered the work of the Catholic Crusade.

The importance of these failings cannot be gainsaid, nor can they be ignored by those of us who wish to bring the Gospel to bear on the problems of our suffering world. But if we are to profit from the mistakes of the Anglican Left, we must first profit from its wisdom. Unlike some contemporary radicals, eager to throw off Scripture, creeds, and prayer as a hindrance to social action, earlier Christian Socialists insisted forcefully that it was just these things which gave substance to Christian hope and sustenance for the long struggle ahead. As Headlam noted perceptively, to abandon the Bible and the doctrine of the Incarnation was not to free Christianity from metaphysics, but to substitute philosophical abstractions for the living and liberating God of faith.[55] If Christians would only take the things they are supposed to believe seriously; if they would but understand that in the Magnificat, which sums up the hope of the Old Testament and heralds its fulfillment in the New, they possess "the hymn of universal social revolution," more would be accomplished than by all the efforts to make the faith of the Church palatable to armchair sceptics.[56]

Not only did the Catholic faith sustain the Anglican Left, it provided guidance as well. Much of what has passed for social action in recent years has been little more than the frantic embrace of whatever cause purported to represent the oppressed. To this weakness for secular fashion, Anglican radicals were largely immune. Maurice and Kingsley chided working-class radicals; Headlam held himself aloof from the Labour party; Widdrington and the Christendom Group criticized the beginnings of the bureaucratic welfare state. Even Noel retained his critical faculties and his independence, bravely holding the banner of the Kingdom before pietists and revolutionaries alike. These Christian prophets were not always correct. But their insistence that the Gospel was the standard by which the Left as well as the Right was to be judged needs to be emulated if we are not to confuse the word of the Lord with mere trendiness.

Most important of all, by holding fast to Scripture and the creeds, the Christian Socialist movement avoided the fatal divorce between prayer and action. The peculiar notion that attention to worship is incompatible with responding to the needs of the poor must be uprooted if either prayer or action pleasing to God is to be possible.[57] The Anglican Left preached revolution, but by revolution it meant more than a change in economic and political arrangements. Maurice and those who came after him had one goal: the joyful Kingdom of God on earth. For it they risked their careers and their reputations. They did so not because they had an exaggerated sense of their own importance or of their ability to change the world, but because they believed in the promises of God. For us, tempted as we are to embrace the despair of our troubled age, that faith and vision is surely their noblest legacy.

4

Early Evangelical Ethics: Preparing for Today

by Peter Toon

Methodism and Anglican Evangelicalism came from the same eighteenth-century womb. By the beginning of the nineteenth century they had minimal contact. Evangelical members of the Church of England sought to lose the image of dissenter or nonconformist and to present themselves as loyal to her faith and practice. John Overton of York spoke for the minority of C. of E. clergy (perhaps about 300) in his lengthy, *The True Churchman ascertained: or an Apology for those of the regular clergy of the Establishment who are sometimes called Evangelical Ministers* (1801). This apologia was welcomed in the pages of the new monthly Anglican evangelical magazine, *The Christian Observer*, which was closely related to the 'Clapham Sect' and to London evangelical clergy.[1]

The Christian Observer professed loyalty to 'vital Christianity' (a common expression for the 'Clapham Sect') and to the principles and structure of the Established Church. So it is no surprise to find that the achievements of John Wesley and George Whitefield, the great evangelists, were viewed as mixed blessings:

> They were instruments under Providence of awakening many to righteousness, and of exciting among the clergy a new degree of attention to some of the great doctrines of our religion. ... However ... Whitefield, naturally vehement, carried some doctrines to an extreme; he made religion too much to consist in agitation and *he entered little into the detail of Christian duties*. He also descredited his cause, especially in the eyes of persons of the higher class, by great coarseness and vulgarity ... Wesley taught the doctrine of perfection, and of sudden conversion. ... Both gave much needless offence; both had low ideas of the duty of subjection to the authorities of the Church of which they were members; both considered themselves rather as apostles. ... The one introduced a general

85

negligence of Church order and a too incautious zeal for doctrinal truth, which has, in some degree, degenerated into conceit; the other, naturally enterprising, yet cool and persevering, politic in his views, and systematic in his plans, laid the foundation of a new Church. . . .[2]

The Anglican evangelicals at Clapham, Cambridge and in other centers wished to be faithful both to the evangel and to the national Church. Furthermore they desired to make their faith appealing and relevant to the middle and higher orders of society.

Together with loyal commitment to the doctrines and parish structure of the Church went a joyous attachment to 'the excellencies of our truly evangelical liturgy,' *The Book of Common Prayer.*[3] In November 1811 Charles Simeon preached four sermons in Cambridge to attentive undergraduates and then published them as *The Excellence of the Liturgy.* He referred to the Prayer Book as 'a composition of unrivalled excellence,' needing only 'the exercise of our devout affections to render it a most acceptable service before God.'[4]

Being devoted children of mother Church, what was it that made them evangelicals? One writer explained:

The term 'evangelical' is applied by men of discrimination, to all, of whatever party (i.e. Calvinist or Arminian) who earnestly enforce the doctrines of original sin, salvation by grace through faith in the Redeemer, and the necessity of regeneration by the Holy Spirit.[5]

The editor of *The Christian Observer* had this to say:

Earnestly solicitous that men should learn that it is of infinitely greater moment to be real Christians than acute controversialists, the conductors of *The Christian Observer* wish that their work should constantly exhibit the important doctrines of the ruined state of man by nature and of his recovery by divine grace; of justification by faith and the sanctifying influence of the Holy Spirit; of the unsearchable love of Christ, and of the obligation of every one no longer to live for himself but for Him who died for him—that the uniform tendency of their publication should be to awaken the careless sinner; to enlighten the understanding by a just display of the duties we owe to God and to man; and to enforce upon the conscience the awful sanctions of the Gospel.[6]

Over a decade later, Daniel Wilson, minister of St. John's Chapel, London (and soon to become a bishop in India) compared the Orthodox (= high-church) and evangelical clergy in this manner:

> They both agree in the fundamental tenets of the unity of the Godhead, the mystery of the Trinity, the divinity and atonement of the Saviour, the person and diety of the Holy Ghost, the immortality of the soul, and the future judgement. They both agree in admitting the inspiration of the Holy Scriptures, and the authorty and purity of our national Church.

He noted that their differences were "in the use and application of what they believe."

> The pious and devout Churchman feels himself a miserable and lost sinner; feels his only hope to be in the meritorious Cross of the Lord Jesus; feels himself in need of the renewing and sanctifying influence of the Holy Spirit; feels the supreme value of his eternal salvation; feels the necessity of renouncing his own moral goodness in point of merit; feels the value of time, the nearness of death, the unutterable importance of eternity, the danger of a worldly spirit, the madness of indifference to religion and the reasonableness of an immortal preparing for immortality.[7]

In other words the evangelical felt what he believed and sought to put into practice what he felt and believed. And as we shall see this practice included much more than evangelism and the support of foreign missions. As William Wilberforce affirmed, the evangelical was interested in, and committed to, 'real' or 'vital Christianity.' This is reflected in his influential book, *A Practical View of the prevailing religious system of professed Christians, in the higher and middle classes of this country contrasted with real Christianity* (1797). To put it simply the evangelicals actually took Christianity very seriously at a time when many or most of the members of the national Church were apparently nominal Christians.

At the heart of evangelicalism was the experience of conversion to God, involving a sense of personal guilt for sin and a desire for divine forgiveness. This experience came to people in different ways, sometimes suddenly, more often gradually. As a result of being reconciled to God, adopted into his family and given the joy of salvation, there was in each true believer a commitment to vital Christianity. No group of Protestants has so emphasized the importance of the indissoluble relation of faith and works as did the Evangelicals of Clapham and Cambridge. Most Evangelicals did not want to be known as either Calvinists or Arminians, for they saw truth in each of these apparent extremes. Of course neither or these words were used in an academic sense to describe the teaching of Calvin and Arminius; instead they referred to two contrary schemes of doctrine inherited from seventeenth- and eighteenth-century debates. Charles Simeon was happy to be called 'a Bible Christian' and others were content to be known as 'practical' or 'prudent' Calvinists. This was a way of emphasizing that while they wanted to affirm the priority of God's grace in conversion they also wanted to emphasize their repudiation of antinomianism and their commitment to practical good works.[8] Few wanted to be called 'Arminian' because this word has associations of human merit counting for salvation.

1.

It may be argued, with justice, that the early Anglican evangelicals (c. 1790–1820) displayed a greater concern than any of their successors to maintain both in theory and in practice a sound and dynamic relationship between, on the one hand, belief, faith and trust, and, on the other, good works, personal morality and social ethics. To argue this does not require that we forget or deny that men such as Wilberforce and women like Hannah More were in important respects children of their time in their social attitudes. Let us admit that we all wear unsheddable cultural skins and that some skins are thinner than others. Those of the Clapham Sect and their supporters were certainly colored by social and economic presuppositions which they did not question.

For people of their station—the middle and higher classes of society—the personal and social ethics propagated by the evangelicals were radical. These spiritual and moral principles proceeded from deep conviction and utter sincerity and were closely integrated into a sense of being redeemed from sin and set free to serve the Lord in his world. The evangelicals judged that they were living in a time of crisis for Europe and especially for Britain, and so their serious call to faith and love was intensified by their evaluation of the context in which they lived.

Wilberforce wrote his *A Practical View* with a deep sense of the moral crisis facing Britain and in the belief that disaster and divine judgment could be avoided by the intercession of the serious-minded Christians of the nation. But before there could be fervent and effectual prayer there had to be serious and vital Christianity. Near the end of the book he wrote:

> Let true Christians, then, with becoming earnestness, strive in all things to recommend their profession, and to put to silence the vain scoffs of ignorant objectors. Let them boldly assert the cause of Christ, in an age when so many who bear the name of Christians are ashamed of him: and let them consider as devolved on them the important duty of serving, it may be of serving their country, not by busy interference in politics (in which it cannot but be confessed there is much uncertainty), but rather by that sure and radical benefit, of restoring the influence of religion, and of raising the standard of morality.
>
> Let them be active, useful, generous towards others; manifestly moderate and self-denying in themselves. Let them be ashamed of idleness as they would be of the most acknowledged sin. When Providence blesses them with affluence, let them withdraw from the competition of vanity; and, without sordidness or absurdity, show by their modest demeanour, and by their retiring from display, that, without affecting singularity, they are not slaves to fashion; that they consider it as their duty to set an example of moderation and sobriety, and to reserve, for nobler and more disinterested purposes, that money which others selfishly waste in parade, and dress, and equipage. Let them evince, in short, a manifest moderation in all temporal things; as becomes those whose affections are set on higher objects than any which this world affords, and those who possess within their own bosoms a fund of satisfaction and comfort, which the world seeks in vanity and dissipation. . . .
>
> Let them pray continually for their country in this season of national difficulty. We bear upon us but too plainly the marks of a declining empire. Who can say but that the Governor of the universe, who declares himself to be a God who hears the prayers of his servants, may, in answer to their intercessions, for a while avert our ruin, and continue to us the fulness of those temporal blessings, which in such abundant measure we have hitherto enjoyed? (Chap. 7, sec. 4.)

Certainly Wilberforce attempted to practice what he preached, and so did his colleagues who met with him at Clapham and in other places. Not only did they seek to improve their own personal faith and morals but they undertook many activities in order to restore the influence of Christianity and to raise the standard of morality in the country and in its dealings with other countries. The causes, societies and groups they founded, sponsored or funded cover a large spectrum.

There are still those who accuse the early evangelicals of a contempt for this life. How such an able writer as Canon Raven could have done this is difficult to imagine, but the myth continues.[9] Responding to this criticism, E. M. Howse, the historian of the Clapham Sect, states:

> The Clapham Sect, the leading evangelicals of their day, did not divorce religion from life. They linked religion to life. They linked it to hunted Negroes on the coast of Africa, on the high seas, and in the plantations of the West Indies. They linked it to standards of political conduct, to the corrupt manners of society, and to the debauched mobs of their time. They linked it to the wretches condemned by game laws, and oppressed in filthy prisons. They linked it to the ragged children condemned otherwise to ignorance, and by philanthropic and benefit societies they linked it to the improvident and unfortunate poor. Their efforts were sometimes casual and their methods were often awry, but at every point at which they did touch life, it was their religion that led them to the contact. The religion may, indeed, have been otherworldly centred, but the circumference of its action embraced a weltering area of humanity, of which most contemporary religion was comfortably oblivious.[10]

Possibly they took on too much. Possibly they ought to have begun to question the very structures of society as well as relieving the problems caused by those structures. There were many "possibles." The fact is that they responded to need because of the love of God in their hearts. Though they spoke as men and women of their time they achieved what others of their generation had no mind or desire to achieve. And what they achieved, they achieved, so they firmly believed, in the name of Jesus Christ their Saviour and Lord. Their ethics were never only theoretical. Indeed, in some cases, they only were conscious of their moral principles by examining what they were involved in. The fact that all men were made in the image of God; the belief that Christ died for all the human race; the conviction that the moral law and the offer of salvation applied to each person, and the sense of mission from God to the world which they had, caused them to act, and having acted sometimes to reflect on what they were involved in.

Fundamental to all the moral thinking of the Evangelicals was the concept of Providence. Their writings, letters and recorded speeches in Parliament contain frequent references to Providence (very rarely to "the providence of God"). Providence, with the capital "P," was shorthand for "God, the moral Governor of the world, who is actively involved in the history and life of nations as their Judge and Saviour." Their belief could be expressed in terms taken from moral philosophy (as we shall see below) but it was more than an intellectual concept. It was a heightened sense of the presence and involvement of God in his world and a conviction that events were to be explained in terms of God's character and purpose for mankind.[11] This was a faith and a religious experience modelled on and akin to that of the prophets and psalmists of ancient Israel and Judah. And it was intensified by their personal appropriation of salvation from Christ. They looked for the hand of God in all events and claimed to discern the general pattern of the divine movements. Certainly many of their contemporaries also referred to "Providence." What distinguished the evangelicals was the seriousness with which they held to this conviction of God's personal involvement in the affairs of their day, and the intensity of their efforts to see justice implemented in the affairs of men.

2.

The personal ethics of the Evangelicals are clearly presented by Thomas Scott, whose *Commentary on the Bible* (1792) was extensively used well into the next century. He was the interpreter of Scripture for most of the Clapham Sect and Evangelicals throughout the country.[12] Some of the results of his exegesis and interpretation of the Bible are collected in his *Essays on the Most Important Subjects in Religion* which went through many editions. Several of these essays are on ethical themes. The roots of Scott's moral theology go back through selected Nonconformist and Anglican writers of the eighteenth century, through certain Puritan writers on practical divinity, to the writings of various Protestant reformers of the sixteenth century. Yet he is no slavish follower of any man, and having received both the Anglican and Calvinist traditions of practical and moral theology, he sought to interpret the demands of God in Scripture with the help he received from the writers of past days.

Like Calvin and the Puritans he perceived the grace of God in the Ten Commandments and viewed them not only as an expression of the general moral law (discoverable in part by natural reason) but also, when spiritually interpreted, as the guide of the committed

Christian life. Essay iv is a brief exposition of the Decalogue. The moral law of God "has its foundation in the nature of God and man, in the relations which men bear to him and to each other, and in the obligations that result from these relations: on which account it is immutable in its requirements, and demands obedience from all mankind, as far as they have opportunity of becoming acquainted with it." This means that its contents have to be made known and, as far as possible, made the basis for public life and government legislation.

The moral law of God is also spiritual, reaching into the depths of the heart, mind and conscience. This is why love to God and to the neighbor is the summary of the law, for the demand for love begins deep in the heart and is expressed through the whole person.

> The law is also spiritual: that is, it takes cognizance of our spirits, or our most secret thoughts, desires, and dispositions; and demands the exact regulation of the judgment, will and affections, in conformity to the holy excellencies of the Lord our God. It principally requires LOVE, or the entire affection of the soul, without which the best external obedience is condemned as hypocrisy.

Thus the exposition proceeds on the assumption that the first part of the Decalogue relates primarily to the love of God in heart and life, while the second part relates to the neighbor as the object of genuine love. Conscious that no person could possibly in heart and in practice perfectly obey the law, Scott insisted that the law is given to us as a rule of duty in subserviency to the Gospel. From the grace given with the Gospel we are enabled to begin to obey the law in heart as well as in general external obedience; and when we fail and are penitent there is the grace of forgiveness.

It was on the basis of the law of love (love of the neighbor) that Scott opposed slavery as it was found in the world of his day. He fully recognized that slavery, with specific safeguards, was allowed by the law of Moses (e.g. Deut. 15:12–15). Included in the safeguards was the promise of emancipation after six years. In his *Commentary* he wrote:

> Slavery was almost universal in the world (i.e. ancient near East); and though, like wars, it always proceeded of evil, and was generally evil in itself, yet the wisdom of God deemed it better to regulate, than to prohibit it; we should not, however, judge of the practice itself by these judicial regulations, but by

the law of love. Slavery like war, may in some cases, in the present state of things, be lawful: for the crime which forfeits life no doubt forfeits liberty; and it is not inconsistent with the moral law for a criminal to be sold and treated as a slave, during a term of time appropriate to his offence. In most cases, if not in all, it must be inconsistent with the law of love (comments on Exodus 21:2–11).

This was a sounder exegetical approach than that of a few keen Evangelicals who in their enthusiasm to condemn slavery on biblical grounds neglected to mention that slavery of a kind was allowed by God to exist in Israel.

Two essays (xviii and xix) expound "the disposition and character peculiar to the true believer." In the first essay the "temper" of the believer before God is delineated. In other words godliness is described—that disposition to behave toward God according to the glory of his perfections and our relations and obligations to him. First there is *humility* "most essential to the Christian temper and as radical to every part of it." Then there is *submission* to God, to the truth of his revelation in Scripture, and to the demands of his will. A third branch of the Christian temper is the *fear of God*, a "reverential fear of the divine majesty, authority, holiness and glory which produces solemn awe, humble adoration and a serious reflecting frame of mind." The *love of God* is essential—an admiring love of the divine perfections as displayed in the works of God, especially in his redemption of the world by Jesus Christ. Finally there is *spiritual mindedness*, the disposition to see primary and true happiness in spiritual things and to find great joy in communion with God.

In the second essay the true Christian temper as it respects brethren and neighbors is delineated. Because the believer gains patience, contentment and cheerfulness in his relation to God he displays *an indifference to the world and the things of the world.* This is not an indifference to people or their needs but "to the world and its honours, friendships, wealth, decorations, splendour and of indulgences, whether of the senses, appetites, or the passions of the mind." Further, it does not mean a refusal to participate fully in human society: rather it means to participate in it as a child of God, reflecting the standards and ideals of the kingdom of heaven. Another characteristic of the Christian life-style is *benevolence or philanthropy.* The principle of God's love in the heart tends to "enlarge the heart in good will to men: to soften it into compassion: to subdue envy, enmity and resentment, and to kindle an ardent desire after the present and future happiness of the human species, however distinguished and separated, or whatever their character and conduct towards us may be."

Another effect of evangelical principles is *a disposition to be harmless and blameless*. The serious Christian will seek to prevent anything which increases the sum total of human misery or vice. Here we may let Scott speak for himself as an example of the detail given in his ethical teaching:

He will habitually aim to be just and honest in all his dealings; not grasping at gains which custom may have sanctioned, but which strict probity forbids; not taking advantage of any man's ignorance or necessity, to circumvent or exact from him; not evading taxes, and so leaving his neighbour to bear a disproportionate part of them; not insisting on his utmost due, when it would distress those who owe it; not keeping, by a continual fraud, that property which has unjustly been obtained, when it is in his power to make restitution; not living extravagantly, or engaging in perilous schemes, and thus contracting needless debts, to the injury of his creditors and family: not taking his neighbour's work without wages, or oppressing the poor to increase his wealth, or support his luxury; not concurring in any plan for getting money, by methods which enslave the persons, expose the lives, or endanger the souls of men; nor using the too customary impositions of trade, which are everywhere condemned in Scripture, however pleaded for by men professing to believe it, and who substitute the rule of doing as others *do* to us instead of doing as we would they should do to us. In short, he will conscientiously render to God, to rulers, and to all the different members of the community, their dues; rather choosing to give up his own right, than to infringe upon that of another.

Further, he will pay the strictest regard to truthfulness and faithfulness in all that he says and does. "He cannot consistently trifle with so sacred a matter as truth for the sake of jest, a humorous tale, or a compliment: much less to gratify anger, malice or avarice, or in flattery, slander or religious controversy."

The last disposition of the Christian temper he mentions is *to love mercy and to be kind and liberal in doing good*. Active kindness, however, does not consist merely in giving to others: "a man may express much love by denying his own inclination or foregoing his own ease, that he may serve others." And, in endeavoring to do good and harm no-one, he will be ready to forgive and to seek after peace.

A general impression gained from reading this ethical material is that Scott was a careful student of both the human heart (especially as found in the middle and upper classes of society) and the practical exhortations of the New Testament. He made the effort to bring the two together, believing that the forgiven man, in the power of the Holy Spirit, could begin to put these moral rules into practice. Though Scott firmly held that the same demands were made by God upon the unregenerate as upon the regenerate man, he made it his particular task to place before those who claimed to be justified by faith, what their sanctification meant in real terms in day-to-day life. The burden of his teaching is addressed to those involved in business and commerce, because that is where the strength of Anglican Evangelicalism was found at the beginning of the nineteenth century.

Essays xx and xxi are "on the believer's attention to relative duties." These are the duties arising out of the basic relationships in human society. "When the Christian is followed into the retired scenes of life, the habitual effect of his principles may be more precisely ascertained; and his attention to the welfare, comfort and peace of all around him, even at the expense of many personal inconveniences and much self-denial, will prove his piety to be genuine and of most salutary tendency." Again, Scott is quite clear that the depth of God's demand is not any the less if one is not a serious-minded Christian. Rather, the genuine Christian has a particular motivation:

> . . . believers are influenced by the constraining love of Christ, a sense of immense obligations received, a desire of adorning and recommending the Gospel and unfeigned love to all around them, producing a permanent attention to everything connected with their present and eternal welfare.

The motivation of those who have not the power of the Gospel in their lives usually arises from the fear of punishment and hope of reward (from God). Yet the proximity of ethical exhortation and doctrinal teaching in the New Testament is a reminder that the Gospel gives both the right mental attitude and the necessary spiritual power to fulfill relative duties to those who submit to the Gospel of Christ.

The first area is *the reciprocal duties of husbands and wives*. Here Scott's main thrust is the way in which husband and wife are to relate to each other. He has little to say about such topics as divorce (where he adopts the traditional Calvinist approach, allowing divorce after adultery by one partner). Much of his practical advice must have arisen from his work as a pastor and counselor. His aim is to make each partner aware of the right kind of attitudes, behavior-patterns and activities required in order to make marriage into the kind of relationship intended by God. This, he maintained, would be the easier if marriage were approached in the right way from the beginning. A couple planning marriage "cannot consistently treat this momentous matter with a childish levity, or hearken to the corrupt suggestions of worldly convenience, avarice, or irrational attachment; or to the fascinations of wit, beauty, or accomplish-ments of any kind, in preference to piety." When the marriage has taken place "the married persons should consider each other, not only as the objects of their own choice, but also of the Lord's choice for them; and should constantly desire and pray to be perfectly satisfied with it." He is at pains to insist that even if one partner fails in his/her obligations, this does not mean that the other partner is excused. Again it is to be noted that Scott is not thinking of mar-riages which have broken down but he is thinking always of the improvement in quality of those who remain together, and he is convinced that the reception and outworking of Gospel principles will bring a quality of life obtainable in no other way.

The second area is *the reciprocal duties of parents and children.* Already in essay iv (on the Decalogue) he has expounded what honoring parents means. Children "ought to love the persons of their parents; respect their characters, counsels, and instructions; consult their interest, credit and comfort; conceal their infirmities, bear with their tempers and humours, alleviate their sorrows and rejoice their hearts as far as possible; and, when they are grown old and incapable of maintaining themselves, the children are bound, if able, even to labour for their support, as the parents did for them when they were infants." In essay xxi Scott is more concerned with the relation of a keen young Christian to his (nominal Christian) parent.

> In general children are not required to preach to their parents: at least every word should be spoken with modesty, tenderness, and unassuming gentleness; and they should rather aim to induce them to hear sermons, to read books, or to converse with pious and prudent Christians, than themselves to give instructions, or engage in arguments with them. ... For parents will seldom become docile scholars to their own children, especially if they teach in magisterial and reproving language.

The most conclusive argument children can use to bring their parents to genuine faith is "an uniform conscientious conduct, in obliging attention, silent submission to undeserved rebukes, diligence in business, fidelity to every trust resposed in them, and a disinterested regard to the temporal advantage of the whole family."

The duties of parents to their children cannot proceed unless selfishness is not followed. "From the very first, wise and conscientious parents will do nothing, for the sake of ease, indulgence or any other selfish purpose, which may endanger the life, health, understanding, or morals of their children; as far as may be, they will personally attend to every thing relating to them; and be very careful not to entrust them to those, whose care and attention are merely the result of interested motives." The need for discipline is clear:

> The word of God directs parents to rule their children, during their tender years, by compulsion; and to repress their self-will and rebellious spirit by correction; that they may be early habituated to obedience and submission; which will be of the greatest advantage to them in their whole lives, both in secular and religious matters.

Indeed, the more a man studies human nature, and repeats the experiment of bringing up children, "the fuller will be his conviction, that all attempts to educate children without correction, and to treat them as rational and independent agents, before they are capable of using their reason or liberty, spring from forgetfulness of their innate depravity, and oppose the wisdom of man to that of God: and let modern manners evince with what success this has been attended." It was because Wilberforce was concerned about the lack of discipline in family and social life that he saw the need for something to be done about it. "God Almighty has set before me," he said in 1787, "two great objects, the suppression of the slave trade and the reformation of manners."[13] Scott and Wilberforce agreed that the right place to start was in the home; however, when that foundation had not been laid it was necessary to take such action as was possible to bring discipline and respect into society.

Following the imposition of loving discipline parents must not neglect to maintain their moral control over teenage children in terms of sound advice and good arguments. It is also required of parents that they make their children feel happy in their company so that they are ready to ask for advice and help when necessary.

But the greatest duty of parents is to set the right context and thereby to help to bring their children to true faith and genuine Christian commitment. Too many parents are "accessory to the murder of the souls of their own offspring."

After brief comments on the duties of brothers and sisters to each other, Scott moved on to *the reciprocal duties of servants and masters*. This of course presupposes a type of society which has virtually disappeared from western Europe and north America but which is found in many other parts of the world today. Scott's commitment to "Providence" meant that he did not question the way society was ordered. Rather he sought to improve the quality of relations within the God-ordained orders of society.

> The believer who is "called being a servant" or who finds it necessary for him to enter upon this kind of life, should remember that God has constituted these different situations in society, for the same reasons as he has allotted to the several members in the body their distinct offices: namely, for the common benefit of the whole: and that he has chosen servitude as the best situation for him and requires his unreserved sumission to it.

Also:

> If pious servants are favoured with a situation in a religious family, they should remember that equality in Christian privileges by no means implies equality in domestick life: instead therefore, of behaving with an unbecoming familiarity, or neglecting their master's orders, as if they "despised them," they should "count them worthy of all honour. . . ."

Further,

> The Christian servant will especially aim to "adorn the doctrine of God our Saviour" by cheerful obedience to every lawful command, diligence in all the duties of his station, and faithfulness to the trust reposed in him; remembering that his maintenance and wages are the price which he receives for his time, and strength and skill.

Scott took the teaching about household slaves from the New Testament and adapted it to the household servants of the Georgian age.

Like the New Testament writers Scott has also advice for masters in their treatment of their servants.

> In general, such a master will not expect more work from his servants than they can well perform; nor deprive them of time for relaxation and retirement. He will deem it his duty to give them adequate wages, and to make their situation as comfortable as he can. He will provide them with things suitable to their station, when in health, and be very tender to them in sickness. . .

Further, he will not abandon them when they are old and infirm. Especially will he be concerned about their spiritual welfare and their observance of the Lord's Day as a day for worship.

Of course Scott recognized that there were other relative duties arising from such relations as rulers/magistrates to people, of the rich and the poor, of the young and the old, and of the pastor and his flock. Comments on these are found in various points in his *Commentary* and occasional writings. However, we have looked at enough of his teaching to recognize that it represents an attractive, Gospel-centered, puritanical (in the best sense of the word) form of Protestant (moderate Calvinist) moral theology. He saw no reason to work for the changing of the order of society, but he saw many reasons, in the light of the Gospel and the moral law, for improving the relationships within that order. With penetrating clarity he saw what being a serious-minded Christian meant in society, in the home and in business. In a sense he sought to produce a quality of life arising from the Gospel which served as an "oil" to keep the machinery of relationships within the God-ordained order lubricated. But more than this, he did aim at the glory of God. He did seek to maintain a healthy relationship between, on the one side, the joy and power of the Gospel, and, on the other, the duties arising from Christian ethics. Regrettably not all Evangelicals in the second half of the nineteenth century were able to keep the healthy balance he and his colleagues managed to create. Embroiled in one controversy after another they tended to separate the Gospel from ethics and even within ethics they concentrated too much on spiritual duties at the cost of social and political concerns.[14] Thus up to the present day Evangelicals have tended to speak of evangelism *and* social concern, viewing these things are parallel concerns rather than as two parts of the one obedience to Christ for which the Gospel calls men.[15]

3.

In the person of Thomas Gisborne (1758–1846) the Evangelicals possessed both a philosopher and an eloquent preacher.[16] He was at St. John's College, Cambridge, with Wilberforce, and their friendship, after a lapse of some years, was restored when Gisborne was a clergyman and Wilberforce was beginning his great work for the abolition of the slave trade. Gisborne's home at Yoxall in Staffordshire became a second Clapham, for not only was he tied to the Clapham Sect by reason of common faith and convictions, but he had married the sister of Thomas Babington, one of the Sect.

We are interested in Gisborne because he wrote *The Principles of Moral ... Philosophy ...* (1789) which was read both before and after the turn of the century.[17] His popular ethical teaching, in a refined, sermonic form, was also widely disseminated in his *Sermons on Christian Morality* (1809). He was not a brilliant or outstanding philosopher: rather he was a man with a very good mind who devoted himself to moral philosophy and evangelical principles. He was certainly *an*, if not *the*, intellectual guide of the Clapham Sect and hundreds of other Evangelicals throughout the country. Much of his guidance was given in long personal conversation or in carefully constructed letters.

The primary purpose in writing *The Principles of Moral and Political Philosophy Investigated* was to challenge the validity of the ethical teaching of William Paley, Archdeacon of Carlisle and author of the well-known *Evidences of Christianity.* Gisborne sought to provide a better philosophy which was in harmony with the evangelical understanding of divine Revelation. He understood Paley in *Principles of Moral and Political Philosophy* (1785; 17th ed. 1805) to teach that "a man is bound to the observance of each moral rule, as long as he thinks such observance generally expedient; that he is permitted, and even obliged in conscience, to disregard any moral rule, whenever in his opinion the violation of it will be attended on the whole with beneficial consequences; and that with respect to *every* moral rule cases may occur, in which expediency will *actually* require the violation to take place." Like the ethics of Jeremy Bentham it was a system of expediency and utility (hence utilitarianism) and had obvious popular attraction (which lasted nearly to the end of the nineteenth century). Gisborne claimed that it would be "cheerfully be embraced by those whose indolence desires a rule of conduct easy to be retained, and of universal application; by those whose vague opinions and ill-governed passions are averse to absolute and immutable restraints; and by those who affirm, that a moral agent should, in every case, be permitted to determine for himself, unfettered by any dictates of revelation, what actions will promote on the whole his happiness or misery."[18]

For reasons of space we cannot follow Gisborne's detailed criticisms of Paley's position except to note the one criticism that it is in direct opposition to the moral teaching of revelation. Neither, regrettably, can we follow his arguments to reject the widely accepted principles of honor and social custom as viable and acceptable foundations for true morality. We must concentrate upon his positive teaching. This begins with the statement of "the natural rights of human beings" as creatures made by God:

1. Every man has originally a right, by the gift of God, to the unrestrained enjoyment of life and personal freedom; and to such a portion of the unappropriated productions of the earth as is necessary for his comfortable subsistence.

2. He, therefore, who deprives another of these gifts, or restrains him in the enjoyment of them, except such deprivation or restraint is sanctioned by divine authority, is guilty of an act of injustice to the individual, and a sin against God.

3. Every man originally has authority from God to deprive another of these gifts or to restrain him in the enjoyment of them in the following cases, and in those only.
   1st, When in so doing he acts according to the express command of God.
   2dly, When he proceeds in such deprivation and restraint so far, and so far only, as is necessary for the defence of the gifts of God to those whom he is bound by natural ties to protect, or those by whom his aid is solicited or to whom it is deemed acceptable, against attacks unauthorised by God.
   3dly, When he proceeds to such deprivation or restraint in consequence of the consent of the individual suffering it.

4. Every man sins against God, who does not act in such a manner with respect to the use, defence, and disposal, of his rights, which have been established in the preceding propositions, as he is of opinion will, on the whole, fulfil most effectually the purposes of his being.[19]

Most of the book is an exposition of these principles with an application of them to particular cases—e.g. punishment, slavery, property and engagements (promises). Though he believed that these principles arose from within what may be called natural theology, he maintained that they were wholly in accord with the teaching of the Bible for the conduct of society.

As the topic of slavery was a major public issue in the 1790s his remarks on this subject will serve to illustrate his teaching. If slavery is "the condition of a person who is compelled to labour at the will of another without any previous contract" then a person may be forced (on the basis of natural justice) to be a slave only on one of two possible grounds—for indemnification or for punishment. This slavery must cease as soon as the just purposes for which it was imposed are obtained. Further, the master has no absolute right to possess the service of the children of the slave. He may only possess their service to the extent and for so long as a child would normally be under the direction of his parent. If the master has rights, he also has duties:

> Not having the right to endanger the life or health of the slave, except so far as the danger is the unavoidable consequence of the reasonable service of the latter; he is obliged in justice either to provide food, clothing, and other necessaries, for the slave, or to allow sufficient time and opportunities for the other to provide them. He is also bound in the sight of God to consult by benevolent precautions in his general conduct the preservation of the health of the slave, and the recovery of it when impaired; and particularly to superintend his morals, and to furnish him with the means of religious instruction; to treat him on all occasions with kindness and forbearance, more especially to be mild in exacting labour and inflicting punishment; and not to give or sell the slave to any person, whom he does not think likely faithfully to perform the duties of a master.[20]

Thus it is possible to reconcile natural justice and slavery. Whether in fact slavery was practiced anywhere in the world according to such justice Gisborne does not say. Like Scott he accepted that the institution of slavery according to justice was acceptable in a world where there was sin and evil.

To accept slavery as theoretically justifiable did not mean that one had to accept the African slave-trade as according to natural justice:

> Whoever has *honestly purchased* from the *proper owner*, either in Africa or the West Indies, a slave, whom, after *serious enquiry*, he *believes in his conscience* to have been deservedly condemned to that state for either of these ends (indemnification or punishment) has not violated justice in the transaction.

Nor, supposing that his conviction continues, and that he faithfully discharges the duties of a master, will he act unjustly in exacting the labour of the slave during the term for which he was condemned (whether it were for a limited period or for life), nor in disposing of him for the whole or any part of the term to any other person, whom he has reason to think disposed and likely to treat the slave properly.

Having in mind the information so often put before the House of Commons concerning the nature of the African slave-trade he went on:

But whoever has defrauded the former owner of a slave in the original purchase; whoever has accepted or exercised a power over the liberty of another, without having made full and impartial inquiries whether that liberty is justly forfeited, and is also justly at the disposal of the seller; or without being convinced in his conscience that the fact is so; whoever detains the slave in bondage directly or indirectly a moment after the conviction has been done away; or a moment after the conclusion of the time for which slavery may justly be continued; whoever does not faithfully discharge the duties of a master, or transfers his slave to another whom he does not think likely to discharge them, commits in each of these cases a flagrant sin against God: and, in most of them, as flagrant an act of injustice to man.[21]

By these statements the African slave-trade was condemned on various counts. As he asked, "Does he [the slave owner in West Indies] not know that the wretched beings whom he purchases are almost universally the victims of avarice, treachery and rapine?" For many reasons "the trade ought instantly and universally to be abandoned." And Gisborne gave full support to Wilberforce to bring the trade to an end.

In the fifth edition of *Principles* (1798) there is a long appendix, "Remarks on the late decision of the House of Commons respecting the Abolition of the Slave Trade," written on 12 June 1798, and accompanied by a short letter to William Wilberforce. The Appendix contains a tract written by Gisborne in 1792 after the House of Commons had decided that the slave-trade should be gradually abolished. The content of the tract is a series of moral arguments against the idea of gradual abolition and in favor of instant abolition. The second part of the Appendix explains that little or nothing has improved in the six years since the tract was written, and it includes an impassioned plea to stop the slave-trade before God, the Almighty Judge, causes Providence to act against the interest of Great Britain.

However we evaluate Gisborne's intellectual contribution—and few in modern times appear to have read his writings of ethics—what we must concede is that his work, with its warm reception within evangelicalism, does show that the evangelicals not only faced up to the real challenge posed by utilitarianism but also sought to provide an alternative moral philosophy in harmony with the word of God. This is not to be underestimated when a constant tendency in evangelicalism is always toward activism and away from intellectual pursuits.

A growing amount of work by historians is being done on the beliefs and activities of the evangelicals of the nineteenth century.[22] There are good biographies of people who were deeply involved in philanthropic endeavors.[23] But little work has apparently been done to make clear the actual moral assumptions and (where articulated) principles of the evangelicals whose clergy in 1853 were reckoned to constitute one-third of the whole.[24]

Over the decades since 1960 the confidence which evangelical Anglicans in England have felt within their own denomination has shown itself by an increased involvement in ethical discussions, as in other aspects of church life.[25] This is particularly noticeable in the sphere of social ethics. From the turn of the century this had been a "no-go area," inhabited by high churchmen of the Christian Social Union, or liberals preaching a Social Gospel. As awareness has grown that evangelicals are no longer a beleaguered minority in the Church of England, so they have been willing to leave the safe ethical territory of personal morality (in which by and large a conservative stance is maintained on biblical grounds) and attempt to reassert an influence in the social and political discussions of the day. In these areas there is a readiness to be more radical, asking what kind of conduct presents the Kingdom of God as a live option in our world today, as an anticipation of the Parousia and age to come; how did Christ and his apostles view the structures of society around them; what criticisms do the standards expressed in Israelite law offer the standards accepted in our cultures; how biblical are the appeals to such biblical events as the Exodus by some "liberation theologians"? In all this the evangelical emphasis on the authority of the Bible, in matters of conduct as well as of faith, is, as one might expect, what gives this movement its particular slant.

In such a brief chapter as this it is not possible to give a full history of this development in Anglican evangelical awareness. I would not wish to imply that every Anglican evangelical is equally happy or involved with the development, or that it is simply an evangelical or simply an Anglican development. Evangelicals of many denominations have responded to the writings of such Mennonites as the American R. J. Sider; third world delegates at the American Sponsored Lausanne Congress on World Evangelisation in 1974 made a great impression on their "first world" colleagues, with their insistence that the gospel included a concern for the social and personal development of the individual and his society, and that this development could be hampered when socio-political involvement was not seen as part of Christian duty. Third World Anglican leaders such as (now Bishop) Festo Kivengere were among those making this point, and evangelical Anglicans such as John Stott among those who brought it back to Britian.

In the last two decades Evangelicals within the Church of England have held two national congresses in 1967 and 1977. After the first, Prof. J. N. D. Anderson wrote one chapter in the report—*Guidelines*, ed. J. I. Packer, Falcon Books, London, 1967. In that he covered the whole area of morality, personal and social. He reminded evangelicals of their antecedents, in men like Wilberforce and Shaftesbury, and suggested that contemporary evangelicals need to rethink some of their accepted views in social fields. In the decade which followed David Sheppard, now Bishop of Liverpool, wrote *Built as a City* (1974) from his experience as a missioner and bishop in East and South London. In it he examined the church's task when faced with the moral challenges of powerlessness among the city dwellers of our generation. A group of younger evangelicals, encouraged by theological college staff began a series of stimulating ethical studies (Grove Ethics Booklets, Bramcote, Nottingham, 1973 ...) which have sought to encourage ethical thinking and awareness among evangelicals and others, initially within an Anglican constituency. In the spheres of personal morality the Nationwide Festival of Light, many of whose leaders have been members of the Church of England, has championed a responsible Christian approach to sexual and family morality. Thus, when the second National Evangelical Anglican Congress met in 1977 one of the three preparatory books written to lead into the congress was devoted entirely to ethical issues (*Obeying Christ in a Changing World, 3: The Changing World*, ed. by Bruce Kaye, Collins Fontana, Glasgow). The study group on 'Power within Democracy' at that congress proved one of the most lively, however, and the divisions in thinking on social ethics among evangelical Anglicans (as in the Episcopal church more widely) are evident in that one group within the working party threatened to throw out what they felt to be a series of left-of-center resolutions proposed by the steering committee, and so the final report (Falcon Books, London, 1977) contains an alternative statement, of a more individualistic cast.

It would be wrong to claim that ethics is now a major emphasis in Anglican evangelical thinking, though it is much more prominent than at the middle of the century. There are evangelicals holding prominent positions in the Church of England's Board for Social Responsibility, and in some of the British Universities. The subject remains, however, neglected at theological college level. It is something which usually goes along with pastoral studies in a subsidiary way.

II. Contemporary Theory

5

Thoughts After Lambeth

by T. S. Eliot

The Church of England washes its dirty linen in public. It is convenient and brief to begin with this metaphorical statement. In contrast to some other institutions both civil and ecclesiastical, the linen does get washed. To have linen to wash is something; and to assert that one's linen never needed washing would be a suspicious boast. Without some understanding of these habits of the Church, the reader of the Report of the Lambeth Conference (1930) will find it a difficult and in some directions a misleading document. The Report needs to be read in the light of previous Reports; with some knowledge, and with some sympathy for that oddest of institutions, the Church of England.

The Conference is certainly more important than any report of it can be. I mean that each Conference has its place in the history of Lambeth Conferences, and that directions and tendencies are more significant than the precise formulation of the results obtained at any particular moment. To say that a significant direction can be traced, is not to applaud any aimless flux. But I suspect that many readers of the Report, especially those outside of the Anglican communion, are prepared to find (or prepared to condemn because they know they will not find) the clear hard and fast distinctions and decisions of a Papal Encyclical. Of such is Mr. George Malcolm Thomson, whose lively pamphlet in this series[1] has given me food for thought. Between a Lambeth Conference Report and a Papal Encyclical there is little similarity; there is a fundamental difference of intent. Perhaps the term "encyclical letter" for the archiepiscopal communication heading the Report is itself misleading, because it suggests to many minds the voice of final authority *de fide et moribus;* and to those who hope for the voice of absoluteness and the words of hard precision, the recommendations and pious hopes will be disappointing. Many, like Mr. Thompson, will exclaim that they find only platitudes, commonplaces, tergiversations and ambiguities. The Report of the Conference is not intended to be an absolute decree on questions of faith and morals; for the matter of that, the opinions expressed have no compulsion until ratified by Convocation. The Report, as a whole, is rather the expression of the ways in which the Church is moving, than an instruction to the faithful on belief and conduct.

Another consideration which we must keep in mind, before venturing to criticise the Report, is the manner of its composition. Some of the Report is to me, I admit at once, mere verbiage; some parts seem to me evasive; some parts seem to me to be badly expressed, at least if the ordinary uninstructed reader is acknowledged; one or two recommendations I deplore. But it ought not to be an occasion to us for mirth that three hundred bishops together assembled should, on pooling their views on most momentous matters, come out with a certain proportion of nonsense. I should not enjoy having to commit myself on any subject to any opinion which should also be that of any two hundred and ninety-nine of my acquaintance. Let us consider the quantity of nonsense that some of our most eminent scientists, professors and men of letters are able, each for himself, to turn out during every publishing season. Let us imagine (if we can imagine such persons agreeing to that extent) the fatuity of an encyclical letter produced by the joint efforts of Mr. H. G. Wells, Mr. Bernard Shaw and Mr. Russell; or Professors Whitehead, Eddington and Jeans; or Dr. Freud, Dr. Jung and Dr. Adler; or Mr. Murry, Mr. Fausset, the Huxley Brothers and the Reverend Dr. Potter of America.

With this comparison in mind, it is, I think, profitable to dispose first of those sections of the Report which are most insipid, and of that which has received most popular notice. I regret that what seem to me some of the best parts of the Report, such as the section on *The Christian Doctrine of God*, have been neglected in favor of those sections about which readers of the penny press are most ready to excite themselves. But if one is writing about the Report, one must be willing to offer one's own comment on these already over-commented sections. The report on "Youth and its Vocation" suggests that the bishops had been listening to ordinary popular drivel on the subject, or ordinary popular drivel about what the bishops themselves are supposed to believe. They begin with a protest which for any intelligent reader should be unnecessary. "We desire at the outset to protest emphatically against the contention that the Youth of today are, as a whole, less moral or less religious than youth of previous generations." It ought to be obvious that the Youth of today are not "as a whole" more or less anything than the youth of previous generations. The statement, not having much meaning, need not occupy much attention. "There are signs of a great intellectual stirring among the rising generation." One could wish that this journalistic hyperbole had been avoided. There can hardly be a great intellectual stirring among a whole generation, because the number of persons in any generation capable of being greatly stirred intellectually is always and everywhere very, very small. What the bishops might have said, I think, with justice, is this: that one does find here and there among educated young men a respect for the Church springing from a recognition of the intellectual ability which during two thousand years has gone to its formation. The number of persons interested in philosophy is always small; but whereas twenty years ago a young man attracted by metaphysical speculation was usually indifferent to theology, I believe that today a similar young man is more ready to believe that theology is a masculine discipline, than were those of my generation. If the capacity for faith be no greater, the prejudice against it is less; though one must remember to congratulate youth on finding themselves in this situation, before admiring them for taking advantage of it. I hope at this point that of the fifty bishops who committed themselves to the *dismal trope* that "youth of this generation . . . has admittedly struck its tents and is on the march," there was a large minority of dissentients. That is one of the troubles of the time: not only Youth but Middle Age is on the march; everybody, at least according to Fleet Street, is on the march; it does not matter what the destination is, the one thing contemptible is to sit still.

Youth, of course, is from one point of view merely a symptom of the results of what the middle-aged have been thinking and saying. I notice that the same fifty bishops refer guardedly to "the published works of certain authors whose recognized ability and position give undue weight to views on the relations of the sexes which are in direct conflict with Christian principles." I wish that they had mentioned names. For unfortunately, the only two authors of "recognized ability and position" officially disapproved in England are Mr. James Joyce and D. H. Lawrence; so that the fifty bishops have missed an opportunity of dissociating themselves from the condemnation of these two extremely serious and improving writers.[2] If, however, the fifty were thinking of Mr. Bertrand Russell or even of Mr. Aldous Huxley, then they are being apprehensive about what to

me is a reason for cheerfulness; for if Youth has the spirit of a tomtit
or the brain of a goose, it can hardly rally with enthusiasm to these
two depressing life-forcers. (Not that Mr. Huxley, who has no
philosophy that I can discover, and who succeeds to some extent in
elucidating how sordid a world without any philosophy can be, has
much in common with Mr. Russell.) I cannot regret that such views
as Mr. Russell's, or what we may call the enervate *gospel of happiness*, are openly expounded and defended. They help to make clear,
what the nineteenth century had been largely occupied in ob-
scuring, that there is no such thing as just Morality; but that for any
man who thinks clearly, as his Faith is so will his Morals be. Were
my religion that of Mr. Russell, my views of conduct would very
likely be his also; and I am sure in my own mind that I have not
adopted my faith in order to defend my views of conduct, but have
modified my views of conduct to conform with what seem to me the
implications of my beliefs. The real conflict is not between one set
of moral prejudices and another, but between the theistic and the
atheistic faith; and it is all for the best that the division should be
sharply drawn. Emancipation had some interest for venturous
spirits when I was young, and must have been quite exciting to the
previous generation; but the Youth to which the bishops' words
apply is grey-haired now. Emancipation loses some of its charm in
becoming respectable. Indeed, the gospel of happiness in the form
preached by Mr. Russell in middle age is such as I cannot conceive
as capable of making any appeal to Mr. Russell in youth, so medio-
cre and respectable is it. It has nothing to offer to those born into
the world which Mr. Russell and others helped to create. The elders
have had the satisfaction of throwing off prejudices; that is, of
persuading themselves that the way they want to behave is the only
moral way to behave; but there is not much in it for those who have
no prejudices to reject. Christian morals gain immeasurably in
richness and freedom by being seen as *the consequence of Christian
faith*, and not as the imposition of tyrannical and irrational habit.
What chiefly remains of the new freedom is its meagre impov-
erished emotional life; in the end it is the Christian who can have
the more varied, refined and intense enjoyment of life; which time
will demonstrate.

Before leaving the not very remunerative subject of Youth, I must
mention another respect, not unrelated, in which Youth of today
has some advantage over an earlier generation. (I dislike the word
"generation," which has been a talisman for the last ten years;
when I wrote a poem called *The Waste Land* some of the more

approving critics said that I had expressed the "disillusionment of a generation," which is nonsense. I may have expressed for them their own illusion of being disillusioned, but that did not form part of my intention.) One of the most deadening influences upon the Church in the past, ever since the eighteenth century, was its acceptance, by the upper, upper middle and aspiring classes, as a political necessity and as a requirement of respectability. There are signs that the situation today is quite different. When, for instance, I brought out a small book of essays, several years ago, called *For Lancelot Andrewes*, the anonymous reviewer in the *Times Literary Supplement* made it the occasion for what I can only describe as a flattering obituary notice. In words of great seriousness and manifest sincerity, he pointed out that I had suddenly arrested my progress— whither he had supposed me to be moving I do not know—and that to his distress I was unmistakably making off in the wrong direction. Somehow I had failed, and had admitted my failure; if not a lost leader, at least a lost sheep; what is more, I was a kind of traitor; and those who were to find their way to the promised land beyond the waste, might drop a tear at my absence from the roll-call of the new saints. I suppose that the curiosity of this point of view will be apparent to only a few people. But its appearance in what is not only the best but the most respected and most respectable of our literary periodicals, came home to me as a hopeful sign of the times. For it meant that the orthodox faith of England is at last relieved from its burden of respectability. A new respectability has arisen to assume the burden; and those who would once have been considered intellectual vagrants are now pious pilgrims, cheerfully plodding the road from nowhere to nowhere, trolling their hymns, satisfied so long as they may be "on the march."

These changed conditions are so prevalent that any one who has been moving among intellectual circles and comes to the Church, may experience an odd and rather exhilarating feeling of isolation. The new orthodoxy, of course, has many forms, and the sectaries of one form sometimes speak hard words of others, but the outline of respectability is fairly clear. Mr. Middleton Murry, whose highly respectable new religion is continually heard to be "on the march" round the corner, though it has not reached us yet,[3] is able to say of his own version: "The words do not matter. If we can recreate the meaning—all the words of all the religions will be free to us, and we shall not want to use them." One is tempted to suggest that Mr. Murry has so many words in his employ already, including some of his own creation, that he has no need to summon others. A writer still more respectable than Mr. Murry, because he is a Professor at an American University, is Mr. Norman Foerster, the fugleman of Humanism. Mr. Foerster, who has the honest simplicity to admit that he has very little acquaintance with Christianity beyond a narrow Protestantism which he repudiates, offers Humanism because it appeals to those "who can find in themselves no vocation for spiritual humility"! without perceiving at all that this is an exact parallel to saying that Companionate Marriage "appeals to those who can find in themselves no vocation for spiritual continence." It is true that to judge from his next paragraph he has at the back of his mind some foggy distinction between "spiritual humility" and "humility" plain, but the distinction, if present, is not developed. One can now be a distinguished professor, and a professional moralist to boot, without understanding the devotional sense of the word *vocation* or the theological sense of the virtue *humility*; a virtue, indeed, not conspicuous among modern men of letters. We have as many, as solemn, and as splendidly-robed prophets today as in any decade of the last century; and it is now the fashion to rebuke the Christian in the name of some higher "religion"—or more often, in the name of something higher called "religion" plain.

However low an opinion I held of Youth, I could not believe that it can long be deceived by that vacuous word "religion." The Press may continue for a time, for the Press is always behind the times, to organize battues of popular notables, with the religion of a this and of a that; and to excite such persons to talk nonsense about the revival or decay of "religion." Religion can hardly revive, because it cannot decay. To put the matter bluntly on the lowest level, it is not to anybody's interest that religion should disappear. If it did, many compositors would be thrown out of work; the audiences of our best-selling scientists would shrink to almost nothing; and the typewriters of the Huxley Brothers would cease from tapping. Without religion the whole human race would die, as according to W. H. R. Rivers, some Melanesian tribes have died, solely of boredom. Every one would be affected: the man who regularly has a run in his car and a round of golf on Sunday, quite as much as the punctilious churchgoer. Dr. Sigmund Freud, with characteristic delicacy of feeling, has reminded us that we should "leave Heaven to the angels and the sparrows"; following his hint, we may safely leave "religion" to Mr. Julian Huxley and Dr. Freud.

At this point I may make a transition from Youth to another point in the Report, at which I feel that the bishops also had their eyes on Youth, On page 19 we read:

"Perhaps most noteworthy of all, there is much in the scientific and philosophic thinking of our time which provides a climate more favourable to faith in God than has existed for generations."

I cannot help wishing that the bishops had consulted some of the able theologians and philosophers within the Church (such as Professor A. E. Taylor, who published an excellent article on the God of Whitehead, in *Theology*) before they had bestowed this benediction on our latest ramp of best-sellers. I do not disagree with the literal sense of the pronouncement which I have just quoted. Perhaps it is rather the tone of excessive amiability that I deprecate. I feel that the scientists should be received as penitents for the sins of an earlier scientific generation, rather than acclaimed as new friends and allies. And it may be an exceptional austerity or insensitiveness on my part, but I cannot consent to take climatic conditions so seriously as the phrase above seems to allow us to do. I do not wish to disparage the possible usefulness of the views set forth by Whitehead and Eddington and others. But it ought to be made quite clear that these writers cannot confirm any one in the faith; they can merely have the practical value of removing prejudices from the minds of those who have not the faith but who might possibly come to it: the distinction seems to me of capital importance.

One characteristic which increased my suspicion of the scientific paladins of religion is that they are all Englishmen, or at least all Anglo-Saxons. I have seen a few reported remarks on religion and philosophy from the lips of such men as Einstein, Schroedinger and Planck; but they had the excuse of being interviewed by Mr. Sullivan; and the remarks were chiefly interesting, as I imagine Mr. Sullivan intended them to be, for the light they threw on the minds of these interesting scientists; none of these men has so far written a popular book of peeps into the fairyland of Reality. I suspect that there is some taint of Original H. G. Wells about most of us in English-speaking countries; and that we enjoy drawing general conclusions from particular disciplines, using our accomplishment in one field as the justification for theorizing about the world in general. It is also a weakness of Anglo-Saxons to like to hold personal and private religions and to promulgate them. And when a scientist gets loose into the field of religion, all that he can do is to give us the impression which his scientific knowledge and thought has produced upon his everyday, and usually commonplace, personal and private imagination.[4]

Even, however, in the section on Youth, we may find some wise and true sayings, if we have the patience to look for them. "The best of the younger generation in every section of the community," we are told, "and in every country of the world, are not seeking a religion that is watered down or robbed of the severity of its demands, but a religion that will not only give them a sure basis and an ultimate sanction for morals, but also a power to persevere in reaching out after the ideal which in their heart of hearts they recognize as the finest and best." I wish that this might have been said in fewer words, but the meaning is sound, and cannot be repeated too often. There is no good in making Christianity easy and pleasant; "Youth," or the better part of it, is more likely to come to a difficult religion than to an easy one. For some, the intellectual way of approach must be emphasized; there is need of a more intellectual laity. For them and for others, the way of discipline and asceticism must be emphasized; for even the humblest Christian layman can and must live what, in the modern world, is comparatively an ascetic life. Discipline of the emotions is even rarer, and in the modern world still more difficult, than discipline of the mind; some eminent lay preachers of "discipline" are men who know only the latter. Thought, study, mortification, sacrifice: it is such notions as these that should be impressed upon the young—who differ from the young of other times merely in having a different middle-aged generation behind them. You will never attract the young by making Christianity easy; but a good many can be attracted by finding it difficult: difficult both to the disorderly mind and to the unruly passions.

I refer with some reluctance, but with positive conviction, to the much-discussed Resolution 15 on marriage and birth control. On one part of the problem there is an admirable analytical study by the Master of Corpus in *Theology* for December, 1930. I can only add one suggestion to that statement, without attempting the problems of casuistry which the Master of Corpus discusses with great skill. I feel that the Conference was not only right and courageous to express a view on the subject of procreation radically different from that of Rome; but that the attitude adopted is more important than this particular question, important as it may be, and indicates a radical difference between the Anglican and the Roman views on other matters. I regret, however, that the bishops have placed so much reliance upon the Individual Conscience; and by so doing jeopardized the benefits of their independence. Certainly, any one who is wholly sincere and pure in heart may seek for guidance from the

Holy Spirit; but who of us is always wholly sincere, especially where the most imperative of instincts may be strong enough to simulate to perfection the voice of the Holy Spirit?

The Resolution shows pretty clearly both the strength and the weakness of the Report, and the strength and weakness of the Anglican Church. The recognition of contraception is, I feel sure, something quite different from a concession to "modern" opinion. It was a courageous facing of facts of life; and was the only way of dealing with the question possible within the Anglican organization. But before asserting the distinct character of the Anglican Church in this way, the bishops must have taken a good deal of thought about it; all the more astonishing that they did not take a little more thought, and not proceed to a statement which seems to me almost suicidal. For to allow that "each couple" should take counsel only if perplexed in mind is almost to surrender the whole citadel of the Church. It is ten to one, considering the extreme disingenuity of humanity, which ought to be patent to all after so many thousand years, that only a very small minority will be "perplexed"; and in view of the words of the bishops it is ten to one that the honest minority which takes "competent advice" (and I observe that the order of words is "medical and spiritual") will have to appeal to a clergy just as perplexed at itself, or else stung into an obstinacy greater than that of any Roman clergy, by the futility of this sentence.

In short, the whole resolution shows the admirable English devotion to commonsense, but also the deplorable Anglican habit of standing things on their heads in the name of commonsense. It is exactly this matter of "spiritual advice" which should have been examined and analysed if necessary for years, before making any pronouncement. But the principle is simple, though the successful application might require time. I do not suggest that the full Sacrament of Confession and Penance should be imposed upon every communicant of the Church; but the Church ought to be able to enjoin upon all its communicants that they should take spiritual advice upon specified problems of life; and both clergy and parishioners should recognize the full seriousness and responsibility of such consultation. I am *not* unaware that as opinions and theories vary at present, those seeking direction can always find the direction they seek, if they know where to apply; but that is inevitable. But here, if anywhere, is definitely a matter upon which the Individual Conscience is no reliable guide; spiritual guidance should be imperative; and it should be clearly placed above medical advice—where also, opinions and theories vary indefinitely. In short, a general principle of the greatest importance, exceeding the application to this particular issue alone, might have been laid down; and its enunciation was evaded.

To put it frankly, but I hope not offensively, the Roman view in general seems to me to be that a principle must be affirmed without exception; and that thereafter exceptions can be dealt with, without modifying the principle. The view natural to the English mind, I believe, is rather that a principle must be framed in such a way as to include all allowable exceptions. It follows inevitably that the Roman Church must profess to be fixed, while the Anglican Church must profess to take account of changed conditions. I hope that it is unnecessary to give the assurance that I do not consider the Roman way of thought dishonest, and that I would not endorse any cheap and facile gibes about the duplicity and dissimulation of that Church; it is another conception of human nature and of the means by which, on the whole, the greatest number of souls can be saved; but the difference goes deep. *Prudenti dissimulation uti*[5] is not a precept which appeals to Anglo-Saxon theology; and here again, the Anglican Church can admit national (I do not mean nationalistic) differences in theory and practice which the more formal organization of Rome cannot recognize. What in England is the right balance between individual liberty and discipline?—between individual responsibility and obedience?—active co-operation and passive reception? And to what extremity are divergences of belief and practice permissible? These are questions which the English mind must always ask; and the answers can only be found, if with hesitation and difficulty, through the English Church. The admission of inconsistencies, sometimes ridiculed as indifference to logic and coherence, of which the English mind is often accused, may be largely the admission of inconsistencies inherent in life itself, and of the impossibility of overcoming them by the imposition of a uniformity greater than life will bear.

Even, however, if the Anglican Church affirmed, as I think it should affirm, the necessity for spiritual direction in admitting the exceptions, the Episcopate still has the responsibility of giving direction to the directors. I cannot but suspect that here the Roman doctrine, so far as I have seen it expounded, leaves us uncertain as does the Anglican. For example: according to the Roman doctrine, which is more commendable—prudent continence in marriage, or unlimited procreation up to the limit of the mother's strength? If the latter, the Church seems to me obliged to offer some solution to the economic questions raised by such a practice: for surely, if you lay down a moral law which leads, in practice, to unfortunate social consequences—such as over-population or destitution—you make yourself responsible for providing some resolution of these consequences. If the former, what motives are right motives? The latest Papal Encyclical appears to be completely decisive about the question of Resolution 15—at the cost of solving no individual's problems. And the Resolution is equally, though perhaps no more, unsatisfactory. The Roman statement leaves unanswered the questions: When is it right to limit the family? and: When is it wrong not to limit it? And the Anglican statement leaves unanswered the questions: When is it right to limit the family and right to limit it only by continence? and: When is it right to limit the family by contraception?

On the other hand, the fact that Resolution 15, as I take it, is wrong *primarily* in isolating and treating as independent a question which should be considered as a detail subsumed under the more general question which should have been treated first—that of Spiritual Direction and Authority; this fact does I think indicate one recurrent cause of weakness. When the episcopal mind sees that something is self-evidently desirable in itself, it seems inclined to turn first to consider the means for bringing it into being, rather than to find the theological grounds upon which it can be justified; and there are traces of this zeal here and there in the suggestions towards Reunion and fraternization. For instance (p. 117 of the Report), it is suggested that a bishop might authorize and encourage baptised communicant members of churches not in communion with our own, to communicate in his diocese with Anglicans "when the ministrations of their own Church are not available." It is true that this is to be done only under special and temporary local conditions; and it does not form part of my purpose to doubt that under the conditions which the bishops must have had in mind, such intercommunion is most desirable. But what does the suggestion imply? Surely, *if* dissenters should never communicate in Anglican churches, or *if* in certain circumstances they should be encouraged to do so, two very different theories of the Sacrament of the Altar are implied. For the innovation proposed, theological justification is required. What is required is some theory of degrees of reception of the Blessed Sacrament, as well as the validity of the ministration of a celebrant not episcopally ordained. My objection therefore is not to the admission of dissenters to the Altar—and I do not wish to attack what has not yet been defended—but to the propagation of this practice before theological justification has been expounded. Possibly theology is what Bradley said philosophy was: "the finding of bad reasons for what we believe upon instinct"; I think it may be the finding of good reasons for what we believe upon instinct; but if the Church of England cannot find these reasons, and make them intelligible to the more philosophically trained among the faithful, what can it do?

Where is american Moral Theology Today in light of this essay?

6

Revising Anglican Moral Theology

by Timothy F. Sedgwick

Does Anglicanism have a normative, distinctive, and adequate moral theology? It is often asserted that such a moral theology grew out of the Oxford Movement and is represented by such figures as James Skinner, Kenneth Kirk, and Herbert Waddams. This chapter challenges such an assertion on all three counts. The moral theology associated with the Oxford Movement is not normative because it does not reflect the diversity of positions to be found in the Caroline Divines; it is not philosophically and theologically distinctive because it took its basic presuppositions directly from nineteenth century Thomism; and it is not adequate because it does not present a historical understanding of human life. In this situation, the Roman Catholic moral theology which has emerged since Vatican II presents Anglicanism with an opportunity and a challenge.

A 1977 Anglican symposium on ethics concluded, "In our proceedings the Anglicans, under questioning from other Christians, became aware that they were not altogether clear among themselves about the bases, the convictions, the history, from which Anglicans have typically proceeded in dealing with questions of the private and the public good."[1] The problem is not that there are no systematic Anglican ethicists. One need only look at Richard Hooker or Jeremy Taylor, the Cambridge Platonists or Joseph Butler, Samuel Taylor Coleridge or F. D. Maurice, William Temple or Kenneth Kirk. Rather, the problem is what is Anglican about such ethicists, at which points do they agree on fundamental convictions, and what then is the way in which one should proceed from fundamental beliefs to moral judgments? The answer to these questions is important in order to establish what is Anglican identity and to identify the sources and develop the method that will enable moral guidance.

My interest in this chapter is to open discussion about the moral life in terms of Anglican identity. Specifically, I want to engage one segment of the Anglican tradition, the tradition of Anglican moral theology that has developed since the second half of the nineteenth century, propelled by the interest in Roman Catholicism after the Oxford Movement (1833–1845). This literature proposes a normative definition of the content of the Christian moral life and the

121

method by which moral theology should proceed in order to provide guidance for what is called "the cure of souls." By engaging this tradition, one answer to the 1977 symposium will be presented. By analyzing the adequacy of Anglican moral theology in its representation of Anglican history, I will relativize its claim to represent Anglicanism in general. The specific philosophical and theological presuppositions that undergird their understanding of Christian faith and the moral life may then be dealt with on their own merit. Specifically, I will argue that Anglican moral theology appropriated a Thomistic framework which dominated its conception of moral theology and Anglican identity. Those standing in this tradition implicitly had a normative definition of Anglicanism which prevented them from recognizing the diversity of assumptions which prevented them from recognizing the diversity of assumptions which undergird the theologies of the seventeenth century Caroline Divines. The warrants for Anglican moral theology are not then historical, but rather philosophical and theological.

Freed from any simple claim that Anglican moral theology expresses the historical identity of Anglicanism, the critique of the Thomistic philosophical and theological assumptions which ground its thought will be considered. The critique has come largely from contemporary Roman Catholics. Criticisms have focused in three areas: the relationship of Christian faith to morality, the character of moral decision-making, and the nature of the criteria for moral judgments. These criticisms have then raised broader questions about the purpose of the Church in relationship to the moral life. The criticisms themselves are grounded in a change of world view or world perspective, what Bernard Lonergan has called "the transition from a classicist world-view to historical mindedness."[2] It is the historical understanding of human life which opens up and necessitates new ways of envisioning the moral life and so the task of guidance in the Christian life. By presenting this challenge, the intent is, at the very least, to press the questions which Anglicans must ask if they are to assess their heritage critically in order to develop and articulate their present identity and to provide resources for the Christian moral life.

I.

While denying the authority of the church to exercise the disciplinary action that the Roman Catholics used in many matters, Anglican works in moral theology are themselves largely concerned with providing guidance for the priest by developing principles and rules which enable assigning degress of culpability to the penitent. As might be expected with the renewed interest in sacramental confession, Anglican moral theologians after the Oxford Movement appropriated the framework we associate with the Roman Catholic manualists.[3] The first attempt to develop such a moral theology began in England in 1870 when the Fathers of the Cowley Mission of St. John the Evangelist initiated a committee of clergy for the construction of a "Manual of Moral Theology." James Skinner came prepared for this meeting with a rough sketch of the outlines of moral theology. Pressed by the others to publish this outline, Skinner, in spite of his feeble health, managed to revise his sketch and in 1882 publish a detailed *Synopsis of Moral and Ascetical Theology.*[4] This became for those that have followed a normative expression of the structure and character of moral theology.

The development of a contemporary and comprehensive moral theology is credited to Kenneth E. Kirk. He has in fact been called "the outstanding moralist of the modern Church of England."[5] His four major works in moral theology—*Some Principles of Moral Theology* (1920), *Ignorance, Faith and Conformity* (1925), *Conscience and its Problems* (1927), and *The Vision of God* (1931)—are standard references for Anglicans. In *Some Principles of Moral Theology,* Kirk himself claims that Skinner's *Synopsis* "is by far the greatest" contribution to constructing an Anglican moral theology.[6] In fact, all the works by Anglicans assume the framework adopted by Skinner. In 1892 John J. Elmendorf published *Elements of Moral Theology Based on the Summa Theologiae of St. Thomas Aquinas,* and William Walter Webb published *The Cure of Souls,* a manual which develops specific judgments within Skinner's larger framework.[7]

The development of Anglican moral theology may be completed for the late nineteenth and early twentieth century by noting two additional works. In 1878 Edward B. Pusey, himself one of the founders of the Oxford Movement, wrote a long introduction and translation of the Roman Catholic Jean-Joseph Gaume's *Manual for Confessors.*[8] Although not specifically a work in moral theology, this translation and introduction indicates the context in which the call for moral theology arose. In 1924 Francis J. Hall and Frank H. Hallock published *Moral Theology.*[9] Based on lectures given at Western Theological Seminary in Chicago, Hall, like Webb and Elmendorf, attempts to develop the specific content implied in Skinner's *Synopsis.* We may then capture the structure and character of Anglican moral theology by reviewing Skinner's *Synopsis* and then Kirk's development of the assumptions or first principles of this moral theology.

In his *Synopsis*, Skinner "adopts the Scholastic method of *arrangement*."[10] The first part is concerned with foundations. Skinner accepts the Aristotelian division of the soul as consisting of sensate and rational powers which governed by the will move the self toward the end of union with God. The *Synopsis* then calls for a detailed development of a theory of action grounded on right reason. After analyzing choice, moral theology needs to develop the internal rule of action (i.e., the criteria for a good conscience) and then the external rule of action (i.e., a natural law theory). Parts two and three move from this foundation to the specific content of the Christian life. Part two considers the first four of the Ten Commandments, duties toward God. These are to be developed through a consideration of the theological virtues (faith, hope, and love), the cardinal virtues (prudence, fortitude, temperance, and justice), the gifts and fruit of the Holy Spirit, the Beatitudes, the Evangelical Counsels (obedience, poverty, and chastity), the nature of true worship, and the monastic life. Part three takes up the last six of the Ten Commandments, duties toward the neighbor. These all may be understood in terms of justice, giving each person their due. Part four moves from the content of the Christian moral life to the aids for the Christian life, the sacraments. Special attention is given to the sacrament of penance (reconciliation) and to ecclesiastical order, including the criteria for the proper function of the offices of the Church.

Following Skinner's *Synopsis*, the first task in developing a moral theology is the development of a theory of action, including the end of action. This leads to assumptions regarding the nature of conscience and the nature of moral principles and rules. This, as Kirk says in *Some Principles of Moral Theology*, constitutes the study of Christian ethics: "a branch of study preliminary to moral theology—an inquiry into the general principles of all ethics (the nature of happiness, of the voluntary and involuntary, of the moral consciousness and the moral criteria) undertaken with the object of establishing the truth of the Christian doctrine on these points."[11] In other words, as James M. Gustafson designates the subject of Christian ethics, Christian ethics is interested in answering three fundamental questions: the nature of the good, the nature of moral agency, and the nature of the criteria for moral judgment.[12] Moral theology is more narrowly understood in terms of casuistry, a study of the "collection of precedents and considerations . . . intended to guide the Christian in his decisions." Of importance but set aside as a larger concern is what Kirk calls "the wider demands of Christian ethics—those which concern social, national and international intercourse."[13] Such an interest was expressed by Christian socialists at the time of Kirk and is now generally referred to as the concerns of religion and society or Christian faith and culture.

In *Some Principles of Moral Theology,* Kirk states what he sees as the central postulates for a moral theology. Above all, the "two fundamental postulates" are:

> (i) The Soul is free to choose between good and bad, right and wrong, in all its actions: it has what is technically known as free-will. (ii) The Soul, however tainted or corrupted by sin, retains an innate power both of perceiving what is good and right, and of aspiring to it—a conscience, in short; though that power may be grievously weakened and perverted, and in the end may be altogether inhibited by a constant life of vicious habits.[14]

The establishment of these postulates, it would seem, rests with philosophical anthropology, i.e., a philosophical account of human agency. Such postulates could be understood from a number of different frameworks—Aristotelian-Thomistic, Kantian, existential, British action theory, phenomenological. Kirk, however, says quite as a matter of fact that "the truth of these two assumptions rests not with moral theology but with Christian apologetics."[15] This is strange for he has just indicated that the task of Christian ethics is an inquiry into the "general principles of all ethics." What appears to be assumed is that these "two fundamental postulates" would be understood in the same way regardless of the different philosophical framework used to defend the notion of free-will and moral knowledge. As Kirk says:

> Scholastic philosophy adopted almost without question the Aristotelian psychology which, in its garbled Latin dress and with certain later developments, had come down to it; and Roman theologians still think in Aristotelian terms under the influence of St. Thomas Aquinas. The English student may therefore believe himself free to employ in his account of the soul and its properties both the terms and the conclusions of modern psychological research, provided always that these do not, either implicitly or explicitly, run counter to the two fundamental postulates of Scripture and Christian doctrine, without which a Christian science of morality is impossible.[16]

It is difficult to believe, however, that Kirk actually would think that the philosophical framework would make no difference. Certainly the intellectualist tradition of Aristotle and the voluntarist tradition of the nominalist, Protestant Reformers, and contemporary existentialists affirm understandings of free-will and moral knowledge; and yet they do so in ways that make a significant difference in their understanding of the character of the moral life.[17] In fact Kirk holds so closely to the intellectualist tradition with its affirmation that values are objectively knowable that he commits himself to a particular philosophical framework, that represented by Aristotle and Thomas. In spite of Kirk's claim to reject faculty psychology and to claim "that consciousness is an indivisible unit whose 'parts' are no more than logical abstractions,"[18] he actually holds to a faculty psychology which understands reason as an ahistorical capacity to grasp objective truth. Kirk believes, as Frederick Olafson claims regarding the intellectualist thesis, "that value predicates have meaning by virtue of standing for objective qualities or relations that are independent of our feelings and volitions; that rational beings are able to apprehend these qualities; and that true (and false) statements can accordingly be made about them."[19]

This is best exemplified by the fact that Kirk accepts the scholastic distinction between *synderesis* as reason grasping first principles of morality and conscience (*syneidesis*) as the application of the first principles to the concrete situation through practical reason. "The validity," says Kirk, "of general principles of morality is no more here in question than is their origin. For just as moral theology assumes that its principles, whatever their immediate source, have their ultimate origin in the self-revelation of God to man, so too it assumes that these principles (as formulated by the Church under the guidance of the Holy Spirit), have a validity which will be unquestioned by the normal Christian conscience."[20]

Given this objectivist framework regarding the moral content of Christian faith, the "standing problem of all ethics," says Kirk, "is the reconciliation of two apparently opposed principles, which may be called the principle of law and liberty, or of authority and individualism."[21] "Laws—both of nature and of God—will be binding; that is to say, wherever, upon reflection, a case is found to fall wholly and clearly under one of them, there will be no room for further discussion and questioning. The law will be obeyed."[22] As Kirk later claims, moral theology is then "concerned not so much with the highest standards of Christian conduct . . . as with the *minimum* standard to which conduct must attain if it is to be adjudged worthy of the name 'Christian' at all."[23] What keeps this from being simply minimalistic and legalistic is Kirk's claim that such laws have their ground in an ideal which is the vision of God.[24] The Christian life is not simply moved by external obedience to the rule but by the law written upon the heart; the external law is but the objective expression of the act which joins the soul with God.

> Natural law is completed in divine law; and the essence of the divine law is first of all that it is of internal conditions rather than of external acts, and secondly that it is in the main a *lex non scripta*, a law implanted in the soul. The gospel precepts indeed, the Beatitudes, even the decalogue in its Christian reinterpretation, are a part of this new law; they prepare and fit the soul to receive the power of the Holy Spirit; but in essence it is a law of liberty. The ideal Christian, in other words, would be one who, while fully possessed of the principles of morality, need never to call them to mind. He would be so full of the Spirit, so intimately in communion with his Lord, that his actions would spontaneously correspond with the Christian ideal; he would then have no need either to consider them beforehand or to review them afterwards.[25]

The rest of Kirk's corpus can be understood as deepening reflections on the tradition within this basic intellectualist framework. Kirk's second book, *Ignorance, Faith and Conformity,* is a quite narrow study of "invincible ignorance" in order to understand and reconcile the tension between law and liberty. Kirk's own conception of the true nature of Christian faith and the moral life is indicated by his broad generalization that begins the text. "The history of moral theology in the West is in the main a history of successive attempts to adjust the claims of conscience to the claims of law."[26] In *Conscience and Its Problems,* Kirk attempts to show how to apply Christian principles to contemporary society. Again, while recognizing the question of foundations, Kirk proceeds from within a Thomistic framework which he seems to take for granted as most adequate. As Kirk notes,

> It might perhaps have been more logical to have started the detailed approach to moral theology by a discussion of the purpose of life; and to have developed an ideal code of Christian ethics co-ordinated round one central principal—be it the vision of God, the proclamation of the Kingdom, the brother-

hood of mankind or the imitation of Christ. But about the main principles of Christian conduct, as applicable to a civilisation like our own, there is little controversy. Difficulties only begin with the discussion of the subordinate precepts dependent upon these main principles; and such subordinate precepts can only be reached with any degree of assurance and unanimity if the rules of procedure adopted are both wise and commonly accepted. Here, therefore, at the point where controversy presses, a prior study of casuistry is all-essential.[27]

Kirk's framework for understanding the Christian life, the intellectualist framework of Thomas, was apparently indelibly imprinted upon his thinking. When he turned to the broader interest of Christian ethics in *The Vision of God*, he does not investigate philosophical presuppositions but takes the dominant Thomist image and uses it to normatively interpret the Christian tradition. Again the problem of law and liberty is the central focus, understood and reconciled in terms of worship as the end of humanity. The errors of the moral life are the result of losing sight of God and worshiping the external manifestations of true faith. When this happens moral precepts turn Christian faith into a formalism, corporate discipline becomes the worship of the institution, and the experience of God as exemplified by asceticism becomes simply a rigorism against the world.

The few contemporary writings in moral theology by Anglicans also reflect the intellectualist framework of Thomas. R. C. Mortimer in 1947 wrote *The Elements of Moral Theology* as a work which would follow in Kirk's footsteps in introducing moral theology to Anglican readers, especially "the younger Clergy and those training for Orders in the Theological Colleges," and to "afford a starting point . . . for the compilation of an Anglican manual." The book itself follows Thomas in "an enquiry into man's end, into the nature of human actions and their morality, into the law of God to which those actions should conform, into conscience by which man perceives that law and directs his actions, and into the virtues whereby he manifests obedience to God and the sins whereby he revolts from him."[28] More contemporary, Herbert Waddams writes *A New Introduction to Moral Theology* and Lindsay Dewar writes *An Outline of Anglican Moral Theology.*[29] The structure basically remains the same; what is new is the updating of the practical reflections on sexuality, the use of force, the sanctity of life, and the problem of wealth.

II.

The formation of the Anglican Church in the sixteenth and seventeenth centuries necessitated theological justification, vision, and articulation. Public debate nurtured such reflection. We now have an extensive legacy of writings which are identified as the works of the Caroline Divines, most notably Richard Hooker (1554–1600), Robert Sanderson (1587–1663), and Jeremy Taylor (1613–1667). Historical studies have claimed a unity in the moral theology of these thinkers;[30] the Anglican moral theologians have assumed that they are heirs and bearers of this understanding.[31] If, however, the unity of the thought of the Caroline Divines is unfounded, then the claim that Anglican moral theology represents the normative definition of Anglicanism is historically inaccurate. If that is the case, the normative claim and corresponding definition of Anglicanism made by Anglican moral theology are grounded on theological and philosophical reasons which must be assessed on their own merit. First, the unity which is assumed in the Caroline Divines is questioned.[32] Next, the tradition of Anglican moral theology is challenged theologically and philosophically by looking at the questions posed by contemporary Roman Catholic moral theology.

The unity of the Caroline Divines' thought in moral theology has been argued most fully by H. R. McAdoo. His 1949 study, *The Structure of Caroline Moral Theology*, remains the classic work and is the basis of contemporary Anglican moral theologians' claim that their work expresses the understanding of the Divines. McAdoo's central claim is that the Caroline Divines—especially Hooker, Sanderson, and Jeremy Taylor—hold to a "carefully thought-out position, the determining element in which was the recovery and preservation of Catholic truth by the avoidance of the extremes of authoritarianism and of doctrinal anarchy. . . . They maintained that a Church was truly Catholic only when 'lawful authority' and 'just liberty' by a permanent tension saved the faith from the unequilibrium of doctrinal additions or subtractions."[33] Implicit here is a normative claim about both (1) the theological content of Christian faith and (2) about theological method, the means by which this content is understood and applied to the life of the Church. As McAdoo later claims in his study of *The Spirit of Anglicanism, A Survey of Anglican Method in the Seventeenth Century*, Anglicanism "has always regarded the teaching and practice

of the undivided Church of the first five centuries as a criterion . . . , that this undifferentiated Catholicism was the pivot for
Anglican thinking." This substantive claim regarding the content of
Christian faith expresses "itself by a specific theological method."[34]
This method is none other than the appeal to the recognition of the
authority of Scripture, tradition, and reason. Says McAdoo, "This
theological method, varying its stress according to the demands of
different situations, consists in the appeal to Scripture, to antiquity
and to reason."[35]

In terms of moral theology, McAdoo claims, "the verdict of the
Anglican was that the Roman infallibilism tryannizes over conscience by striking at liberty, and the Puritan over liberty by offend-
ing against reason."[36] Hooker, Sanderson, and Taylor all recognized
that the Christian moral life is explicated in terms of its objectivity
as expressed in understandings of law and in terms of its subjectivity
as expressed in understandings of conscience. All reject those who
think that preaching a gospel of justification is a sufficient basis for
ethics. Such a Lutheran approach is libertine, antinomian. On the
other hand, addressing their own context in England of the debate
between Roman Catholicism and Puritanism, all three refused to
believe that the Church through either reason or revelation contains
the definitive content of the Christian life or that the Bible is a
sufficient source for the moral life. For Hooker and Sanderson, the
application of universal principles to the concrete situation was an
act of the individual conscience that could not be judged ultimately
by the Church or dictated by the Bible. Taylor, in turn, recognized
that in many areas Christianity has left us to our "natural liberty."

However, while we may speak of this as an Anglican stance—in
John Donne's phrase, the *via media*—this stance may arise from
several different understandings of the nature and relationship of
Scripture, tradition, and reason. Sykes has commented, Anglicanism "approaches the question [of authority in the Church] from
the point of view of the norms of authority, Scripture, tradition and
reason, not infrequently with a complacent sidelong glance at Ec-
clesiastes 4:12, 'a threefold cord is not quickly broken.' The problem
with this approach is its ambiguity, especially in respect of the third
member of the trio. What, after all, is rationality in theology? The
answers to this are as various as Christendom itself."[37] For example,
one could adopt a Thomistic framework with its understanding of
morality based on natural law open to all persons; or one could
develop a Reformed Protestant approach, Puritan in the broadest

sense, in which reasoning within faith provides the means for sanctification, for growing in faith.[38]

In fact, such differences in method seem apparent in the Caroline Divines. Following a Thomistic framework Hooker can claim that "although man participates in the Eternal Law by means of the inward principle of his being, his distinctively human participation in it is by knowledge."[39] Similarly Sanderson, in focusing on the nature of conscience, can accept the general framework of Thomas and say, "Conscience is faculty or habit of the practical intellect which enables the human mind by a reasoning process to apply the light it possesses to particular moral acts."[40]

In contrast to Hooker and Sanderson who grounded the moral life in reason, aided and confirmed by revelation, Jeremy Taylor takes a more Reformed stance by reversing the relationship between natural law and revelation while using the language of Thomas and the scholastics. The Christian moral life is grounded in revelation. As H. R. McAdoo says of Taylor, "He discerns the essential feebleness of a conception of Natural Law depending chiefly on the appeal to natural reason unilluminated by revelation. Hence he shifts the stress, so that revelation rather than *recta ratio* [right reason] predominates in his thoughts."[41] He, in fact, calls natural law nothing but the "convention of natural reason," "a box of quick silver that abides nowhere."[42] Reason does not reveal to us natural law; its purpose is rather instrumental, to apply the demands given in revelation. "We look no further for tables of law in nature," says Taylor, "but take in only those precepts, which bind us Christians under Christ our lawgiver, who hath revealed to us all his Father's will."[43]

Different theological assumptions appear to separate Hooker and Sanderson from Taylor. For example, the fall is far greater for Taylor than for Hooker or Sanderson. Therefore, Hooker and Sanderson can affirm natural reason's capacity to discern God's order while Taylor denies this capability. Underlying this fundamental theological difference may be a very different conception of God. Hooker is ultimately a rationalist; he has a fundamental belief that the world is rationally ordered. God himself is marked by the law of reason as expressed in the very idea of eternal law. In contrast, Taylor appears to be more of a voluntarist. "God is the lawgiver."[44] We know the law not through reason but through God's will, through God's revelation in Scripture.

These differing theological assumptions are significant in understanding Christian faith and the moral life. The development of moral theology from the point of view of Reformed theology or the point of traditional natural law makes a significant difference. When fundamental sources of authority differ—the primacy of reason in discerning moral obligations or the primacy of Scripture as revealing the will or commands of God—the structure of moral theology is itself modified. For example, the use and function of Scripture will differ, the openness to and the need of secular sources will differ, the understanding of grace in relationship to moral discernment will differ, and the understanding of the character and meaning of sin will differ. These theological differences will then imply differences in liturgy and worship, in preaching and Christian education, and in understandings of Christian responsibility and service to the larger society.[45]

While the Caroline Divines assumed doctrinal context universally accepted in the early Church and expressed in the Creeds, doctrinal content does not provide a means for identity since the interpretation of the meaning of doctrine may vary considerably. To claim an Anglican identity one must argue for a particular theological method by which one understands doctrinal content; or, alternatively, one must indicate the proprium underlying the various theological methods which have been adopted by Anglicans in order to establish their common ground in Christian faith.[46] For example, F. D. Maurice may provide such a proprium by emphasizing that the particular constellation of theological beliefs that we consider normative are not the essence of faith; rather, the proprium is the relationship established with God through Christ.[47]

While McAdoo provides a historically significant summary of the teachings of the Caroline Divines and develops the continuities of their thought, he obscures their theological differences. In fact, he thinks that the differences are matters of emphases, that the Divines were fundamentally of one mind. As he says about his work, the aim is "to show how the Carolines reformed moral theology in accord with their principles, retaining that which conformed to these doctrinal standards of Anglicanism and rejecting or remoulding that which ran counter to them."[48] Wrong in the claim of unity amongst the Caroline Divines, it is erroneous to claim that Anglican moral theology developed after the Oxford Movement is the true heir of Anglican identity. Rather, Anglican moral theology from Skinner to Kirk to Waddams proposes a particular method, that of the Thomistic intellectualist tradition, which holds to a particular understanding of the nature and the relationship between Scripture, tradition and reason. This tradition is not the rightful heir of

Anglican identity but one voice which claims to be normative on theological and philosophical grounds.

In conclusion, Anglican moral theology after the Oxford Move- *Conclu* ment does not express what has been a singular and undivided understanding of Anglicanism. We are then left with the assessment of Anglican moral theology on theological and philosophical grounds. What is called for is a theological and philosophical argument which grounds moral theology itself. As Kirk himself saw, although he failed to act upon his insight, before a moral theology can be written it is necessary to provide a systematic study of the ground of the moral life. This task he called Christian ethics, the investigation of the nature of the good, the nature of moral agency, and the nature of the criteria for moral judgment.[49] The remaining discussion examines the ramifications of this task.

III.

Criticisms of the intellectualist framework which grounds Anglican moral theology—the same framework that dominated Roman Catholic thought after Trent until Vatican II—are grounded in what Bernard Lonergan has called "the transition from a classicist world-view to historical mindedness."[50] The intellectualist frame- *Aquinas* work assumed that values are objective, that they stand for qualities or relations that are independent of us, and which we as rational beings are then able to grasp universally. The fundamental criticism of this tradition has been that its understanding of values is wrong. Contemporary critics reject the intellectualist thesis and make the alternative claim that values are human symbols which express the evaluative understandings which persons have made. Values arise historically and so express a particular historical understanding and vision. H. Richard Niebuhr has developed and called such an understanding of value a relational value theory.[51]

The difference between these two understandings of value is well expressed by Lonergan. The differences, he says, "are enormous, for they differ in their apprehension of man, in their account of the good, and in the role they ascribe to the Church in the world. But these differences are not immediately theological. They are differences in horizon, in total mentality."[52] On the one hand, as is done in the intellectualist world view,

> if one abstracts from all respects in which one man may differ from another, what is left is an unchanging element named human nature. One may fit out the eternal identity, human

nature, with a natural law. One may complete it with the principles for the erection of positive law. One may harken to divine revelation to acknowledge a supernatural order, a divine law, and a positive ecclesiastical law. So one may work methodically from the abstract and universal towards the more concrete and particular, and the more one does so, the more one is involved in the casuistry of applying a variety of universals to concrete singularity.[53]

Here the beginning of understanding is what is believed to be objective and eternal. These universals do not change. It is then impossible to arrive at an understanding and demand for change in moral judgments.

historicist "On the other hand," says Lonergan, "one can apprehend mankind as a concrete aggregate developing over time where the locus of development and, so to speak, the synthetic bond is the emergence, expansion, differentiation, dialectic of meaning and *relativism* meaningful performance."[54] In this modern, historically conscious view, what constitutes the human is not some abstract essences but, in Alfred Schutz's provocative phrase, "growing older together."[55] The human arises from the interplay of shared experience, understanding, judgment, and commitment. Lonergan summarizes this interrelationship by saying: *or meaning*

A common field of experience makes for a potential community; and without that common field people get out of touch. Common and complementary ways of understanding make for a community of mind; and without it there are misunderstanding, suspicion, distrust, mutual incomprehension. Common judgments constitute a consensus; and without it an easy tolerance gives way to amazement, scorn, ridicule, division. Common commitments, finally, are the stuff of fidelity to one another, of loyalty to the group, of faith in divine providence and in the destiny of man; and without such commitments community has lost its heart and becomes just an aggregate.[56]

In this view normative values are not eternal verities objectively known by the intellect but are "the hard-won fruit of man's advancing knowledge of nature, of the gradual evolution of his social forms and of his cultural achievements."[57] Such meanings are not fixed, static, and immutable but shifting, changing, and developing. Our normative values are then perhaps best understood as our probing, testing, and commitment of our life together.

This change reflects at bottom the development of a new "root metaphor" or paradigm by which to grasp and structure our experience.[58] Central to this development is the historicity of life. Because a paradigm provides the means by which experience is grasped, it is not provable. Rather, our experience can only confirm claims regarding the character of the paradigm. What is important for our discussion here is that a change in paradigm, in world view, raises questions regarding the foundation and structure of moral theology. Specifically three interrelated questions are raised which are focused around the three fundamental questions of ethics—the nature of the good, the character of moral agency, and the criteria for moral judgment. First, what is distinctively Christian in relation to the moral life? Second, what is the character of moral decision-making? Third, what are the criteria for moral judgment? The broader question then raised is what is the function of the church in relationship to the moral life?

In the area of the criteria for making judgments, traditional understandings of natural law have been challenged. For example, in developing natural law Anglican moral theology has used the traditional deductive reasoning and understood human sexuality in the same way as Roman Catholic manualists. Using the same argument as given in the Papal Encyclical *Humanae Vitae*,[59] R. C. Mortimer says, "To every human faculty God has ordained its proper end and means. He who acts against what God has prescribed sins. The end of the sexual act is quite clear—the procreation of children. To use it in such a way as to frustrate that end is therefore 'unnatural.' "[60] Kirk uses the same reasoning to discourage use of contraceptives.[61] The ground of such a judgment is simply that the laws of nature indicate that the end of sexuality is procreation. This judgment has been challenged by Anglicans as well as by Roman Catholics on the ground that the end of sexuality is twofold: procreation and the communion between partners. Waddams and Dewar argue that it is unjustified to necessarily place procreation as the higher end and so judge contraception as immoral.[62] For the sake of the relationship between spouses and for the sake of the society, contraception may be approved.

What is significant about Waddams and Dewar, however, is that they still argue in line with traditional natural law thinking. The first principles of the morality of sexuality—procreation and human communion—are objectively given. The debate is how these are to be applied to the concrete, contemporary situation. Dewar will then justify contraception as a probable opinion.[63] Beginning with an a priori principle which is believed to be grounded objectively in nature itself—human sexuality is for the end of procreation—results in a negative judgment against uses of sexuality which are not procreative; or, even when it considers contraception as permissible to prevent procreation because of the higher end of the relationship itself or of the social good, the uses of contraception would appear to be doing evil in order to do good.

The issue of masturbation helps to illumine further the problem with this moral reasoning. From a traditional natural law approach masturbation is condemned as a sin against nature and reason since it is using sexuality without regard to the end of procreation or communion.[64] But, masturbation may be in fact good in the process of a person's sexual development; obsessive preoccupation with oneself may result more from the prohibition against masturbation than from masturbation itself.[65] In both cases, natural law thinking has a physicalist bias that arises from accepting a priori material moral absolutes.[66] Such moral absolutes focus our attention in ways that are less than truly helpful for understanding the meaning of human acts. One wonders if moral laws are so objectively given as the classicist mentality believes.

What therefore becomes most problematic about the traditional natural law approach to morality is that this approach too easily loses from view the very source of Christian life. It begins with principles which express abstract ends of human life rather than the dynamic call which arises from Christian faith. Too often this focus reduces Christian faith to certain minimal demands instead of seeing morality as a response to the gift and new life of faith. This challenge to understand the very nature of the moral life, especially what is distinctively Christian in relationship to morality, may be seen by focusing on the contemporary critique of the intellectualist understanding of moral agency.

As we have indicated, the intellectualist framework understands moral agency in terms of two aspects of conscience. Conscience is called *synderesis* to indicate the human capacity to intuitively grasp the first principles of morality; conscience more specifically conceived (*syneidesis*) is the application of first principles to concrete situations.[67] Interestingly, in spite of their discussion of Freud, both Dewar and Waddams generally accept this intellectualist understanding of conscience.[68] If, however, meaning is constituted historically in and through community then the intellectualist understanding of conscience is both ahistorical and individualistic.

The image which is most often used to capture this new understanding of conscience is the image of response and responsibility. As H. Richard Niebuhr suggests, we have more and more come to understand ourselves not as applying rules to situations but as responding to actions in light of our interpretations and expectations which themselves are given by the community in which we share our lives.[69] Conscience is then understood holistically, more an expression of our identity than an expression of universal law.[70]

The effect of this changing perspective is especially significant in understanding the relationship of Christian faith and morality. Within the traditional perspective of the self as discerning first principles and acting in accord with these moral principles in order to move toward its proper end, Christian faith inevitably is viewed as an ideal, as the final end of human life. Kirk's *The Vision of God* is a classic statement of this understanding.[71] Christian faith is the highest good, that toward which we strive. Morals, as Kirk himself maintains, is then concerned with minimal standards, though the ideal must also always be kept in view.[72] Christian faith is teleologically connected with morality; it is the end which grounds the moral life. Morals tend to be viewed as means, as necessary duties.

When the model of the self is changed and viewed in terms of responsibility, the relationship of Christian faith and morality is also changed. Responsibility emphasizes the dialogical structure and personal character of life. The moral life is lived in response to the call of God, neighbor, and all of creation. Morality is a human creation that expresses our developing identity. Bernard Häring has developed this historical understanding of the self in relationship to moral theology as much as any other Roman Catholic thinker. His three volume moral theology, *The Law of Christ*, which was published in German in 1954, can be seen as initiating and foreshadowing this general change of perspective in Roman Catholicism.[73] He is completing a moral theology which brings the understanding of the self in terms of responsibility into even clearer prominence. As Häring says, a distinctively Christian approach to ethics emphasizes "responsibility as a leitmotif in a way that shows it as expression of creative freedom and fidelity."[74]

Christian faith in this view is not seen as the ultimate end but as the source of our identity. We are formed historically through the influences about us, from family and peers to the images presented in books and on television. Christian faith is decisive as it challenges and integrates these various sources into a whole which finds Christ as the center of life, as the source of our identity. There is here no supernatural knowledge imparted by Christ; there is but one history which is viewed as a unity of meaning from the perspective of Christ. The relationship of Christian faith to the moral life is then understood in light of the ways in which identity is formed. Moral content is not derived from Christian faith in any strict sense. Christian faith motivates the moral life by affecting our identity; it gives a specific orientation to life which affects the way in which a person sees the world, intends the world, and is disposed to act in the world.[75]

Regardless of the point at which one begins to question the intellectualist tradition of moral theology, the whole edifice is brought into question. Questions raised about natural law as criteria for judging action raise questions about moral agency, especially one's understanding of what is meant by conscience. These questions then suggest different ways of conceiving what really is the meaning of the good, religiously and morally. Or if one first questions the meaning of the good, how Christian faith and the moral life are related, then questions about the adequacy of the intellectualist account of conscience and natural law inevitably follow. The importance of these questions is not simply theoretical. The theoretical differences in assumptions regarding the foundations of the moral life make a practical difference in understanding the relationship of the church to the moral life.[76]

When Christian faith is understood in terms of identity and not in terms of supernatural knowledge, then questions of the relationship of religious experience, Christian proclamation, and the formation of identity come to the fore and take on particular significance. The ground for rapprochment between disciplines is set. Spiritual crisis, insight, and growth become intrinisically tied to the development and activation of a Christian moral vision. What has too often been separated—moral theology and ascetic, mystical and sacramental theology—come into dialogue. And, moreover, new conversations develop—for example, between depth psychology and moral theology in terms of the development of identity, motivation, and vision.

In the recent literature written by Roman Catholics the question of ecclesiastical authority is particularly acute since in practice previous to Vatican II the magisterium was considered largely in terms of the authorized legislator in matters of faith and practice. Rather than legislator and judge, the church is now viewed more in the image of pilgrim, as open to the variety of voices from within and from without as witnesses to the needs of the world and the meanings of Christian faith.[77] This changed conception of ecclesiology—admittedly under current attack from within the Curia—represents a rapproachment with the polity that has in fact characterized Anglicanism with its emphasis on a pluralism of visions and witnesses informed by tradition.

More questions, however, are raised than those of authority. When the church is viewed as a pilgrim people, responding to the signs of the time, other changes may be envisioned: renewal of lay ministry; reform of the liturgy as the corporate action of the people of God; revision of the content and structure of theological education; new understandings of the task of the ordained ministry and the character of priestly formation; restructuring of the church in its ministry in the small church, the inner-city, and the suburbs; and the development of resources for ministry to specific needs ranging from spiritual renewal and community change specific groups such as youth, single persons, minorities, and the elderly. It is beyond the scope of this article to indicate the variety of changes that have been proposed in the area of church renewal. However, what should be clear is that changes in viewing moral theology will suggest changes in the shape and character of the church.

In conclusion, Anglican moral theology since the Oxford Movement provides a coherent vision of the Christian moral life, but their understanding does not represent a singular and undivided understanding that begins with the Caroline Divines. Rather, Anglican moral theology's claim to express what is normative for Anglicanism rests on theological and philosophical grounds which are those of the intellectualist framework of pre-Vatican II moral theology. This framework has been found wanting. It ultimately reduces the moral life to minimal obligations which are ahistorical and individualistic. Christian faith is then reduced to an ideal, the supernatural end toward which we strive. This fails to comprehend the dynamic, historical character of Christian faith, that Christian faith is primarily to be understood as gift and that the moral life is both an expression and creation of that gift.

The revisioning of moral theology of contemporary Roman Catholics then offers a challenge and an opportunity. The challenge is most forcefully focused at the philosophical and theological ground for understanding Christian faith and the moral life. Anglican moral theology has asserted rather than argued for the ground of its understanding. This challenge provides an opportunity. To develop the presuppositions that ground moral theology—to develop understandings of moral decision-making, of moral criteria, and of what is distinctively Christian in relationship to the moral life—would provide new resources for developing a moral theology that would be of service to the church. An opportunity is also given for understanding what is normative for Anglicanism. A moral theology argued in terms of its foundations would provide a beginning point for comparing the many voices which constitute the Anglican tradition. When such comparative work is done, it will then be possible to formulate and argue what it is that should be normative for Anglicanism.

7

The *Via Media* As Theological Method

by Theodore A. McConnell

Seneca said that historians were inferior to philosophers because instead of dealing with the moral ills of the human condition they handed down for posterity the actions of bandits. To be certain, the actions of bandits are often the roots of moral ills and so it is necessary to be aware of their actions. Perhaps there is more to commend Seneca's wisdom that one might surmise, for it also suggests the importance of reflection upon moral matters if one is to avoid an appalling captivity to the bandits.

The perspective from which one views moral ills and makes "ethical" decisions is a matter for prudent reflection. For the religion person the guidance of moral theology and the church's teaching is paramount if religion is to function in ordinary living. And so the question of what methods or ways of thinking ought to be employed in moral theology resides at the center of any attempt to understand or depict the ethics of a religious tradition.

In historic terms the *via media*, which was John Donne's phrase but whose heritage traces back to Aristotle's "golden mean," has been the label often adopted in characterizing Anglican approaches to matters of morality and ethics. Anglicanism generally has been regarded and has seen itself as an alternative way between Roman Catholicism and the Reformation and perhaps nowhere is this approach more clearly defined and identified than in the *via media.* Certainly the *via media* is by general consent one of the benchmarks of Anglicanism and it has been very much a part of Anglican moral thought. Here, then, is a way of thinking and acting that represents a distinctive alternative to those of Rome, Geneva and Lutherstadt Wittenberg. That distinctiveness, as this chapter will attempt to suggest, is neither accidental and meaningless nor a matter of simplistic and unresolved compromises. Rather, it is a viable and substantive way whose history and development deserves consideration.

I. Early Formulations

The beginnings and foundations of the *via media* as a theological method can be seen developing in successive stages in the works of Richard Hooker, Jeremy Taylor, Robert Sanderson, and Joseph Butler. Richard Hooker's maxim "all things in Measure, Number and Weight" is one of the most incisive and enduring descriptions of the *via media*. And while there has recently been ample analysis of prior formulations of the method including its earliest forms in Hugh Latimer and the English Protestant reformers,[1] Hooker's economical enunciation of a distinctive method remains primary. As Archbishop Henry McAdoo has reminded us in his indispensible work, *The Spirit of Anglicanism:* "Perhaps the most important thing about Hooker is that he wrote no *Summa* and composed to *Institutes*, for what he did was to outline method. What is distinctively Anglican is then not a theology but a theological method."[2]

The legacy of Aristotle and St. Thomas is the fundamental key for understanding Hooker's development of method. Being firmly convinced of the supremacy of natural law, Hooker attached particular importance to the place of reason and experience in seeking the good. As part of the created order and a reflection of the divine mind, reason and experience in balance provide a clear perception of the good. "Goodness is seen with the eye of understanding. And the light of that eye, is reason."[3] As John Booty has noted, participation is the key to Hooker's understanding of nature and God.[4] An enduring participation and balancing of extremes through the general consensus of humanity reveals the fundamental signs of goodness.[5] "The general and perpetual voice of men is as the sentence of God himself."[6]

In the two degrees of goodness that Hooker believed attainable by humanity is to be found a further manifestation of an emerging *via media*; a consistent balancing of all things in measure according to their order in the universe. The first degree is a general perfection sought by all creatures. And second is that goodness which is a resemblance with God "in the constancy and excellence of those operations which belong to their kind."[7] In steadfastly joining these two and in the balancing of *constancy* and *excellence*, Hooker can be seen adhering to a carefully established middle way. The primary traits of constancy and excellence are forever joined together but always with the significant contextual proviso of "in their kind." Beyond these fundamental principles Hooker did not proceed in his writings to a broad application of method, especially in terms of moral matters. The supremacy of natural law was the guide for decisions, and its inevitable operation in either a descriptive or prescriptive way. As John Booty has made clear in the first chapter of this book, Hooker consistently placed emphasis upon action rather than deliberation. The method, grounded in natural law, was all sufficient in approaching moral choices.

Whereas Hooker's great legacy was that of outlining a theological method, Jeremy Taylor was the first Anglican theologian to apply that method in a significant way. In *Ductor Dubitantium* his exhaustive and detailed exploration of the attributes and actions of conscience displays a consistent attachment to the foundations of natural law. Indeed in many respects Taylor's work can be read as a harmonious continuum flowing from Hooker's deep well. There is an attachment to natural law but Taylor shifted the emphasis from right reason alone to include revelation. This development needs to be remembered in reading Taylor as well as in tracing the history of the *via media*. With Taylor the understanding of natural law was expanded to include relationship and revelation alongside reason. Moreover, in contrast to Hooker, in Taylor one finds little discussion of method. The huge body of applications must be absorbed and examined to discern the even handed and presistent reliance upon the *via media* as method. The method is pervasive but implicit to Taylor, a trait that one can observe frequently throughout the history of Anglican moral theology. Nevertheless, as one reads *Ductor Dubitantium* an unmistakable commitment to the method can be noted.

In his extended examination of faith and reason, for example, Taylor's assignment of weight to everything in its measure is distinct: "There are on both sides fair pretences, which when we have examined, we may find what part of truth each side aims at, and join them both in practice."[8] Throughout the catalog and analysis of virtues, vices and moral dilemmas, Taylor adheres to a balancing that reflects an unshakable conviction that there is no innate conflict between human faculties and the natural law, "for right reason proceeding from nature drives us on to good and calls us off from evil."[9]

But what of evil, which can be perpetually observed and experienced in the affairs of human life? The flaw that leads to evil is not inherent in nature but in human will and a degenerate power that ignores and defies the natural order: "Every man hath enough of knowledge to make him good if he please: and it is infinitely culpable and criminal that men by their industry shall become so wise in the affairs of the world, and so ignorant in that which is their eternal interest; it is because they love it not."[10]

The final and only corrective is a consistent balancing of scripture, tradition and right reason, which insures adherence to the good.[11] In so doing, Jeremy Taylor provided one of the earliest and surely most extensive applications of the *via media* to the countless practical matters of morality. The *Ductor Dubitantium* stands as one of the most complete "manuals," written in that distinctive and elegant style of Caroline thought, and utterly consistent in its application of method. Nevertheless, Taylor's approach was not a rigid and mechanical casuistry but a dynamic and flexible application of fundamental beliefs and convictions. It represents the application of principles in relationship and as such it is one of the earliest examples of a basic characteristic of the *via media*.

Bishop Joseph Butler's rigorous and sustained defense of natural religion and ethics has long been regarded as a model of argument and exposition. In the notable *Fifteen Sermons* and the appendix of his most well-known work, *The Analogy of Religion,* Butler set forth his case for the ultimate reasonableness of Christian morality. The beginning point for ethics, according to Butler, is human reason, and the human goal is to live in accord with one's true nature. For Butler the innate human attributes of self-love, responsibility, natural benevolence and conscience lead to moral behavior. The distinctively Christian dimension of moral action is found in a balancing of private and public interests. The Gospel teachings are regarded as a fulfillment of natural morality. The fulcrum of Butler's ethics rests on the prudent balance of self-love and benevolence which he held to be the innate predilection of human nature. There is no necessary conflict because "to aim at public and private good are so far from being inconsistent, that they mutually promote each other."[12]

Butler's enunciation of the *via media* made in the context of his discussion of human nature, shows a firm attachment to the method: "Is not the middle way obvious? Can anything be more manifest, than that the happiness of life consists in these possessed and enjoyed only to a certain degree, that to pursue them beyond this degree is always attended with more inconvenience than advantage to a man's self, and often with extreme misery and unhappiness."[13]

The theological dimension is a supplementary aspect rather than the foundation of Butler's moral thought. His philosophical deliberations in which the place of reason is always paramount and central, shows a method scarcely different than Aristotle's golden mean. Nevertheless, Butler was intent upon consistently applying this method in a religious context and gave its form to his interpretation of Christian teachings. In Butler one sees a uniquely high point of the rationalist impulse in which the heritage of Greek philosophical method is the foundation for moral thinking.

A pivotal point in the development of the *via media* is to be found in the life and writings of John Henry Newman. As with so much else in Newman's life, the story is a complicated and rather perplexing one, mirroring the tortured path of his religious pilgrimage. Newman's analysis of the *via media* early in his career led to a characterization of the method as *the* distinctive trait of Anglicanism and the veritable cornerstone of its doctrinal and moral theology. And it was with this method that one of the most substantial breaking points in his turning away from Anglicanism to Rome took place. The indispensable source for examining Newman's thought in this matter is his two volume work, *The Via Media of the Anglican Church*, written between 1830 and 1841. A certain "corrective" between the first and second volumes mirrors his turning to Rome, although it is important first to examine his masterful formulation of the theological method.

Newman began his treatise with what was to become a famous dictum: That the *via media* had never existed in anything like its ideal form. "The *Via Media*, viewed as an integral system, has never had existence except on paper; it is known, not positively but negatively, in its difference from the rival creeds, not in its own properties; and can only be described as a third system, neither the one nor the other, but with something of each, cutting between them, and, as if with a critical fastidiousness, trifling with them both, and boasting to be nearer Antiquity than either."[14] Yet Newman insisted that the method was one of substance and not merely eclectic. Its distinctiveness is to be found in adherence to the teachings of the early church and the fathers, as well as the subsequent guidance and fulfillment provided by the Prayer Book, the Articles, Episcopal authority, and natural reason. "Though Anglo-Catholicism is not practically reduced to a system in its fulness, it does exist, in all its parts, in the writings of our divines, and in good measure is in actual operation, though with varying degrees of consistency and completeness in different places. There is no room for eclecticism in any elementary matter. No member of the English Church allows himself to build on any doctrine different from that found in our Book of Common Prayer. That formulary contains the elements of our theology; and herein lies the practical exercise of our faith, which all true religion exacts."[15]

In relying upon natural reason and law, Newman stood in the long philosophical tradition that we have already noted in Anglicanism. The Hellenistic and Thomistic framework is intact, and indeed one of Newman's persistent reminders concerned the manifold importance of reason in achieving the *via media*. What is most needed and most to be sought after is "a sound judgment, patient thought, discrimination, a comprehensive mind, an abstinence from all private fancies and caprices and personal tastes."[16] To secure the *via media* is neither simple nor easily predicted in most cases, because it involves the balancing of so many elements in a discerning manner. "The middle path adopted by the English Church cannot be so easily mastered by the mind, first because it is a mean, and has in consequence a complex nature, involving a combination of principles and depending on multiplied conditions; next, because it partakes of that indeterminateness which . . . is to a certain extent a characteristic of English theology, lastly, because it has never been realized in visible fulness in any religious community, and thereby brought home to the mind through the senses."[17]

For Newman the *via media* is ultimately a living, dynamic, developing phenomena. In coming to know and practice the right and the good, he found that so many parts must be held together— Scripture, reason, tradition, ecclesiastical authority, and conscience. Quite like Richard Hooker, finally there is a persistent admonition to balance and weigh all these things, holding them in proportion. "The true Catholic Christian is he who takes what God has given him, be it greater or less, does not despise the lesser because he has received the greater, yet puts it not before the greater but uses all duly and to God's glory."[18]

Newman's contributions to the definition and exposition of the *via media* are considerable: an elegance of style and rhetorical power; a substantial and thorough outline and exposition of the method for doctrinal and moral theology; a clear enunciation of its ecclesiastical applications; and a power of personal conviction and example that has few equals. As Owen Chadwick has observed, the Oxford undergraduates discovered in Newman "an ethical power which led them to examine the unwonted doctrine and then to revere the teacher. From the pulpit of St. Mary's they learnt obedience, holiness, devotion, sacrament, fasting, mortification, in language of a beauty rarely heard in English oratory."[19]

Ultimately, of course, Newman's turning to Rome embodied a renunciation of the *via media* and a severe judgment concerning its presence and practice within Anglicanism. That judgment continues to be a source of substantial debate and disagreement even as his earlier theological formulation of the method stands as an exemplary model for its proponents.

II. A Developing Theme

F. D. Maurice's life and career was contemporary with that of Cardinal Newman's, although Newman outlived Maurice by eighteen years. It has sometimes been held that Maurice's theology was in large measure the antithesis of Newman's, and nowhere has that been presumed to be more so than in terms of theological methods. (We shall shortly return to the question of whether that opinion can be sustained.) Maurice was, of course, the great opponent of "systems" to the extent that his scorn and contempt for them became almost intemperate. Characteristic of his firm convictions was the famous passage in *The Kingdom of Christ* in which he wrote that "he who endeavors to substitute a Church for systems, must regard with most dread and suspicion the attempt at a complete, all-comprehending system. Hating all systems, he hates those most which are most perfect, because in them there are the fewest crannies and crevices through which the light and air of heaven may enter."[20] At the same time Maurice readily acknowledged the necessity of a method of thinking and a guide to action, and much of his writing was directed toward making distinctions between "systems" and "methods." Systems were to be rejected and destroyed, whereas methods could assist one in finding truth and value.[21]

For Maurice, Christology was the beginning point of all theology and ethics, and the unifying power of the Christ is the underlying principle of his thought. Moreover, he argued against the distinction between natural and revealed theology, although it is probably more accurate to say that for him the natural becomes revealed. Speaking somewhat derisively, Maurice likened the *via media* to an indivisible, equatorial line, clearly something that he regarded as both artificial and contrary to the practice of Christianity. Maurice's objections to systems in theology were based upon his conviction that they resulted in the loss of God, either by burying one under a heap or arguments and reasons or by strangling one with chains of inference.

Maurice was intent upon maintaining the tension between various polarities and insofar as he could be said to have employed anything resembling the *via media*, it was in terms of continuing this dynamic tension. Beyond this, much of his writing suggests a more contextual and less defined approach to ethical matters. "The test of all principles affecting to be moral and human must be in their application to the circumstances in which we are placed."[22]

While it might seem that Maurice represents a departure from much of the Anglican tradition in terms of method, the matter is not quite that simple. To be certain, Maurice was the great despiser of systems, but he did return often to that holding together of seemingly disparate elements that can be said to be a fundamental characteristic of the *via media*. For him, this would have been explained in terms of the distinction between "system" and "method." Maurice is best seen as using his theological method to protest and argue against *systems* of doctrine, specifically Calvinist and Lutheran ones. Nevertheless, a distinction should also be made between Maurice's continuation of the tension and the clearer, more decisive resolution that was characteristic of the balancing of Hooker, Taylor, and Butler. Ultimately, there was not so much a departure as a decisive shift in locus and function with Maurice, a shift that moved the terms of ethical discourse and decision-making to a contextual framework that was anchored in the bedrock foundation of the Christ.

The common judgment of Maurice's thought as antithetical to that of Newman is based upon a superficial reading of the texts, and is not an accurate assessment of the matter. In terms of theological method, Newman probably was closer to Maurice than he might have supposed. As the late Ian Ramsey has written: "when Maurice prefaces his Warburton lectures on *The Epistle to the Hebrews* with a carefully detailed *Review of Mr. Newman's Theory of Development*, his critique was remarkably sympathetic, and the reader has the impression of many common insights, many points of agreement and, I would even dare say, a common metaphysical concept of authority."[23] The two men sought similar things and each deeply believed that he had encountered the form and substance of them. Both Newman and Maurice believed that the authority had been given or revealed; for Maurice, this never transferred into a system, whereas Newman believed that he had discovered a living system into which the authority had been transferred.

William Temple, the ninety-eighth Archbishop of Canterbury and one of the more accomplished philosophers and theologians of this century, devoted considerable attention to ethics and moral questions during his life. While there was some development and change in Temple's thought that can be noted in successive works, when viewed as a whole there is a notable consistency and coherence in his work. The changes are ones of nuance and more in the nature of elaboration and further development of previously stated ideas. (For ethics and moral theology the relevant sequence is to be found in moving from *Men's Creatrix* through *Christianity in Thought and Practice* to *Nature, Man and God.*)

Temple was deeply influenced by and committed to the Platonic tradition and ultimately pursued this heritage through Whitehead to the development of his own process perspective. A restructuring of the classical Hegelian dialectical method was central to Temple's approach to theology and ethics. In this can be noted a shift away from the classical Anglican *via media per se* to a more strictly dialectical methods. In *Nature, Man and God*, Temple's final and most complete statement of this method is given: "When the 'antithesis' has been worked out, and its shortcomings also have become apparent, the time is come for the 'synthesis.' This is not a mere average struck between the two. It is always a reassertion of the 'thesis' with all that has proved valuable in the 'antithesis' digested into it."[24]

This method was a foundation of Temple's thought that was consistently applied throughout his life. In what if any respect it can be said that this method represents a *via media* is a matter for some debate. Putting aside matters of terminology for the moment and concentrating upon the function of the method, it is apparent that Temple's method represents a change in meaning, and to a degree in function, for any *via media*. No longer is the central act of ethical reflection necessarily one of bringing together and balancing Scripture, tradition, and reason. (Concerning Scripture, for example, Temple tended to approach it in a rather simple and uncritical fashion and it did not enter directly into his discussion of method.) Rather, reason, conscience and the actions of the human community are evaluated in a dialectical manner and the final, decisive emphasis was placed upon experience.

Temple adhered to a personalist perspective of value and regarded goodness as a personal quality. Moral worth is not located in actions or things *per se*, but in being valued by someone. In 1917, in *Men's Creatrix*, he wrote: "The intention of the term Good may be known *a priori*, but its extension only by experience; we can only tell what things are good by experience of those things."[25]

In 1924, in *Christus Veritas*, this personalist perspective was elaborated further: "Value exists for subjects; but the subject finds the value only when completely absorbed in the object." He knew that "Man's obligation is not chiefly to admire goodness but to be good."[26] Ultimately no definition of the highest good is possible, but the approach to it can be depicted in terms of a valued object and an apprehending subject. To seek and know involves "a subject-object system, perfectly co-related."[27] In *Nature, Man and God* (1934) this process was further refined: "Value as actual belongs neither to the Subjective nor to the Objective side of the Subject-Object relation, but precisely to that relation itself."[28]

The conclusion or final point of the process of experiencing value for Temple was inherent (by extension) in the relationship to God, the source of all value. God is the unifying principle who creates and controls the entire process. As the good is dependent upon someone valuing something, so the standard of good is experienced in divine self-revelation. For Temple this was a many-sided phenomenon or process that can be observed to have undergone development and progressive revelation. In 1936, he gave clear expression to this in defining Christian ethics: "Christian ethics is very definitely a department of Christian theology; its norm or standard of valuation is to be found in the character of God as He has revealed Himself in nature, in history, in the prophets and their reading of history, and in Jesus Christ."[29] At the end of *Nature, Man and God*, Temple depicted the embodiment of the good as a divine self-manifestation in human personality and spoke of "a finite self whose apparent good is the real good."[30]

Natural law was neither set aside nor degraded by Temple, but was approached in a dialectical context. He tended to follow the Greek philosophical tradition with regard to natural law, ascertaining what had been generally accepted among people as a standard and using reason to determine its function or application in decision-making. In fact, in his final book, *Christianity and the Social Order*, natural law is accorded a significant place in moral deliberations: "It is wholesome to go back to this conception of Natural Law because it holds together two aspects of truth which it is not easy to hold in combination—the ideal and the practical."[31]

The unifying principle and basis of Temple's thought, including his ethics, was a process perspective of reality. The world is a process in which there emerge distinct levels of being. In human life all of the levels are to be found but they only become unified insofar as the person follows God's revelation. It is within this process framework that Temple's personalist view of ethics with its stress upon relationships as the crucible and locus of decision-making was developed. The resolution of ethical matters was a process moving toward unity. Toward the conclusion of *Nature, Man and God*, he moved to a description of the process relationship in ethics as one of "vocation." With the providing of general methods and principles, the work of ethics and moral theology is finished.[32] The final stage of the matter is a process relationship in which the self maintains the various elements of the dialectic in dynamic tension: "What acts are right may depend on circumstances, social history and context, personal relationships, and a host of other considerations. But there is an absolute obligation to will whatever may on each occasion be right."[33] Essentially this method was one of correspondence between mind and matter. For Temple the basis of all valuing was inherent in that relationship—a correlation of reality with knowledge.

With William Temple there can be noted a distinctive development in the understanding and function of the *via media* in moral thought. Here one sees much that is contiguous with Maurice, but also considerably more, including an elaborate philosophical process perspective, a particular kind of dialectic, and a personalist view of value. The *via media* of Hooker, Taylor and Butler, in particular, has undergone significant change in form and substance. The sense in which Temple can be said to have relied upon a *via media* in moral decision-making must, of course, be answered in terms of his method and theology. The characteristic emphasis is less that of authority, reason and scripture and more one of a unified philosphical method. At first idealism, and later realism came to provide the framework for his theology. And his process view of the universe led to a completion of natural theology in divine revelation and more especially in the incarnation.

Bishop Hensley Henson in the 1936 Gifford Lectures, *Christian Morality*, took Butler's identification of morality with natural religion as his starting point. Henson largely followed William Temple's perspective, although the process motif was less explicit than in Temple's writings. Henson adhered to a *via media*, depicting it and all of Christian moral theology in a dynamic, developmental character. For Henson, development and adaption in applying certain unchanging basic principles was the key to Christian moral practice.[34] This emphasis upon development as the unique and distinctive feature of Christian morality was explicitly related to sexuality, the state and war, economics, and race in a rather remarkable work that foreshadowed many contemporary developments in social ethics. Henson sought to demonstrate the practical applications of moral principles. In so doing his reliance upon a *via media* was implicit whereas the emphasis upon development was all-encompassing.

Kenneth Kirk, one of the most noted Anglican moral theologians of the twentieth century, was Regius Professor of Moral and Pastoral Theology in the University of Oxford and subsequently in 1937 became Bishop of Oxford. Following the example of Jeremy Taylor, Bishop Kirk developed a comprehensive and detailed manual of guidance for moral decision-making, but unlike Taylor, Kirk was not an adherent of the *via media.* His theological method was based upon a combination of natural law and what he termed divine law, the essence of which was "first of all that it is of internal conditions rather than of external acts, and secondly that it is in the main a *lex non scripta,* a law implanted in the soul. The gospel precepts indeed, the Beatitudes, even the decalogue ... are a part of this new law."[35] The divine law, functioning as the conscience, complements and completes natural law. "A mature and sensitive conscience, then, should recognize as authoritative the promptings both of natural law ...; and of divine law—the reinterpretation of natural law according to the teaching and example of Christ, as well as the rules by which a Christian life may be brought most fully under the influence of the Holy Spirit."[36]

Kirk made a basic distinction between ethics and moral theology: ethics is concerned with general principles and ideals; moral theology is concerned with minimal standards and concrete cases. Kirk's moral theology has often unjustly been depicted as a rigid and absolutist approach, whereas in fact it was a carefully nuanced and sensitive work that emphasized spiritual growth and direction of the self toward increasing union with God as the seed-bed of morality. This growth of the self through devotion and discipline leads to right decisions made almost as innate reflections of natural and divine law embedded in the conscience.*

Generally speaking, following Bishops Kirk and Mortimer little attention has been given to method in Anglican moral theology and ethics. Some note, however, should be given to the thought of two prominent Anglican philosophers, Austin Farrer and Ian Ramsey, although neither of them wrote extensively on this topic. As acknowledged churchmen and prominent philosophers their works

---

*Another manual of moral theology written in this century is R. C. Mortimer's *The Elements of Moral Theology* (1920). For purposes of this essay there are not substantial differences between Bishops Kirk and Mortimer, other than a recognition that the latter interpreted and adhered to natural law in a somewhat stricter manner.

have been of unusual importance in contemporary Anglicanism and Ian Ramsey's brief six years as Bishop of Durham before his death in 1972, marked a notable period of ecclesiastical and theological leadership.

In Austin Farrer's philosophical writings on theism and epistemology there are clear indications of an approach to moral decision-making that was consistent with a characteristically Anglican incarnational theology in which revelation is required to have a correlation with reason and experience. Truth is never regarded as inherent in objects *per se,* but in the object and its correlates.[37] A clear preference for a relational view of ethics is apparent in Farrer's philosophy: "Practical (moral) judgment does not proceed, then, from facts to inferred probabilities, nor from an addition of probabilities to a firmer probability. It proceeds from suasion to persuasion, from tentative to final response."[38]

Ian Ramsey's comprehensive and systematic exploration of the meanings and functions of words and language used in a religious context stands as a work of paramount importance in contemporary religious thought.[39] Ramsey was intent upon establishing what it is possible to say about God without making logical blunders and in two significant essays published in 1966, he directed attention to the grounds for offering a theological interpretation of value judgments.[40]

For Ramsey, relationship and relatedness is a primary factor in moral decision-making and in this respect his work can be regarded as similar to the *via media* seen in Farrer, Temple and others. With Ramsey, however, there was a distinctive concern with and emphasis upon the function of language and discourse in making decisions. Much of his attention was directed toward clarifying, modifying and discerning the structure of arguments, reasons and discourse. Following careful and rigorous analysis of the language of morals, Ramsey established the nature of relatedness and relationship in moral decisions: "a value-judgment occurs as and when a group of natural properties 'come alive,' 'take on depth,' in this sense disclose a claim emerging from them, a claim to which we respond in a 'free' decision."[41]

Because value judgments have been shown to have the character of being responsive, Ramsey then moved to demonstrate the possibilities for speaking about God in moral decision-making. Much of Ramsey's later work was a meticulous effort to differentiate between human and divine being and activity and the ways in which discourse must be structured to avoid confusing the two spheres.[42]

Another often noted characteristic of the *via media* that Ramsey's perspective embodied was a commitment to a correlation between reason, revelation and experience in order to establish truth. Ultimately this correlation was central to Ramsey's position, although it was expressed in a sophisticated and nuanced language analysis. At the same time Ramsey's discussion of natural law and its "rehabilitation" was a less than definitive study of the problem. His call for an agreed upon deposit of principles largely ignored the function of the creeds and his call for a "key" term invites an objectionable reductionism.

The so-called situation approach to ethics and moral decision-making which attained prominence in the decade of the sixties, in large measure was led by several Anglican writers. The phenomena is analyzed elsewhere in this book and so it only is necessary to comment upon its relationship to the *via media* as a distinctively Anglican method. Chief among the texts of the "situation ethics" movement are those of Joseph Fletcher: *Situation Ethics: The New Morality* (1966) and *Moral Responsibility: Situation Ethics at Work* (1967). Fletcher disavowed all systems and systematic approches to moral decision-making. In a reductionist, if not simplistic approach, he claimed that there are only three methods of moral decision-making: legalistic, antinomian and situational. His descriptions of both the legalistic and antinomian categories indiscriminately place together exceedingly different approaches in a way that presents them as caricatures. The effect is one that blurs and distorts many nonsituational approaches.

While there have been suggestions that the situational approach represents a modern *via media* method, Fletcher has not suggested this and it is difficult to find evidence to support such a conclusion. Rather, the situational approach is an exceedingly eclectic one that, in the last analysis, appears to be self-contradictory, for it posits a solitary absolute ("love") that is entirely relative. Thus we are presented with a relative absolute!

Fletcher's approach was endorsed and promoted by the former Anglican Bishop of Woolwich, John A. T. Robinson. In his popular tract, *Honest To God* (1963), and in subsequent writings Robinson advocated the love principle as the sole one for moral decision-making: "Life in Christ Jesus, in the new being, in the Spirit, means having no absolutes but his love, being totally uncommitted in every other respect but totally committed in this."[43] The extreme relativism of the situational approach was decisively enunciated by Robinson: "For nothing can of itself always be labelled as 'wrong'."[44] Similarly, Fletcher's "absolute" or only principle for moral decision-making is that of "love": "Everything else without exception, all laws and rules and principles and ideals and norms, are only *contingent*, only valid if they happen to serve love in any situation."[45]

A fatal problem here is that "love" denotes so many different and often conflicting phenomena that it is devoid of substance. In the hands of the situationalists, the term remains so linguistically imprecise that it may readily and easily result in numerous logical blunders. In the final analysis Fletcher, Robinson and the situationalists have replaced one kind of absolute with another, less meaningful one. It can be said to be less meaningful for it permits contradictory interpretations that can lead to justification of any desired action. Scripture, tradition and reason may be discarded readily by the situationalist who concludes that the situation "demands" it to preserve the love principle. Simply stated, the approach is tautological. Moreover, the situational approach is radically different from the historic traditions of the *via media* in its insistence upon a solitary principle, in its provision for the discarding of Scripture, tradition and reason and finally, in its decisive denial of divine transcendence and the supernatural.[46] Such a pantheistic idea of God fails to satisfy the minimum deposit of truth that Western Christendom has consistently believed necessary and warranted by Scripture and tradition.

A brief comment should be made regarding the situational approach of the late American Bishop James A. Pike. In two books (*Doing the Truth*, 1955, and *You and the New Morality*, 1967) and numerous lectures, Pike identified his approach as a situational one, although the writings present a less clear-cut identity. Pike devoted considerable attention to the concept of natural law, arguing against its classical expressions. Whereas his writings at times indicate a tendency to use a *via media*, his fundamental and persistent approach to moral decision-making was that of applying legal methods rather than theological ones. Pike referred to the significance of "a reservoir of insight available when particular decisions have to be made"[47] but he never addressed the central point of how to proceed when there are conflicting claims between Scripture, tradition, reason and experience. While Pike's ethical reasoning was eclectic, relativistic and existential, the end again and again he returned to a rigid application of the three-stage syllogism of logic and legal practice.

Strong and decisive challenges to the situationalist's methods and perspectives have come from other Anglican theologians including Herbert Haddams, Lindsay Dewar and John Macquarrie. Waddams' Christocentric approach to moral matters assigned a primary place to a revised notion of natura law. Much of his revision in understanding is directed toward placing natural law under the "law" or Scripture as interpreted by Christ and the Church.[48] While there are traces of the traditional *via media* in Waddams' approach, they are subordinated to the primacy of the teachings of Christ interpreted by the tradition. And much in the manner of Kenneth Kirk, Waddams ultimately relies upon human spiritual growth into increasing love of God and obedience to God to lead to right decisions and actions.

Similarly, Lindsay Dewar has followed Kirk's theological outlook and consistently applied it to morality. The traditional *via media* has not been a primary part of his approach which is best characterized as one in which the locus of moral decision-making resides in an increasing identification with the will of God. The conscience is shaped and developed through devotion and discipline to God and this becomes the reliable guide to right decisions.

Dewar's analysis of the situationalist approaches to morality is among the most comprehensive and decisive of those that have been made. Like Waddams, he has called attention to the absolutely necessary place of tradition, something that has been cast aside and renounced by the situationalists and indeed by those of the reformed persuasion who so often stress individualism—the individual's conscience, the individual's will, the individual's personal perception of God and morality. Dewar's analysis has concluded the matter: "To interpret the ethics of inspiration individualistically is to run counter to the facts of Christian history from the Council of Jerusalem (Acts 15) onwards. The guidance of the Holy Spirit is given in the first place to the Body as a whole, and only in the second place to the individual member of the Body. It was at this point ... that a wrong turn was taken by the theologians at the Reformation; and their successors have followed them, in their approach to morals."[49]

John Marquarrie's theological scholarship has encompassed the entire field including substantial consideration of ethics and morality. Whether in fact Macquarrie's perspective can be regarded as an Anglican one in any historic sense remains open to dispute. More than anything else he has appropriated the entire framework and structure of Heidegger's ideology and method. In more recent writings on spiritual topics, Macquarrie has displayed some evidence of the Anglican heritage, but basically the Heideggerian mold has remained unquestioned. Macquarrie's existential outlook and Heideggerian methodology is nowhere more readily seen than in his discussion of conscience.[50] Similarly, in considering revelation Macquarrie has simply appropriated and translated into theological categories Heidegger's perspective by calling for a "general possibility of revelation" and in depicting revelation in terms of an "unveiling, whereby what has hitherto been concealed from us is now opened up."[51] A third example of this unyielding adoption can be seen in Macquarrie's redefinition of natural law in existential-ontological terms.[52] The dogmatic approach and penchant for all-encompassing systems with interlocking terms and categories of an exclusive nature that is so characteristic of Germanic philosophical and theological enterprises, is antithetical to the Anglican outlook and approach. Perhaps nowhere is this opposition more clearly pronounced than in terms of the *via media*, a method whose essence has been shown to be one of flexbility, development and a balancing and holding togther of Catholic and reformed traditions in a unique style and manner. It should be recognized that Macquarrie has attempted to modify and reinterpret his theology thereby mitigating its intrinsic incompatibility with Anglican methods, but this attempt fails so long as the work remains based upon the Heideggerian foundation. At crucial points such as defining the nature and methods of theology, the idea of revelation, the nature of conscience, and the nature of history, he relies entirely upon concepts and categories borrowed from Heidegger's system. In so doing he has adopted a system that stands in contradiction to the traditions of the *via media*.

III. The Viable Method

In the preceding review of Anglican moral thinking about theological method, some distinguishing traits and characteristics as well as certain shifts in thought have been noted. Generally speaking, Anglicans have tended to follow Aristotle's advice when he wrote in Book II of the *Nicomachean Ethics*: "In reasoning about matters of conduct general statements cover more ground but particular statements are more accurate, for conduct is concerned with particulars." The development and application of the *via media* has emphasized particulars and opposed the building of all-encompassing systems. Throughout diverse periods of Anglican history the method has proven to be useful and applicable to moral decision-making. The great and high points in the formulation of the *via media* are to be found in the works of Richard Hooker, Jeremy Taylor, John Henry Newman and William Temple. Proceeding on from William Temple's time, there has been a noticeable tendency to place increasing emphasis upon relationship and relatedness in defining and applying a *via media.* This, too, is best understood as a modern application of Aristotle's dictum that one only becomes good by so acting: "It is well said, then, that it is by doing just acts that the just man is produced, and by doing temperate acts the temperate man; without doing these no one would have even a prospect of becoming good."[53]

A consistent trait that is apparent in the history of the *via media* is an understanding of the method as a dynamic and living one that allows for change and development while preserving historic essentials of belief and doctrine. The method is not one of synthesis or accommodation as has sometimes been asserted, but rather a substantial and viable way of analysis that is marked by a certain flexibility and dynamic that holds together in due measure and proportion the claims of Scripture, tradition, reason, conscience and ecclesiastical authority. One contemporary writer who has misunderstood and distorted Anglican perspectives has asserted that the *via media* results in postponing and avoiding all weighty issues and critical decisions.[54] The history of the *via media* clearly shows how unwarranted and incorrect is that judgment. It is a judgment based upon gross distortions of history and ignorance of the texts of Anglican moral thought.[55]

The subject of theological method has long occupied a prominent place in theology and as James Gustafson has indicated, in more recent times the concern with method has intensified.[56] Much of this preoccupation has been concerned with the relationship between method and the practice of theology, and the theological landscape is crowded with elaborate attempts to fashion a method "before" proceeding to practice theology. In this regard the question of priority is a misplaced one that has resulted in numerous blunders. These blunders largely have been avoided in Anglican theology because there has been a tendency to see the matters of method and practice as interdependent ones. It is hardly possible to begin doing theology without giving attention to method, but in doing so one is beginning to deal with the substance of theology. Such a conviction is part of what is entailed in saying that the *via media* embodies a certain flexibility, growth and development. In other words, the method is shaped by doing theology even as theology is shaped by the method. This is not intended to be a tautological act, but rather an indication that theological method is formed and developed in practicing theology. To be certain, one sets out with some principles or points along which any inquiry will proceed and these should be precisely articulated, carefully reasoned and backed by warrants because of their priority and influence, but as John Macquarrie has aptly stated, "method and content are inseparable in theology. Any discussion of method in abstraction can be only provisional."[57] It might well be added that because those points of priority are provisional, they can be reshaped in the course of practice *if* the method is sufficiently flexible to permit change and development. And that is what the *via media* has consistently made possible in Anglican moral theology.

The role of reason and experience understood in Newman's subtle sense of "sound judgment" has consistently occupied a prominent place in Anglicanism and the *via media* is no exception in this respect. The distinctiveness of reason's role is of paramount importance in understanding the *via media* for this sets it apart from those religious traditions in which there is a slavish adherence to the biblical words perceived and interpreted individualistically. At the same time the method has prevented an equally slavish devotion to the rationalist impulse. The guiding inspiration of Scripture interpreted by reason and the traditions of the Church Fathers and Saints is the preferred approach and method. *Sound judgment* denotes a discriminating comprehensiveness that is capable of avoiding individualistic preferences and prejudices while holding together diverse elements in due proportion to their "measure, number and weight."

Speaking both historically and methodologically, the *via media* represents a clear-cut way of guarding against the unchecked dangers of individualism in moral decision-making. As such it has provided an alternative to a variety of reformed, free-church and situationalist ideas about revelation and inspiration. Use of the *via media* has insured that balanced weight be given to Scripture, tradition, reason and experience. The resulting exercise of sound judgment as shaped and developed by this fourfold heritage has made possible a prudent and balanced approach which has come to characterize much of Anglican thought.

Growth, change and development within a prudential outlook that recalls and is respectful of history and tradition is yet another way of expressing the nature of the *via media*. As such it has most often come to be a living and active way of making moral decisions. As such it has enabled Anglicanism to avoid the dogmatism and rigidity of a solitary system without ignoring or shunning such basic influences and guides as those of natural law. As such it has provided form and substance to a Catholic tradition that is reformed and reforming but is not of the reformation.

8

Anglicans and the New Morality

by Edwin G. Wappler

When we talk about the new morality and how Anglicans have responded to it, we must be sure of what we mean by the term. So often the expression has been used loosely to indicate anything having to do with changing sexual mores. In this highly-charged framework, those who favor what they think is the approach of the new morality find themselves defending it with a deep personal investment. For them it seems to connote freedom, authenticity, and a liberation from the outdated codes of bygone eras. On the other hand, those who oppose the direction it takes react against it with an even greater vigor, for they view it as an invitation to moral chaos. Anglicans, like just about everyone else, have found themselves on both sides of this angry debate.

But Anglicans have engaged the new morality in another and more significant way. They have thought of it in terms of situation ethics, a method of decision-making which insists that there can be only one absolute norm or ultimate principle, love, which must be applied in the ethical situation. It is primarily a *way* of reaching ethical decisions, not a body of new moral teaching or a call to abandon restraint and discipline. Not all situation ethicists are Christians, but those who are believers inevitably make some form of love their sole absolute. How they will approach an occasion of moral choice is succinctly stated by Joseph Fletcher, the dean of situation ethicists, in these words, "The situationist enters into every decision-making situation fully armed with the ethical maxims of his community and its heritage, and he treats them with respect as illuminators of his problems. Just the same he is prepared in any situation to compromise them or set them aside *in the situation* if love seems better served by doing so."[1]

When we consider how Anglicans have reacted to situation ethics, we are immediately struck by the number of prominent figures in Anglicanism who have identified themselves with the new morality. In addition to Joseph Fletcher, at least the following churchmen have defended the situationist position in print: James A. Pike, W. Norman Pittenger, and O. Sydney Barr in America, John A. T. Robinson, Douglas Rhymes and Harry A. Williams in England.[2] William Spurrier has attempted to reconcile situation ethics and the tradition of natural law, but seems to favor the new over the old morality at the level of his primary ethical commitment.[3]

It is an unmistakable fact, then, that the new morality in its intellectually serious form, situation ethics, has had a significant appeal to Anglican ecclesiastics. Perhaps no other Christian family has had so many ranking figures in the situationist camp. The Anglican tradition has certainly had more than its share of remarkable eccentrics, but it has not been known for its radicals. We may wonder therefore, how such a supposedly staid family of Christians could produce such morally avant-garde offspring. Is there something in Anglicanism which, given the proper external challenge, might lead logically to situationism in ethics? Are there ingredients in the Anglican character and outlook which lend themselves to the development of situation ethics? I believe there are such elements and that they can be broadly identified.

The first of these "congruences" between Anglicanism and situation ethics is a common stress on the _via media_, the golden mean between extremes. Situation ethics tries to provide a middle way between the extremes of legalism on the one hand and lawlessness on the other. Secondly, the familiar distinction between the few fundamentals and the many accessories of religion finds an echo in the situationist claim that love and love alone is what finally matters; all else is more or less dispensable. Thirdly, what Paul Elmer More called Anglicanism's "axiomatic rejection of infallibility" accords well with the situationist mood of ethical relativism. Fourthly, the traditional Anglican theological focus upon the Incarnation rather than the Atonement has brought with it a tendency to teach a high doctrine of man and to stress the possibility of human rationality. This affirmation fits well with the general confidence situation ethics possesses about our ability to discern and choose the loving thing to do in an instance of ethical choice. Finally, the oft-noted Anglican preference for pragmatic and non-systematic approaches to issues in theology or church life is easily discernible in the situation ethicist's tendency to test moral principles by asking, "Do they work for love in the situation?"

Even with this general framework of common ingredients before us, we might still wonder why the new morality did not appear much earlier than the 1960s. Although a question such as this may be finally unanswerable, I believe that we can identify the catalyst as the crisis of faith in a "world come of age." Without the accompanying challenge of the secular theologians and their varying perceptions of the "death of God" plus the multitude of other intellectual bills that became due at that time, it is hard to imagine such a concerted effort at ethical reconstruction taking place. As Anglicans and as worldly Christians, the situationists could not sit by as if they were sectarians and consign the world to the devil. They had to address modernity in language which could be understood, and they had to speak in terms which were both honest to man and honest to God. Ethics was at the cutting-edge of so much in the modern world. What better place could there be to start a radical reconstruction of Christian faith and life?

The State of Anglican Moral Theology When the New Moralists Appeared

The common perception of those who championed situation ethicists in the 1960s within Anglicanism was that the old morality was not in a strong position to influence contemporary life. Moral theology, or as it was styled in the seventeenth century, "practical divinity," was no longer the vital and popular concern it has once been in Anglicanism's golden age. It was not central to the average church member's daily existence, nor did it influence in any spiritual depth the thinking of those in need of more guidance. Part of its problem had to do with its inability to adjust to the urban industrial world and the complexity of social relationships in that environment. It preferred to speak to individual ethical problems. Because the traditional socio-economic teachings of the Church were regarded as obsolete for present day conditions, they were gradually forgotten. Religion became increasingly a personal and private affair. In like manner, the focus of moral theology was on the cultivation of personal virtue, not on the achievement or maintenance of justice in society.[4]

Even at the personal level, however, moral theology was often ineffective. Its characteristic style was the deductive and rational method of the Aristotelian-Thomistic tradition in Christian thought. Its tendency was to become dry and rationalistic, leaving behind human emotion as a less worthy constituent of character. Moreover, under the influence of an unfortunate development in post-Tridentine Roman Catholicism, the temptation arose to separate moral and ascetical theology, to divide ethical activity from the life of prayer, to

differentiate between realities of discipleship which classical Anglican moral theology had thought of as inseparable.

Anglican moral theology, even when its insights were applied to
modern society by theologians of the stature of F. D. Maurice,
Charles Gore and William Temple, did not succeed in recapturing
its former place at the center of cultural life, although it did much
to remind the Church of elements within its own tradition which
had been almost forgotten in the early industrial decades of the
nineteenth century. The same partial success attended the revival of
moral theology attempted by Kenneth Kirk in the twentieth century. Had the old tradition any life left in it? Was not moral
theology as a discipline hopelessly bogged down in *a priori* thinking
in an age more and more impressed by empiricism? Could the
Christian life ever be systematized without becoming dessicated
and legalistic?

Bishop Kirk was himself acutely aware of moral theology's problems in the modern world. He insisted that the theologian must be
on guard against the temptation to press his analyses of character
and its parts to mathematically accurate conclusions. He acknowledged that "human conduct and divine grace are fields which admit
only of the widest generalizations, and to every such generalization
there must be innumerable exceptions." Yet he defended the contemporary need for the discipline, especially in the Anglican context. He argued that the principle danger of modern religious
thought was not over-analysis but vagueness. Kirk believed that the
modern tendency to skip definitions was much more than just an
intellectual deficiency. It was having serious practical results on
faith and morals, for such a failure "finds its natural outcome in a
prevailing indifference both as to the truths of doctrine, pure and
simple, and to those of morals. It has resulted in a widespread
abandonment of any ideals of absolute truth or of absolute goodness; in an individualism according to which each man may believe
what he likes and do what he likes without reference to any external
criterion except a vague social convention. . . . That this is the
prevailing tone of mind of the English laity, at all events, cannot be
denied."[5]

As Kirk had read the situation in the 1920s, the problems of laxity
and indifference were far more serious than any danger posed by a
revival of the legalisms of yesterday. Moral theology's challenge was
to try to steer a middle course between over-rigidity of definition
and vagueness of unthinking piety. "It requires," he wrote, "such a
degree of exactness as will ensure to the priest clear guidance in

dealing with the problems that beset human conduct, without giving him the arrogance and obstinacy which are bred by a sense of absolute rightness." Ideally, the character of moral theology would feature a combination of certainty on some matters and open-mindedness on others. "But," said Kirk, "for the present day the certainty is more needed than the open mind, and we should turn again to Scripture, Christian experience, and the agreed results of free inquiry into human character, to reestablish for the guidance of conduct truths whose validity had not so much been questioned as forgotten."[6]

Kirk's sentiments about the ethical climate of his time remind us that pastoral considerations have always figured prominently in the moral theological tradition. Historically, moral theology developed in response to the need of the Church to offer guidance to its flock, those who accept the teachings of the Christian faith as authoritative and trustworthy. Moral theology assumes that Christians live out of a deep sense of loyalty to their tradition, that they can and do turn frequently to the Church for moral guidance, and that they expect and welcome this guidance as necessary to their progress in the Christian life. Because the Church has normally provided pastoral guidance through its clergy, moral theology has often been written for the parish priest whose duty it was to give advice to his parishioners. Kirk followed in this path and addressed himself primarily to clergymen, although he regarded his writings to be of interest to anyone who wished to become better acquainted with the Church's moral heritage.

Not everyone in the Anglican world greeted the attempt to revive moral theology with enthusiasm. Many thought that twentieth century conditions of life precluded, even for the devout, the kind of recourse to pastoral guidance necessary for the effective implementation of its teachings. Even Kirk himself expressed some doubts as to whether the effort to revive it would prove fruitful. Yet he persisted in his work of renewing and reapplying the basic insights of moral theology to the needs of the Church, trying in the process to remain simultaneously faithful to the witness of the New Testament, the Thomistic inheritance, and the modern context of morality. His authentic liberality as a thinker was overshadowed by the more rigid traditionalist approach of Robert C. Mortimer, his successor as Regius Professor of Moral and Pastoral Theology at Oxford, and chief moral theologian of the Church of England.[7] Mortimer's efforts were supplemented more recently by those of Herbert C. Waddams.[8]

And so the tradition of moral theology was preserved and in a measure renewed in contemporary Anglicanism. Yet despite a noble attempt at a revival, Christian morality, on the whole, remained a rather impotent force in shaping modern society and was less and less influential in the ethical thinking of many individuals, including churchmen. The stage was set for a new initiative in moral thought.

How the Situationists Indicated the Moral Tradition and How They Proposed to Correct It

The essential judgment made by the Anglican situationists was that the moral tradition of the Church (and the theological background presupposed by that moral system) was obsolete in the contemporary world. Because of the new context of modernity in which the Church had to work, it was impossible to defend and explicate the traditional system of morality without a drastic reformulation of its letter and spirit. This reformulation or reformation was mandatory if the Christian faith was to have any influence, other than a negative and waning one upon contemporary life. However, before a new reconstruction in ethics could take place, the old morality had to be indicted for its crimes against the human spirit. This prosecutorial task was undertaken with obvious relish by the new moralists, who accused the old morality of being legalistic, overburdened with minutae, hypocritically dishonest, divorced from real life, and scornful of human moral potential.

For Joseph Fletcher, the most systematic of the new moralists and the only professional moral theologian among them, the great cause of the tradition's failure was that it had been wedded to legalism. Fletcher regarded legalism, the absolutizing of principles, and not antinomianism, the individualistic and unprincipled approach to decision making, as the primary danger to be avoided in the moral life. While many contemporary critics were concerned to point to the collapse of all norms and values into a relativistic whirl, Fletcher did not view the threat of antinomianism as of more than potential peril. Legalism had been the common path which traditional morality had trod over the centuries and it remained the number one enemy of ethical progress.

According to Fletcher's understanding of situation ethics, there was only one law, the law of love. He stated flatly that Christian situation ethics reduced law from a statutory system of rules to the claim of love alone. He made this radical simplification on the basis of the example of Jesus and St. Paul who "replaced the precepts of the Torah with the living principle of *agape—agape* being *goodwill at work in partnership with reason.*"[9] This is the kind of love which seeks the neighbor's best interest with a careful eye to all factors in the situation. It is stated definitely for the Christian in the dominical summary of the Law, "Thou shalt love the Lord thy God with all thy heart, and all thy soul, and all thy mind. . . . And. . . . thou shalt love thy neighbor as thyself."[10]

While Fletcher regarded an addiction to legalism as the worst failing of the moral tradition, other situationists gave other answers to the question of what was wrong with the old morality. James Pike thought that the stance of the Church vis-a-vis the modern world was wrong because the Church was trying to carry too much "excess baggage" into the twentieth century. As his quarrel with the Church grew, he found himself throwing more and more of its doctrinal and moral baggage overboard in a self-declared effort to save the sinking ship of faith, while he simultaneously took on some baggage of his own, including a collection of quite untraditional beliefs and practices such as spirit communication with the dead.

In an early phase of his criticism of the tradition, Pike described the problem as he saw it in these words, "There are many people within the fold who have not really grasped the heart of the Christian message because they are bogged down by too many doctrines, mores, precepts, customs, symbols, and other traditions, with no sense of differentiation between the relative essentiality and non-essentiality of the respective items." Christians should be able to distinguish the essential matters of faith and practice from the peripheral issues, but too often they cannot and do not do so. Pike felt a duty to participate in the contemporary task of theological reconstruction, and he noted frankly, "Reconstruction involves some destruction as well as some construction."[11]

Before Pike could go about stating the Gospel, he had to rescue it from the corruptions of over-belief and false absolutism. He felt that he had to define "what it is not—though presumed to be." This task of pruning was organized under three headings often thought to be essential for religion: "The Three C's—Creed, Code, and Cult."[12] Not surprisingly, there emerged from his analysis of these elements the position which he had outlined in the introductory chapters of his book, *A Time for Christian Candor,* that there is only one absolute, God, and all particular facets of faith, morality, and worship are relative to that Reality.

While James Pike was struggling to set forth the essential "treasure" of the faith in distinction to the "earthen vessels" of tradition, another Anglican bishop was concerned on the other side of the Atlantic to make his own preliminary efforts at restating the Christian message for the present-day. John A. T. Robinson was striving above all, he said, to be "honest to God," the title of his unexpectedly popular exposition of contemporary issues in theology and ethics.[13] The crucial matter for theology was one of honesty before the face of modernity, a radical recasting of Christian truth consonant with a new style of thinking.

Robinson did not find this task to be a simple or a painless one. He found himself divided in thought and sympathy between traditional conceptualizations of the Church's faith, with some of the practices which had derived from this way of thinking, and a radically different approach which brought into question many elements of belief and piety which had been inherited from the past. Yet, more and more, he found himself unable to believe in what he called the "supranaturalist" statement of Christianity. The chief defect of the supranaturalist view is that it posited a separate realm for spiritual reality and regarded God as a distinct individual Person who dwelt there.[14] This widespread misunderstanding of God's relation to the world brought about a whole series of fundamental distortions in theology, piety, and ethics which were now being called into question by perceptive people inside and outside of the Church.

The volume of this questioning had reached such a magnitude in the present day that every part of Christian faith and life heard itself challenged. Nowhere is this challenge more obvious than in ethics, Robinson noted, for "it is impossible to reassess one's doctrine of God, of how one understands the transcendent, without bringing one's view of morality into the same melting pot." "But," said Robinson, "there is no need to prove that a revolution is required in morals. It has long since broken out; and it is no 'reluctant revolution'. The wind of change here is a gale." Undeniably then, the present task of the theologian or theologically minded moralist was to relate the revolution in ethics to the radical shift away from the supranaturalist point of view, and this is what Robinson attempted to do under the heading of the new morality.[15]

A morality of authoritarian law and suspicion of the flesh was holding the allegiance of fewer and fewer people, argued Douglas Rhymes. Young people especially found it almost impossible to accept, whether or not they had any relationship to the Church. On this point Rhymes believed he could speak from experience as a parish priest and pastor to youth. The legalism and hypocrisy of the old morality were being increasingly scorned, and Rhymes thought that was ultimately to the good. On the other hand, a more authentic Christian morality, that of Jesus, remained to be restated to the modern world. This morality was based on a high doctrine of human nature, which in turn derived from the Incarnation. From this perspective, Rhymes asserted, "We should be proud of man. Man is a great being. Man is the child of God able to be perfect as his Father in heaven is perfect. And so, he concluded, "Whether man *has* come of age, as the Bishop of Woolwich [John A. T. Robinson] seems to think, is a debatable point, but he is certainly meant to come of age."[16]

All champions of situation ethics agreed that theology and morality's great summons in the present era was to address "modern man" on his own terms. That the Church had not done so in any significant measure was also apparent to them, and until it did so, Christian faith and life would remain a fading option in the contemporary world. Although the times might have long called for a reappraisal of doctrine and morality, little was attempted in the post World War II world until the 1960s.[17] Once the task of reconstruction was joined, the question became one of method. Shall the debate stay comfortably within the confines of the academic community among the theologically informed, or shall it try to engage the widest possible audience?

The essayists of *Soundings* (1963) made their statement to the modern world in a form familiar to Anglicans who could recall such earlier collections as *Essays and Reviews* (1860), *Lux Mundi* (1889), *Foundations* (1912), and *Essays Catholic and Critical* (1926). The efforts of the *Soundings* group found a new response in Anglican theology and ethics in the writings of Robinson and Rhymes. Although Fletcher and Pike had already appeared to be headed in a similar direction several years earlier, the net result of the questions raised by the Cambridge essayists was to encourage still more probing of the conventional Christian approach in faith and morals. Within a few years' time the theological and ecclesiastical mood changed from one of rather defensive complacency to one of radical questioning and criticism. Abruptly the priority shifted to rethinking the Christian message and then communicating it as boldly as possible to the dominant secular mentality. Nearly all of those Anglicans who became involved in championing the new morality were skillful communicators and able popularizers. Unlike the scholarly dons of *Soundings,* they chose to address themselves to a broad audience, not only because of their ability to reach such an audience, but also because of their conviction that the time had come for the questions they were raising to be brought out of the academic cloister into the thinking of the average person.

As the proponents of the new theology and the new morality moved to try to meet the challenge they perceived to exist in the contemporary spiritual climate, they could not help but reveal the extent to which they themselves had been influenced by the same trends they felt were dominating others. They too were contemporary men, not clerics who were insulated by virtue of an impregnable faith from the process of secularization which had been going on about them. Thus, as they sought to make a revitalized religion available to modern folk, they could not exclude themselves from being among those to whom they were speaking. The line between past and present, between the traditional and the contemporary, between the world and the Church, ran through their own minds and hearts.

All of those who put forth a situationist solution, therefore, give the impression of being themselves caught up in the contemporary crisis of faith. Yet they were all confident that there was a way out, a way to rediscover an authentic Christian posture, which could speak persuasively to the modern mind because it could be, in a large measure, the work of that mind freed from the shackles of convention and able to return again to the original inspiration of Jesus. The new morality was meant to be a new breakthrough of Christian influence upon modern society. Divinity, so long consigned to the seminary or to the clerical study, was to become "practical" once again, engaging the world with a fresh power and relevance.

Understanding and Appraising the New Moralists

With all the talk among situation ethicists about newness and the need to be contemporary, it is easy to forget the great debt to the past which was owed by the new moralists. Joseph Fletcher frankly admitted in the foreword of his well known exposition of situation ethics, "(1) that the 'new morality' is not exactly new, either in method or in content, and (2) that as a method . . . its *roots* lie securely, even if not conventionally, in the classical tradition of Western Christian morals." In other words, said Fletcher, "it's an old posture with a new and contemporary look." What made it seem so new is that it was "a radical departure from the conventional wisdom and prevailing climate of opinion."[18] Similar sentiments could be found in the works of other situationists. They saw themselves not so much as innovators as restorers.

The roots of the new morality were meant to be in Holy Scripture, especially the New Testament, and in the moral theological heritage too. We have already noted the strong tendency of situation ethicists to appeal to the teaching of Jesus or St. Paul. What may be less obvious is their debt to the moral tradition, except in the case of Fletcher who constantly drew upon the tradition in making his points. In Fletcher's earlier writings there are many references to moral theological concepts, especially those pertaining to social ethics. In his more recent writings on situation ethics he continued to be concerned to trace its concepts back to such well-known moral theological categories as casuistry and equity and to regard his work as the fulfillment rather than the repudiation of what this discipline was trying to do.[19]

Even when there was no clear debt to the moral tradition there was a debt to the broader context of Christianity in the case of all the Anglicans who espoused the situationist position. At some stage of their careers most of them had served as pastors, after being nurtured in the household of faith. They all had a familiarity with the resources of the Christian life which went far beyond that of the average Christian, much less that of the typical citizen of the secular city. Their ethical posture required a spirituality to nourish it which was deeper than that experienced by most churchgoers. One of them, Douglas Rhymes, was vividly aware of the need to create a new spirituality to undergird the new morality, and he tried to provide guidance in that direction.[20] In any event, without the resources of the Christian faith to draw upon, the new morality could not have flourished. It needed both the Church and the Christian heritage to come into being, to enter into critical dialogue with the past, and to have anything substantive to offer to the future.

Beside the thought patterns peculiar to the Anglican tradition in which they were nurtured, the situationists were exposed to at least to other significant sources of opinion of which they in turn became conduits to the lay public. The first of these influences came from the behavioral sciences, psychology and sociology, and to a lesser extent, psychiatry and psychoanalysis. However, rather than appropriating specific insights or elements from this important source of knowledge and opinion, we find the situationists more captivated by the skeptical mood and empirical method of the behavioral sciences.

A second broad area of thought which influenced the Anglican situationists (and was then mediated by them to others who read them) was that of ecumenical Protestant theology and ethics. Insights from Barth, Bonhoeffer, Tillich, Brunner, Bultmann, and the Niebuhr brothers crop up repeatedly in the writings of the situationists and become grist for their intellectual mills. This influence is especially apparent in the works of John A. T. Robinson and Joseph Fletcher. Less commonly did those proclaiming a situational position in ethics draw upon philosophical theology or metaphysics, although Norman Pittenger closely linked his ethic of love's supremacy with a thorough-going commitment to process thought.

One of the reasons why the situationists are important is that they have helped introduce these new currents into the Anglican thought world and into the popular consciousness. To say this is not to say that Anglican thought was unfamiliar with such major intellectual influences as those of the behavioral sciences or ecumenical Protestantism. It is rather to assert that the situationists (1) forced Anglican thinkers to engage these outside sources more directly and urgently, and (2) brought the general public into a discussion which had been going on for some time behind seminary walls. The public discussion of the new morality which ensued went through all denominations and caused a significant hub-bub. The argument was concerned to relate what had been received from the past to what was being said now and to what the non-theological world was asserting. Unfortunately, it was superceded in the public consciousness by other concerns before bearing significant fruit in a new theological-ethical consensus.

In attempting to relate the contribution of the situationists, especially Fletcher, Pike, Robinson and Rhymes, to that of the secular theologians we might find enough common themes to subsume them under that general category of theological thought. Yet they were more eclectic and more pastoral than theologians such as Harvey Cox or Paul Van Buren. They also seem more Anglican, with a more immediate concern for the Church and a greater ability to set their own thinking in the midst of its daily needs. Nevertheless, they decisively broke out of a kind of "Anglican ghetto" mentality. The world and its agenda became very much a matter of concern. Often the stock answers of the moral tradition were rejected as useless, and the situationists turned to other Christians or to the behavioral sciences for what they perceived to be better answers. In so doing, they emphasized the right and duty of each individual to construct a more adequate understanding of theology and morality than that which the tradition was conveying.

In taking seriously this last result of the work of the situationists, there is validity to looking at their influence in terms of the thesis set forth by Thomas Luckmann in *The Invisible Religion*.[21] In his book Luckmann asserts, "that we are observing the emergence of a new social form of religion characterized neither by diffusion of the sacred cosmos through the social structure nor by the institutional specialization of religion."[22] What we are seeing today is religion as a private vision, an individual matter. Religion is becoming invisible in modern industrial society because it is becoming more and more a private quest for meaning rather than an institutionally or socially guided experience.

While Luckmann did not go into detail about the ethical sphere of influence of the churches, his thesis implies that morality, like religious belief, must be personally endorsed rather than institutionally given if it is to be regarded today as valid. Assuming that Luckmann is correct in the broad outline of his thesis, we can then understand situation ethics as a logical concomitant in the ethical sphere of this cultural trend to individualism in religion. Just as "the dominant themes in the modern sacred cosmos bestow something like a sacred status upon the individual by articulating his autonomy" in the religious realm, so they must also be functioning along the same lines in morality.[23]

We must however, be careful to note here that the stated intention of situation ethics was *not* to set forth a purely autonomous or individualistic ethic. They intended to portray a theonomous or God-centered position with love as the ethical equivalent of the divine will. Nevertheless, they were often heard by the general public (and by some theologically sophisticated critics as well) to be proclaiming a gospel of individual choice because they declared themselves so vociferously in opposition to externally given codes as absolute guides in morals. But at their best and their truest, they were not preaching autonomy, however much they may have sounded as if they were in their more polemical and less guarded moments.

When we refer to the three terms, heteronomy, autonomy and theonomy, what we are considering is a kind of spectrum with freedom to act on one end, the autonomous pole, and the obligation to obey the law, the heteronomous pole, on the other. Our contention is that situation ethics is neither autonomy (antinomianism) nor is it heteronomy (legalism). It is instead an attempt at theonomy in ethics, with love as the functional equivalent of God in the moral realm. St. John's dictum, "God is love," implies this deduction. God is love, when He is thought of ethically. Love in situation ethics is the supreme value, for it is the divine way we are commanded to follow.

Whoever acts according to love, whether Christian or non-Christian, is following a theonomous source rather than asserting his will in an autonomous fashion or refusing to take responsibility for his actions by obeying an extrinsic standard as if it were absolute. In situation ethics the question of conscience is resolved in favor of doing the most loving thing, whether according to the law or against the law. Thus, Fletcher concluded, "Christian ethics or moral theology is not a scheme of living according to a code but a continuous effort to relate love to a world of relativities through a casuistry obedient to love; its constant task is to work out the strategy and tactics of love, for Christ's sake."[24]

At first glance situation ethics seems to offer a simple or even superficial rule for moral behavior. Yet as we ponder its implications we see how incredibly demanding the position actually is. If we are to apply love in the situation we must be both steeped in the moral wisdom of the race (what Fletcher called the *Sophia*) and profoundly at one in intention with God. This expectation implies a thorough grounding in both moral and ascetical theology. Viewed from this angle it is an ethic for saints rather than an invitation to moral anarchy, a method which none should attempt without the most serious of motives to live the Christian life. Despite its theoretical simplicity, the casuistry of love demands more and not less from its adherents.

Some critics of situation ethics protest that the danger of legalism is less relevant today than the threat of normlessness. Granted that legalism is a perennial peril in ethics, do we want to make it our number one target in a world which seems notably to lack standards of morality? A more urgent need may be the recovery of a sense of heritage and a new appreciation of the experience of previous generations. Moreover, just as the student of the new physics of Einstein, Planck and Heisenberg must also be familiar with Newtonian science, so the new moralist must be knowledgeable about the old morality before he is competent to embrace the fulness of his ethical freedom as a situationist. This analogy from physics suggests that as there is a need to respect Newton's laws even if their theoretical framework has been superceded, so the moral experience of past ages must be heeded and pondered by anyone who would presume to exercise the right of judging them by love's canon.

Love alone is not enough. Love must be spelled out, and it is the task of moral theology to attempt that elaboration. Even when the love of Christ is hailed as the supreme principle in ethics, we still have the task of describing *how* that love shall take shape in our own actions. As we go about the task of pondering how we can best serve love, we inevitably find ourselves having recourse to what others have said, so that our moral thinking may be enriched, deepened and broadened beyond the narrow confines of our own perception and experience. Situation ethics betrays its own high calling when it tries to commend itself as a short-cut to goodness where "all you need is love."

Conclusion

In attempting to understand situationism against the background of Christian thought, perhaps the most adequate way to see the new moralists whom we have discussed is to regard them as contemporary representatives of an Anglican neo-liberalism. Like the earlier theological liberals, the situationists attempted to modify supranaturalism with an emphasis on the immanence of God. They agreed implicitly and sometimes explicitly that a doctrine of man must stress his potential for divine sonship and free moral agency. They shared the liberals' concern for the primacy of personal over all other values. Moreover, there was a strong Christocentric emphasis in the thinking of John A. T. Robinson and Douglas Rhymes, if somewhat less in Fletcher. Sometimes this tendency slips to a preoccupation with the human Jesus as moral teacher, just as it did amongst the older liberals. Like the older liberals, the situationists tended to regard ethics as the most important expression of religion. The earlier liberals insisted on the legitimacy of applying the test of rationality to biblical and doctrinal matters. The exponents of situation ethics extended that effort into the realm of morality, although some of them have also attempted more sweeping theological reconstruction. Certainly they are at one with the older liberals in welcoming secular learning and secular comradeship in a common search for truth.

One way to describe situation ethics, therefore, would be to see it as the appropriate moral deduction from liberal theology. Just as more traditional moral theology was an outgrowth and a derivation from what may be broadly labeled as Thomistic Anglicanism, so situation ethics is the moral theology of contemporary liberal Anglicanism. In the development of situationism we see an inevitable carrying out of some of the main theological insights originally proposed several generations ago by spokesmen who were often ignored in Anglican circles during their heyday. It is the first attempt at a systematic statement of morality which takes as its basis the pragmatic, empirical, relativistic, and personalistic stance of liberalism rather than the rationalistic, deductive, absolutist, and principle-centered framework of traditional thought.

Yet the dichotomy between the two approaches of situation ethics and traditional moral theology should not be overdrawn. Like theological liberalism situation ethics is best seen as an attempt to renew and recover the essential elements of Christianity obscured by the growth of tradition, not as a totally new initiative without precedent. It is an attempt to update moral thought, to bring moral theology more decisively into the modern era, and to give it a contemporary rather than a classical or medieval philosophical basis.

The moral theology of the future will be built out of elements of the old and new moralities with each contributing something of its genius to the final result. From the past will come a loyalty to the corporate wisdom of the Church, a caution and thoughtfulness in decision-making, and a renewed respect for the experience of living as this has been preserved in maxims of conduct. From the present will come a heightened sense of our responsibility as individuals answerable to God and man for moral choices, a greater confidence and freedom in action, and a deeper appreciation of the peculiarity and complexity of each ethical situation. It is necessary to continue the dialogue between the old and the new so that out of the dialectical process a more adequate statement of moral theology may emerge.

Old and new moralities, like old and new theologies, always have something in common if they are worthy of the name of Christian. They have Christ, and the essence of Christian living has always been, in some sense at least, the *imitatio Christi*. The most important contribution of the new moralists has been to insist that Christian ethics reexamine its tradition against the standard of the loving Christ and be prepared to part with that which cannot with certainty be related to his love. The same imperative was felt by the old moralists, for Bishop Kirk himself wrote that "the Christian life is *not so much a life of following rules, as a life of following Christ.*"[25] Prayer and ethics, devotion and doing, are indeed the inside and the outside of the same reality. There is then a source of unity in ethics and in the life of the Church which can mysteriously hold together both old and new, "Christ Jesus himself . . . the cornerstone, in whom the whole structure is joined together and grows into a holy temple in the Lord."[26]

III. Contemporary Practice

Contraception and Natural Law: A Half-Century of Anglican Moral Reflection

by Harmon L. Smith

The historical and cultural roots of Anglicanism lie deep within a "reformed Catholicism," profoundly influenced by an English temperament. Our heritage embraces not only classical Catholic Christianity and distinctive aspects of the Continental Reformation, but also the Anglican preference for a mediating "both/and" rather than a divisive "either/or." From the many-branched tree of the Anglican Communion sprung from these roots, one might reasonably expect that the fruit of its moral theology would be somehow hybridized; but just how the moral teaching of this Church has incorporated and now represents its seminal elements deserves periodic examination.

A brief review of the ways in which one aspect of this moral teaching has been treated—by several representative moral theologians who have called themselves Anglican, together with official statements from Lambeth Conferences—is instructive for understanding how Anglican moral theology tends to get shaped. The issue before this paper is contraception, and the questions about how this Church and its theologians have treated it are far-ranging.[1]

In the beginning, so to speak, Anglican moral theology was largely indistinguishable from Roman Catholic moral theology in both method and content. Although Anglicans did not share the Roman Catholic separation of moral and ascetical theology, or the post-Tridentine devaluation of individual liberty and conscience in the name of law,[2] a broadly Thomist understanding of natural law was clearly retained. Thus, from the publication of the first four books of Hooker's *Laws* (1594) onwards, natural law theory has had a secure place in Anglican moral theology. That place, however, has become increasingly tenuous and uncertain.

Two Anglican authors from opposite sides of the Atlantic have offered opposite opinions about the steady diminution of the importance of natural law in Anglican moral theology. Speaking before the Church Assembly on July 4, 1963, the Bishop of Exeter, Dr. R. C. Mortimer, complained that

> The great work of the schoolmen in reformulating the concept of the natural law as they found it in Aristotle, and the making of it a basis and a support for the New Testament revealed ethic, has been far too long ignored in Anglican circles. . . . What is urgently needed throughout the whole of Christendom is a reformulation in modern terms of the concept of natural law, . . . [3]

Three years later, Dr. Joseph Fletcher, then Professor of Social Ethics in the Episcopal Theological School, maintained that

> In ecumenical circles there is a widespread but erroneous impression that the natural law doctrine is a fixed feature of Anglican theology. . . . However, there has always been a measure of ambiguity in the Anglican treatment of natural law. . . . They had no difficulty in believing that God wills what is right and good . . . but they were uneasy about the *epistemology* of the classical doctrine. . . . This is the heart of the problem—in the natural-law theory of ethical knowledge, we can postulate the presence of right and wrong objectively in the nature of things, *de rerum natura*, if we appreciate that kind of metaphysics. But this does not entitle us to claim that we *possess such 'values' cognitively.* . . . The natural law may persist as an ontological affirmation, but it is dead as an epistemological doctrine. [4]

Why one laments, and the other celebrates, the demise of natural law will become clearer as we examine the ways in which some Anglican moral theologians—among them, Mortimer and Fletcher—have treated natural law with reference to contraception. [5] While I do not presume to think that this chapter can answer fully all of the relevant questions, I do propose to isolate some features of the arguments in order to consider whether they can serve as a single source for an authoritative Anglican moral theology. This method, in other words, may help to answer the first of our two principal questions, namely, whether there are sources for Anglican moral theology which either provide its specific difference or ensure its orthodoxy.

Traditional Opposition to Contraception on Grounds of Natural Law

Opposition to contraception among Anglicans rests generally on the same grounds that it does among Roman Catholics, except that Anglicans do not make similar appeals to the Church's authority and teaching office. Roman Catholic parenesis has fewer problems with natural law because of the credibility granted to both papal infallibility *ex cathedra* and the magisterium. Nevertheless, Anglican arguments have depended heavily upon traditional natural law theory. That argument, from Hooker onwards, proceeds as follows:

Laws are principles of order which direct things to their proper end and good. All things are subject to law because "All things that are have some operation not violent or casual. Neither doth any thing ever begin to exercise the same without some foreconceived end for which it worketh."[6] Beings may accordingly be divided into classes or kinds which correspond to the ways in which they participate in this lawful movement toward their ends. There are three principal kinds or classes of beings:

1. Inanimate beings tend toward their end automatically; provided, of course, that nothing intervenes to interfere with their natural tendencies. These beings are governed by "natural laws" in the modern sense of that term, that is, they exhibit observable patterns of chemical and physical endurance, change, development, and decay.

2. Animal life comprises the second class of beings. These beings move themselves toward their end instinctively; though they, too, of course, are subject to the first sort of natural laws. (As we will see as we go farther, the higher classes include and build upon the lower ones.)

3. Finally, there is the class of beings which moves toward their end freely. These are, in a sense, *auto-nomos,* a law unto themselves, inasmuch as reason grasps that there is an end and that its pursuit and achievement is good. So these beings rationally participate in their movement toward their appropriate end.

Each of these three distinct, but related, classes of beings has a traditionally defined end. The end of inanimate things has been thought to be maintenance of themselves in being. The end of irrational animate beings is especially maintenance of the life of the species (which implies maintenance of the life of individual members of the species). As the end of mere beings is the good of the maintenance and perfection of mere being, and as the end of living beings is the good of the maintenance and perfection of their life, so the end of rational beings is the good of the maintenance and perfection of their reason. Despite these distinct and proper ends, the classes are also related: as the maintenance of animal life requires the maintenance of mere being, so the maintenance of rational life requires the maintenance of both animal life and mere being.

It is argued further that human life indispensably includes all three levels of being, and that men and women pursue their good properly when they pursue the goods attached to each and all of these. Proper human action is therefore action which is governed by this threefold natural law. Sometimes, however, an action which serves one end may conflict with another. For example, the pursuit of food (which is necessary for animal health and well-being) may oblige one to neglect schooling and intellectual development. In such cases, when the obligations of different levels conflict, it is the lower and more basic end which ought to be pursued: food comes before schooling, having a body is requisite to having a mind. The lower is thus the necessary precondition of the higher. Without food, one cannot perfect one's reason; likewise, one cannot pursue comfortable or humane existence if one does not preserve mere existence.

All three of these levels of being are involved in human sexual intercourse; and the 1549 English Prayerbook doubtless speaks of intercourse as well as matrimony when it enumerates the reasons, causes, and ends to which marriage is ordained:

> One cause was the procreation of children, to be brought up in the fear and nurture of the Lord, and praise of God. Secondly it was ordained for a remedy against sin, and to avoid fornication, that such persons as be married, might live chastely in matrimony, and keep themselves undefiled members of Christ's body. Thirdly for the mutual society, help, and comfort, that the one ought to have of the other, both in prosperity and adversity.[7]

Entirely congenial with traditional natural law theory, procreation is named the first end since it conserves and extends the human species in mere and lively existence. Survival is requisite to all being and achievement. The other ends of marriage—satisfaction of sexual desires in an orderly and lawful way, promotion of a couple's mutual concern, care and love—follow. It should be pointed out that the latter goods are not diminished by their position in the sequence; they are more specifically human than mere reproduction, yet less fundamental; they represent comprehensive human obligations which embrace and entail simple natural obligations as well.

It is for this reason that proponents of traditional natural law theory often argue that every act of human sexual intercourse must be *aptus ad generationem*. This does not mean that human coitus is evil if it does not result in conception[8]; or that a couple may not engage in sexual intercourse if they are infertile for whatever cause; or even that they may not plan to avoid sexual intercourse during the fertile period of the woman's menstrual cycle while engaging in it at other times. It means rather that nothing may be done to prevent impregnation *if that can result* from the act at the particular time it occurs. It is in that sense that traditional natural law advocates have argued that procreation is inseparable from intercourse, and that the act is perverted if it is deliberately turned away from this end. (I should also say, but parenthetically, that it has been further argued that it is wrong to sunder this act from this end even when one decides that procreation is not the primary end, inasmuch as every act of human coitus should be apt for, and not positively directed away from, generation *and* physical pleasure *and* expression of love and unity.)

The *aptus ad generationem* view is still held officially by the Roman Catholic Church, as it is also affirmed by some Anglicans and Evangelicals. The once vehement opposition to contraception by Anglo-Catholics (even of liberal Catholics such as Charles Gore), has, however, diminished considerably in recent decades as a rather broad range of contemporary Anglican thinking on contraception has emerged. This pluralism of positions has not been discouraged by the vagueness and indecisiveness of the few official or semi-official Anglican documents which have been produced.

Official Anglican Statements

Prior to 1930 the Anglican Communion appears to have stood strongly opposed to contraception. Lambeth Conferences in 1908 and 1920, and the Episcopal Church's House of Bishops in 1925, addressed the issue publicly and passed similar resolutions which the world certainly interpreted as stout condemnations of contraception. But Kirk suggests that while these condemnations appear to be strong, they are in fact ambiguous in that they refuse to "lay down rules which will meet the needs of every abnormal case."[9] In any event, the Lambeth Conference of 1930 did use "abnormal cases" as justification for altering what was generally understood to be the Anglican Communion's position on contraception.

Resolutions 13 and 15 of the 1930 Conference state that there may be a moral obligation to limit family size, and that the "primary and obvious method" for doing this is complete abstinence.[10] However, Resolution 15 states that "where there is a morally sound reason for avoiding complete abstinence, the Conference agrees that other methods may be used, provided that this is done in the light of . . . Christian principles." After heated debate, and opposition led by Charles Gore and the Anglo-Catholic wing, Resolution 15 was carried by 193 votes to 67, with many abstentions.

Resolutions seldom offer much in the way of argument. In this instance there was an explanatory report (Number II, "The Life and Witness of the Christian Community"), but it carried of course only the authority of the committee which reported it, and cannot therefore serve as a controlling guide for interpreting Resolution 15. That lacuna is regrettable because the ambiguities of this resolution are many and profound. It is far from clear, for example, what constitutes a "morally sound reason for avoiding complete abstinence," or even whether there can be such a reason. Nor is it transparent what "other methods" are; except, presumably, that they are in accord with "Christian principles," a term which itself is as poorly defined as the other. So ambiguous in fact is this resolution that the best tactic for opponents of contraception might have been to support it fully and then insist that "Christian principles" always exclude "artificial" contraception, in which case the resolution would permit only "rhythm" (i.e., partial abstinence) and no other method!

Most theologians thought that this resolution gave official support to those who would use "artificial" contraceptive methods in extraordinary cases. Since complete abstinence is said (but without explanation) to be the primary and obvious means for preventing pregnancy, an "extraordinary case" presumably entails a long-term condition (making temporary abstinence insufficient) and grave risk (ruling out the use of very fallible "natural" methods). Kirk and Mortimer later attempted to define, or at least give examples of, such extraordinary cases; but Church members were meantime offered nothing more official for guidance than the term itself and a vague reference to Christian principles.

The 1958 Lambeth Conference merely reiterated the resolutions of 1930, but with a significant addendum: the right and duty of determining proper family size, it was asserted, rests on the conscience of parents.[11] Perhaps, in the absence of other direction, this is not an unexpected development; still, it served to exacerbate the problem all the same. On the one hand, the Church permits "artificial" contraception only as a second choice in extraordinary cases; on the other hand, the Church leaves the decision to parents and does not provide any help in determining when the use of contraception is justified.

Beyond this action, the 1958 Conference also produced a detailed report on the family which presented three different positions on contraception,[12] each of which is more permissive than the traditional Roman Catholic position in that they do not absolutely exclude so-called "artificial" means. In the end, the report concludes that "the responsible use of contraceptives by married persons" is morally right.[13] The criterion for judging "rightness" is that the act of coitus, with or without contraceptives,

> ... must above all have integrity as a responsible personal act—although ... it is manifestly impossible to define in advance the precise general conditions which ensure integrity, since many factors are involved which elude or defy definition. A valid conception of the 'given' structure of *coitus*, therefore, must take fully into account the fact that personal and relational factors are 'given' no less than the physiological and biological factors—and that the former must not be separated artificially from the latter.[14]

This conclusion is a remarkably lucid statement of the "appeal to totality," which was to be explicitly rejected by *Humanae Vitae* (cf. esp. paragraphs 3 and 11) ten years later. Critics of such an appeal to "personal and relational factors" argue that it quickly plunges one into a radical situationism; but whether this is true, the report's conclusion certainly makes contraception less exceptional than some would want it to be. Moreover, since only the couple concerned can be presumed to be sufficiently aware of these "personal and relational factors," this conclusion also accounts for the bishop's failure to elaborate in detail their understanding of the circumstances which would warrant the use of contraceptive devices. In the final analysis, the circumstances which vindicate the use of contraceptives are less extraordinary than one might suppose (given the 1930 resolution), and they are primarily (and, in practice, probably exclusively) the business of the couple involved.

The 1968 Lambeth Conference found itself confronting the papal encyclical, *Humanae vitae*; and its response was to quote three resolutions (112, 113, and 115) from Lambeth 1958. It is useful to cite here the two brief paragraphs which preface the iteration of these resolutions:

Responsible Parenthood
22. This Conference has taken note of the papal encyclical letter *Humanae vitae* recently issued by His Holiness Pope Paul VI. The Conference records its appreciation of the Pope's deep concern for the institution of marriage and the integrity of married life.

Nevertheless, the Conference finds itself unable to agree with the Pope's conclusion that all methods of conception control other than abstinence from sexual intercourse or its confinement to the periods of infecundity are contrary to the "order established by God." It reaffirms the findings of the Lambeth Conference of 1958 contained in resolutions 112, 113, and 115 which are as follows. . . .[15]

Now we have come quite a long way, some think 180-degrees, from the strong opposition to contraception of Lambeth 1930; but the Church's official position is still somewhat more conventional than that taken by some of its moral theologians.

Mortimer and Kirk

Kenneth Kirk and R. C. Mortimer are, I think, transitional figures who, by milder condemnation, showed some relaxation of traditional opposition to contraception.

Mortimer's statements on natural law are essentially the familiar and established ones, as is indicated by his sources: Romans 1:28, Hooker's *Laws* I, viii; and St. Thomas' *Summa Theologia* I, II, q. xciv.[16] He recognizes that deductions from the basic principles of natural law may err, and that they therefore require constant rethinking and reformulation. All the same, Mortimer displays an ˙unshakeable confidence in both the existence of, and human access to (through conscience), the natural law:

Murder, theft, adultery are everywhere recognised as wrong in general and in principle. They are easily seen to be destructive of society and inimical to quiet, peaceable and happy living. They have, in fact, no proper place in the scheme of things. Denounce these practices, and men may resent it but will not dispute it. Demonstrate that this particular action proposed violates one of these generally recognised precepts of the natural law, and you have sufficiently demonstrated its wrongness, and it will be done with a bad conscience. Whilst there is a great need to-day for fresh hard thinking on the application of the natural law to new conditions and circumstances, and for effort to elucidate its content, there is an ever greater need for a clear and constant reaffirmation of those precepts which are known and which are still easily applicable, but from which men turn away to their own ruin, under the influence of selfish passion, and to the flagrant violation of which their consciences are becoming increasingly hardened. There is much in the old statement of the natural law which needs no revision. The old rules of honesty and justice, of chastity and neighbourliness, are as true and as binding as ever they were. ... They are the law of God for man ... they constitute a clear, challenging and objective criterion of right and wrong, above and aloof from the confusion and perplexing claims of mere expediency.[17]

Despite such a fulsome affirmation, Mortimer does not simply regurgitate the tradition of Thomas and Hooker, or of such modern Roman Catholic manual moral theologians as Davis and Lehmkuhl. He is reluctant, for example, to condemn actions as being intrinsically wrong without any consideration of their consequences. He agrees with the tradition that one may not do evil in order that good may result; but he claims that when it is certain that a good result will supervene on a bad, the quality of the object of the action is modified by that very fact and certainty.[18] On Mortimer's view, certain or virtually certain results are capable of changing not only the rightness or wrongness of an act *in concreto* but also the very kind and quality of the act. The bearing of this line of reasoning upon contraception will become evident when we examine the conclusions reached by both Mortimer and Kirk.

Kenneth Kirk appeared more interested than Mortimer in the epistemological problems involved with assertions concerning immutable divine law, whether natural or revealed. After presenting four grounds on which some claim to base such immutable laws,[19] Kirk proceeds to show that these grounds are really not at all secure. When, for example, the established principles are no longer very general and formal, they become problematic. Historical study reveals frequent and broad shifts in what is thought to be clearly and obviously and eternally mandated by God and nature.[20] Moreover, scriptural foundations for traditional claims are shaken by variety of the conclusions of exegetes and by modern biblical criticism.[21] Even Church consensus can only indicate that a given formulation of immutable divine law *approaches* the perfection and immutability of what it attempts to express.[22]

The result of such considerations as these is a conclusion "that the moral law, though absolute in ideal character, is often distressingly relative and fallible in its promulgation."[23] In practice, this means that the only laws which are to be treated as immutable, divine laws are those which "sane and mature minded Christians" do not question; a kind of *consensus fidelium*.[24] These, as it turns out, are both few in number and quite general in content. Beyond these are many mutable laws and fluctuating formulations. As a result, the Church in each generation has "the duty of a constant, painstaking, conservative but brave revision of her moral code," a duty which in fact she has often fulfilled.[25] But then this is a duty which is arguably no less imperative for the state and all human institutions in fidelity to conscience and cultural relativism.

Kirk's caution in treating natural law theory and claims appears to be related to his rather high view of ecclesial authority. In practice this means that if a principle has long been taught as binding on Christians, he is circumspect in dealing with it: the older and more widespread a teaching, the less warrant we have to discard or even question it.[26] Thus, while he has a critical perspective on the way in which traditional moral theology founds its teaching, he also tends to reproduce its conclusions (in however milder, more chary a form).

These loyalties—respect for tradition, a high view of ecclesial authority, but a willingness withal to make prudent changes—are reflected in Kirk's conclusions in the matter of contraception. In brief, those conclusions are the following: (1) The traditional condemnation of contraception as *a priori* unnatural is fallacious.[27] It rests either on hard-to-defend intuitions or an the fallacious identification of "natural" with "artificial."[28] Neither can the traditional condemnation be supported by appeal to social needs; the Church does not and should not condemn practices not otherwise objectionable simply by reference to undesirable social consequences.[29] (2) One may legitimately be in doubt in this matter, since even now the traditional view is held by many. But since the matter is vital, the principle *in dubito, libertas* does not apply, and we are left practically and in effect with a prohibition of the practice. The doubt, however, is such that a confessor may take advantage of the mitigations which confessors are wont to do and not refuse absolutism and communion to those who are practicing contraception.[30] (3) On the other hand, one may whole-heartedly accept that contraception is legitimate in abnormal cases. This is the most practically difficult of the positions possible since it requires continuing effort to determine what are "abnormal cases." (4) The Lambeth Conference of 1930 appears to have made the position described under #3 a legitimate one for Anglicans to hold. It is highly desirable, in that case, for the Church to begin providing some authoritative guidelines lest in their absence gross laxity arise.[31]

Mortimer's conclusions are roughly the same. What is an Anglican to do in view of strong and compelling opposition to traditional and Roman Catholic prohibition of contraception? Mortimer says that if one thinks the use of contraceptives probably right in abnormal circumstances (e.g., should one have a hereditary, transmissible disease, or a "wife is unable to bear a further child without grave danger to her life"), and if one be in such circumstances, "here surely ... there is a real probability that the use of contraceptives is right."[32] It deserves noting that Mortimer treats this as a case in which doubt (together with certain circumstances) makes the action right, provided that the agent does not think it more probable that the action is wrong. Kirk, in contrast, thinks that doubt in this matter is sufficient to leave one effectively committed to prohibition.

Both Mortimer and Kirk reject the view that contraception is *a priori* unnatural; at the least, their conclusions assume that the traditional argument can be reasonably doubted. Withal, both recognize not one but two legitimate positions within Anglican moral theology: (a) one may have doubts and conclude that contraception is to be rejected, or (b) one may argue that contraceptives probably or definitely may be used in abnormal circumstances.

Three Contemporary
Anglican Moral Theologians

Because they are currently more widely known and discussed, the contributions of Joseph Fletcher, John Macquarrie, and Herbert Waddams to the matter at hand can be treated more concisely.

I have already indicated the general features of Fletcher's rejection of natural law theory, but a somewhat extended citation from his essay on "The Ethics of Natural Law," which is exemplary for its succinctness and lucidity, will be useful here:

This is the heart of the problem—in the natural-law theory of ethical knowledge we can postulate the presence of right and wrong objectively in the nature of things, *de rerum natura*, if we appreciate that kind of metaphysics. But this does not entitle us to claim that we *possess* such "values" cognitively. Such epistemological complacency has become impossible since the establishment of cultural relativism by Edward Westermark in his *Origin and Development of the Moral Ideas* in 1912. On the basis of the "radical monotheism" in Christian theology, we may believe (heuristically postulate) "natural laws," but we cannot pretend to *know* them as universals or as universally obligatory. The natural law may persist as an ontological affirmation, but it is dead as an epistemological doctrine. This is an age of relativism in Christian terms of humility: the old "canon" of rationality has been shaken by depth psychology; the old "canon" of the occidental perspective has been superseded by a global or even interspatial perspective; the old "canon" of logic and language has been replaced by nondiscursive and symbolic reason. In the same way, the old "canon" of a hierarchy of values has been converted into a *spectrum*—a sliding scale of ethical relativities and a pragmatic temper. With some this becomes *de gustibus non est disputandum* or an "absolute" relativism, but it cannot become so for Christians because of Jesus Christ, the man who is the measure of all things. As Brunner put it, the *Why* is always the same, no matter how much the *What* may vary. The point is that the *What* does vary.[33]

The problem, in a word, is not so much with the objective reality of the will of God, but with human discernment; not with ontology, but with epistemology. And, in Fletcher's view—which is correct, so far as I know—this problematic aspect of natural law theory has been recognized by Anglican theologians from the seventeenth century onwards.[34] In the present, "the question is: Is the moral quality or 'value' of a thing or action intrinsic or extrinsic, inherent or contingent? Is it 'in' a right act or policy, or does it happen *to* it?"[35] Fletcher's opinion is well-known: "The situational method ... holds that whatever is most loving in the situation *is* right and good—not merely something to be excused as a lesser evil."[36]

The bearing of the situational approach upon fertility control is, in Fletcher's view, clear and straightforward:

The problem is: Should we use rational controls for humanly chosen purposes in fertility? ... the problem of every culture, as of every person, is growth and change. What was once viable and functional may become quite maladaptive when circumstances change. ... The only issue as to the morality of birth control arises around the means employed, not about the end sought. . . . The churches suffer from a typical incoherence and ethical superficiality.[37]

With customary candor and clarity, Fletcher concludes his essay with "five propositions," which have been somewhat abbreviated as follows:

1. *Making babies is a good thing but making love is, too,* and we can *and should* make love even when no baby is intended. . . .

2. The best way to make love without making babies is to prevent their conception; the next best way is to prevent fertility itself; and the least desireable way is to end a pregnancy already begun. *But any of these methods is good if the good to be gained is great enough to justify the means.*

3. . . . to be artificial or against nature is often the highest good, in terms of moral values. In short, the natural-law ethic is self-contradictory, problematic, and dead as Queen Anne.

4. Only one thing is *intrinsically* good, that is, inherently and always good and right, regardless of circumstances; and that one thing is love, namely, concern for others. . . . This is *theological* relativism, based on the proposition that *God is love* and *only* God *un*conditional and absolute.

5. Finally: if there are people who believe that any of these things is wrong and sinful, let them conduct themselves accordingly. But let them not try to deprive their neighbors, who see it differently, of *their* freedom and responsibility. . . .[38]

There is no mention here of the "abnormal case," or probabilism, or extraordinary circumstance; but other features of the 1930 Resolution 15, of the 1958 Lambeth commitment to parents of the right and duty to determine proper family size, and of the relaxation of traditional opposition and milder condemnation by Kirk and Mortimer are developed and extended by Fletcher to their logical conclusions. What began as advocacy for the liberty of conscience to work through the intimacies and intricacies of contraception in conscious fidelity to spouse, Church, and self has become, in situationism, the radical freedom of an autonomous self to decide *for itself* whatever is most loving (and therefore right and good) in its situation. What began as rather timid ecclesial response to an urgent and important issue, both within and without the Church, has become a matter of individual self-determination within a pluralistic religion ethos.[39]

Neither John Macquarrie nor Herbert Waddams rejects natural law, but both make substantial modification of it. In his essay, titled

"Rethinking Natural Law,"[40] Macquarrie has provided a clear (though brief) Anglican effort at rehabilitating natural law theory. He begins with a hermeneutical circle:

> Christ interprets for the Christian the meaning of authentic humanity or mature manhood, but he is acknowledged as the Christ or the paradigm of humanity because men have interpreted him as such in the light of an idea of authentic humanity that they already bring to him and that they have derived from their own participation in human existence.[41]

This means that while Christ may contradict our concrete condition, he nevertheless fulfills what we already can recognize deep within us. So all human moral striving—Christian and non-Christian alike—can and is to be affirmed on the ground of a doctrine of creation.[42]

Macquarrie criticizes those who reject the notion of a perduring natural law by arguing that such a repudiation leaves one vulnerable to legal positivism (like that of Nazi Germany) or to sheer moral relativism. What is needed to avoid those disastrous alternatives is recognition that there is a moral order not created by man which lays a demand on him, that there is an ontologically founded morality.[43] But the traditional formulations of natural law theory are not adequate, especially insofar as natural law theory is supposed to supply a body of unchanging rules. Macquarrie contends that such rules as there be from natural law are actually very general and formal; indeed, natural law "is not so much itself a 'law' as rather a touchstone for determining the justice or morality of actual laws and rules."[44] This is so because man's nature cannot be identified with some former, concrete, unchanging state; "natural" does not equal "primitive." Instead, man's nature is forever developing. But this development is not arbitrary or accidental; it is directed, it has a constant tendency.[45]

One evidence of this non-arbitrary character can be observed in the fact that most major moral codes agree to a remarkable extent in their major principles. But beyond all else, Macquarrie believes that the direction of human nature is toward self-giving love; a love which is creative and free and developing (and so cannot be fully expressed in rules). Seen above all in Christ, that loving humanity becomes transparent to the divine; and that is why

> what is distinctive in the Christian ethic is not its ultimate goals or its fundamental principles, for these are shared with all

serious-minded people in whatever tradition they stand. The distinctive element is the special context within which the moral life is perceived.[46]

Such a love explains St. Thomas' statement that man, as free and rational, is a creature that is itself provident. And that is how it can happen that a person who refuses to go out of himself (i.e., to ex-ist) in free self-giving love will surely lose his life in the vain effort to preserve it as a static possession.[47]

One of Macquarrie's applications of his rethinking of natural law is (happily for us) directed to the issue of contraception. In sum, and consistent with his general approach, Macquarrie argues that man's nature is to go out of himself and assume control over crude nature for human ends; doing this, man comes to control and humanize immature nature. So, for example, he comes to control population in a self-conscious way rather than relying on chance, disease, or war: "Given that human nature is not static but, by its very biological basis, must develop itself by way of 'extensions,' the pill is just as natural a method of birth control as is the so-called 'rhythm' method."[48] Or again, "the pill and the condom are now part of his (man's) nature."[49] These changes in human nature are not, however, without important consequences, and Macquarrie recognizes that new problems are created by new possibilities; his own illustration is that contraceptive techniques now permit human sexual intercourse and procreation, formerly inseparable, to be separated. How in light of this, he asks, is one to rework the old defences of chastity and continence?[50] Macquarrie does not venture an answer for us, except to reaffirm his confidence in ever-changing "man's self-understanding" to "sharpen his image of mature manhood." So, in the end, there is no distinctive content or "what" which derives from a Christianly understood natural law, but only the "special context" and criterion of Jesus Christ, "the one whose christhood is a self-transcending manhood."[51] Such advice as this is surely consistent with Macquarrie's entire position; but its sheer formalism, and corresponding absence of decisive material principles, does nothing to advance a *consensus fidelium* or narrow the gap between individual conscience and communitarian accountability or instruct us about what is (and is not) harmonious with the "special context" and criterion of Jesus Christ.

Herbert Waddams, in interesting ways, both augments and pares Macquarrie's approach; but first he distinguishes two meanings of natural law. (1) The first meaning locates in the order of nature, created by God and observed by man. The tendency here is to divide morality into natural (the cardinal virtues) and supernatural (the theological virtues) levels. The natural is a base on which the supernatural builds in this traditional view; but Waddams notes that conversion is a matter of the inner man and may not affect observable behavior, so that nothing changes. On the other hand, conversion transfigures the whole man, so that everything changes. Waddams' point here is not to argue that there is no virtue except among Christians, but only that all good is a result of participation in Christ's life. That participation may come from creation, or it may come from the reflected light of a Christ-saturated culture, or it may come from personal conversion and faith. Withal, and however it comes, only the last is fully acceptable.[52]

(2) Waddams' second meaning of natural law entails the natural sense of right and wrong, including a universal sense about particular moral issues. While recognizing a general, natural sense of right and wrong, he nevertheless judges it to be of negligible importance in deciding concrete moral problems. He warns about leaving Christ out of the picture until the issue has been decided, and then points to the epistemological difficulties of traditional positions based on natural law claims. These, he thinks, tend to physicalism (an example of which is the Roman Catholic position on contraception), that is, they erroneously subject moral claims to physical structures.[53]

Altogether, Waddams' view of reason as the organ of natural law is much more minimalistic than Macquarrie's; and he seems quite willing to do what Macquarrie explicitly refuses to do, namely, absorb all ethical inquiry and effort into Christian ethics and moral theology.[54] This is warranted, Waddams holds, because the objective end of man and the subjective means of achieving that end are the same fulfillment of human potentialities. This consummation comes about when the individual complies with the laws of growth and health which are given with his nature and his situation. And this is ultimately done when the individual is united with God in Christ. Whether this power to respond is a vestige of some original and prevenient empowerment or the result of an immediate act of divine grace alone is a peripheral matter. The effect is the same: man is capable of hearing the call to such unity, and so is not entirely bereft of choice.[55]

Waddams rejects Mortimer's argument on contraception and significantly modifies Macquarrie's view. The tradition permits "rhythm" family planning because what prevents conception in that method is outside, external to, the act itself. Oral contraceptives do not fail that test, because Waddams finds it hard to see that the distinction between "natural" and "artificial," or internal and external, contraceptives is sufficient to constitute a *moral* difference. In the end, he subscribes to the notion that "It is only by holding a rigid view that the prevention of children is always a sin when the sexual act takes place that the use of contraceptives can be morally condemned."[56] In fact, Waddams argues, God has given men freedom to make decisions in areas under their power to control, and there is no *a priori* reason to suppose that he objects to the exercise of this freedom in the area of contraception.

> Those who oppose contraceptives sometimes seem to imply that in the absence of their use God is given a free choice as to whether conception shall take place or not, and that he makes up his mind in every case separately, and issues a kind of separate *fiat* or *non-fiat*. This appears to reflect a crude idea of God and an inadequate concept of human freedom, for it is the meaning of human freedom that God has put it into the power of men to make their own decisions in fields which are under their control.[57]

Waddams' general emphasis on the specifically human (in the case of human sexual intercourse, on the unitive end of this action) leads him to conclude that there are many cases in which contraceptive devices, including especially the "pill" but also sterilization, may be licit; and, while his sense of ecclesial magisterium seems much weaker than Mortimer's, he appeals to the 1968 Lambeth resolution in support of his argument.

A Conclusion and Hypothesis

This brief review of the ways in which a single aspect of the Church's moral teaching has evolved over the past fifty years discloses a number of changes in Anglican moral theology in both method and content. We have surely moved from more traditional to more modern views regarding the morality of contraception. We appear to be considerably less dependent on natural law as historically formulated and argued, and readier to concede to personal preference. We seem less subject to formal ecclesial instruction and guidance, and more amenable to individual conscience. We have moved from a fairly unitary position in 1930 to much more pluralistic views *within* the Church in the 1960s and 1970s; from a kind of

"Catholic" orthodoxy to various expressions of "theonomous personalism."[58] There is, as we have seen, a very broad spectrum of opinion among those who profess and claim to be Anglican; and there does not appear to be a single source, but many and varied sources for both argument and conclusion.

Among what may be many reasons for these changes, I think that Joseph Fletcher is correct when he says that the Church's use of natural law is *not* founded on natural law but on implications derived from Christian beliefs: the natural law maxims worked out by theologians came from doctrine, not nature.[59] As conceived by Aristotelianism, the concept of natural law was not a part of God's redemption which is known (or even augmented) by revelation; instead, natural law was that knowledge of right and wrong which is a part of God's providence and available to unaided human reason alone. It is also "unwritten," which means that nature's unchanging law is change, but change *within the naturally ordained telos of each species.*

The criterion for "the good" within Christianity is revelation, and that is important for distinguishing Christianity from Aristotelianism. An equally important, but too infrequently acknowledged distinction stands between Aristotelianism and Darwinism: the latter has no view of telos within species, so that natural process is open-ended and there is nothing beyond or outside natural process which can possibly serve as criterion for "the good." On Darwinian terms, "the good" is simply survival.

It is therefore mistaken *ex hypothese* to endow the natural knowledge of either Aristotelianism or Darwinism, which is by definition changing and changeable, with the kinds of immutability, certitude, and finality which attach to special revelation. We have tried, to be sure; but our attempts have chiefly served to show our inability (or unwillingness!) to learn how we can be definite without claiming also be to definitive.

To say that the Church's use of natural law derives from doctrine and not nature does not, however, oblige the implication that moral theology *qua se* is thereby ruined and to be abandoned in favor of a secularized individualism (and, hence, secularized pluralism). The simplism, which so comfortably resolved the tension between immanent and transcendent by making them virtually coterminous on the transcendent's terms, is also at work among revisionists of traditional natural law theory. In the latter case, the tension is relaxed by a simple reduction of the transcendent to the immanent. That is the Darwinian hypothesis, and the predicate of social Darwinism as well.

But the facts of the matter are that human sexuality *is* intervention in "the way things are naturally." Government, law, medicine, education, religion—all of these are directed by *human* agency to *humanly directed* purposes and ends. The advocates of naturalistic positivism (except for proponents of totalitarianism) are reluctant, however, to acknowledge the logical methodological consequences of social Darwinism and insist (arbitrarily, so far as I can tell) upon holding onto some quite general and always nonspecific "principles," which are supposed simultaneously to be distinct from mere personal preference and peculiar idiosyncrasy while nevertheless dispossessed of any authority which would make them otherwise. Our problem at this conjunction is how to be decisive in some personal sense which both takes account of, but is not tyrannized by, existential circumstance and manages to transcend "mere nature" without cutting the self off from the boundaries and limitations of the human condition.

The clue to individualism and its social expression in pluralism, is that we have somehow lost our corporate and communal moorings, that there is no agreement among us about what is central and basic upon which most of us would be in accord most of the time. This condition, the loss of an authoritative tradition, constitutes the modern world at its core. This is an obvious and acknowledged situation in Christianity, where some Christians locate the key-concept in Resurrection, some in Nativity, some in Salvation by faith, some in unconditioned *agape*, and some in something else. This is also the obvious and acknowledged situation in the world-at-large—in politics, economics, social organization, and the rest.

So Anglicanism struggles with not two but three points of view: a Catholic tradition, a Reformed perspective, and the autonomous reason of a modern scientific outlook. Our examination of contraception has shown some of the difficulties of attempting to embrace ancient and traditional ways of thinking in the face of modern ways of treating the data. The question is how Anglicanism can come to grips with the radical character of modern thinking. The story of Anglican moral theology since Jeremy Taylor is increasing awareness of the discordant character of these three points of view; but we have not yet happily reconciled these three components, and the prospect for doing so is far from certain. Indeed, how far are we from merely coming to terms with, much less successfully reconciling, our theological traditions with modern autonomous reason is indicated by the following inscription, published by the Church and prominently displayed in newspaper ads and parish houses: "Jesus came to take away your sins, not your mind."

Because Anglicanism has historically located its unity in its liturgy, and especially the Eucharist, it appears to be a doctrinal and moral microcosm of catholic Christianity; but now the meaning of "catholic" signifies the common condition of christianity rather than an undivided church. How to preserve and extend institutional wholeness amid diversity of belief and behavior will likely continue to claim attention within Anglicanism so long as it earnestly and devoutly understands and intends itself to be a *via media*, at once Catholic and Reformed—and modern. This essay has suggested that Anglicanism currently participates in the same loss of an authoritative tradition as every modern institution; and that the celebrated Anglican *via media* is thereby rendered extremely problematic, if it is not in fact defunct. Meantime, our liturgy—especially the Eucharist—displays the practical intention to acknowledge the incorporation of human life into divine grace. The *consensus fidelium* in Anglicanism therefore appears to be located in neither precept nor praxis, but liturgy; and it may be that Anglican moral theologians, so much influenced by and accountable to the modern secular academy, might do well to examine the liturgy as not only the context for worship but also for parenesis and moral action.

10

Politics, the State, and Christian Character

by William Muehl

Some years ago the distinguished Harvard biblical scholar Frank Moore Cross took part in a panel discussion of Christian faith and political responsibility. At one point in the proceedings a member of the audience rose and in a voice quivering with indignation said, "Professor Cross, surely you, as a student of the Bible, know that religion and politics do not mix!"

In the manner of one who has encountered this suggestion too many times and learned to be patient with it, Cross answered, "As a student of the Bible I know that one cannot finally separate religion and politics."

It would be difficult to find any less appropriate basis for asserting the neat division of religion and politics than the Bible. In the Old Testament the two are rarely differentiated and never in any truly significant fashion. The priests and prophets of Israel did not feel free merely to *advise* the nation's political leaders on matters of public policy. They spoke openly and often in the name of God directly to the people about myriad vital issues related to economic, social, political and foreign policy matters. And in their turn the judges and kings of Israel delivered their state edicts as reflections of the divine will, revealed to them without mediating agency.

Far from inaugurating some new dispensation in which religion and politics were carefully separated, as the indignant gentleman quoted above obviously supposed, the emergence of Israel as a nation gave birth to the concept of theocracy, direct rule by God rather than the will of the king or his subjects. This phenomenon was, of course, made possible, almost inevitable, by the radical monotheism of the Jews. Their conception of a single, consistent, self-disclosing divine power over all creation gave them less leeway than their polytheistic neighbors enjoyed to distinguished sacred from secular authority. People who inhabit a universe ruled by multiple, warring deities not unnaturally find it necessary to erect political mechanisms for adjucating the conflicting claims of those gods. And such mechanisms inevitably arrogate to themselves an inherent power which, however often it verbalizes piety, tends to govern in terms of self-validating political standards.

When, however, God is seen to be one and omnipotent there is little basis for establishing a secular political structure. The task of those who rule here on earth is simply to discern and enforce what God wills. And when it is believed also that one of the primary concerns of the divine will is the survival and prosperity of the nation as a Chosen People those revelations having to do with public policy are as likely to be presented to kings as to priests.

Thus, it is altogether false to assume that the biblical norm establishes some boundary line between religion and politics. It does precisely the opposite and unites spiritual and temporal power as reflections of the same authority over both human life and the natural order. As the late H. Richard Niebuhr said, "The separation of church and state may be an historical necessity, but it is surely not a divine ordinance."

This fact of life was not seriously questioned by many thoughtful people until very recently in history. Kings were understood to derive their power from God and were frequently crowned and consecrated by religious hierarchs. Bishops, priests and minor clerics in most of the major churches of the west were appointed by or with the concurrence of magistrates representing the state. Decrees promulgated by governments invoked divine sanctions upon their enforcement and often professed to reflect the will of God in detailed ways for particular situations. Bills of indictment against alleged criminals drew richly upon the language of theology. And one of the major tasks of the political arm of society was to enforce orthodoxy and stamp out heresy.

The interaction of church and state in such ways did not represent merely some sort of cynical accommodation or mutual back-scratching, although it often served unworthy ends. Its primary justification was the quite biblical assumption that there is a single truth binding upon all creation and that this truth must by its nature determine the policies of both church and state.

The abuses which sprang from particular unions of religious and secular authority do not need description here. They were numerous and egregious. Religion was corrupted by the demands of political expediency, and governments were used to compel submission to various kinds of ecclesiastical presumption. The name of God was invoked on behalf of brute tyranny, while worldly priests often called upon the state to secure them in their self-indulgent privileges.

It was precisely the infirmity of the traditional union of church and state which led to the first great effort to separate the two, the First Amendment to the Constitution of the United States, which stated flatly that "Congress shall make no law respecting an establishment of religion or prohibiting the free exercise thereof." The founders of the Federal Republic were determined to prevent the organic union of church and state from the abuses of which many of them or their immediate forebears were refugees.

Most of the men who worked upon the drafting of the Constitution of the United States were fully conscious of the substantive relationship that had always existed between religion and politics. That is, they understood that the concepts of right and wrong upon which public policy is based had their origins and development in religious interpretations of the human condition. As one studies the literature of politics during the federal period in American history one encounters abundant evidence of the founding fathers' dependence upon the divine sanctions that had always served to validate the political process.

Unfortunately, however, the very integral nature of the relationship between religion and politics had allowed even thoughtful people to take their connection for granted and treat it as something self-evidently good and self-perpetuating. It was felt to be unnecessary, even dangerous, to provide some formal arrangement by which this stylistic association could be preserved in the years ahead. It was assumed by the rationalist spirit of the age that certain modes of human behavior were obviously "good" and would be fostered by any responsible community and that other kinds of conduct were obviously "bad" and to be restrained.

The fact that most of these "self-evident" value judgments sprang from centuries of church-state interaction was ignored. The state simply drew upon a reservoir of received values in formulating public policy and took for granted the sanctions by which men and women were to be motivated to obey the law.

With the passage of time, however, the reservoir of received values, the moral consensus based, albeit unconsciously, upon the long experience of Christendom began to run dry. Partly because it was shut off from its wellspring in religion and partly because the growing complexity of a rapidly changing society posed problems with which the dwindling reservoir was unable to deal creatively. Once the words, "Thus saith the Lord," had ceased to be even a ritualistic formula politics lost its moral guidelines. And as an agrarian society turned into one of high technology even the re-membered and respected precepts from the past lost their relevance for daily life. While it may strike all sensible people as self-evidently true that theft and murder are wrong, questions regarding abortion and the proper uses of nuclear energy do not yield to the maxims of common sense.

The realization that social consensus about basic value judgments was no longer strong enough to guide and inspire public policy developed slowly in the American mind. And even when the aware-ness became undeniable a deeply entrenched commitment to the separation of church and state made it seem almost treasonous even to acknowledge the problem. Some Christian groups made effective use of legislation to discourage vices particularly offensive to their denominational polity, always in the name of self-evident virtue, while vigorously condemning the efforts of other groups to do likewise. But the notion that certain modes of behavior naturally commend themselves to all right-thinking people and do not reflect explicit religious judgments was slow to die and continued to nour-ish the illusion that value judgments in the realm of public policy authenticate themselves and can be both justified and enforced without reference to religious sanctions.

The advent of the Welfare State, however, made it increasingly difficult to sustain the myth. Year by year, between 1932 and 1980, the government at various levels accepted responsibility for what had previously been regarded as intimately personal human rela-tionships. Matters that our grandparents had settled arbitrarily and behind locked doors in the family home were thrust into the public arena and made the legitimate subjects of political debate and adjudication.

The rapid proliferation of such governmental interventions into the private sphere made it impossible for zealous Christians to ignore the religious implications of the changes taking place on every hand. When the state begins to authorize or even require changes in sexual mores, family authority, educational standards, the care of indigent neighbors and related subjects it inevitably begins to impinge in obvious ways upon deeply held moral values. And the pretense that it does not, far from calming the fears of religious men and women, only serves to intensify their indignation.

So there broke upon the American scene the phenomenon loosely called "The Moral Majority." Led by clergy of various backgrounds and motivations large numbers of Christians became acutely conscious of the degree to which political decisions were influencing aspects of life traditionally regarded as the province of church, family and individual conscience. The laws relating to birth control, abortion, the sanctity of marriage, homosexuality, parental authority, life prolongation and termination options and similar issues were perceived as making assumptions about human nature and purpose which challenged or even flouted the Bible.

The result of the current contretemps has been the fracturing of the American community and the disclosure of deep divisions within most religious traditions. Those identified as The Moral Majority insist that public policies related even tangentially to moral values must take serious account of this nation's Christian history. Those who regard themselves as "liberals" argue that any effort to base political action upon religious precepts violates the First Amendment to the Constitution and constitutes, in effect, the establishment of a religion. The whole picture is blurred by the fact that at several critical points the defenders of religion advance the causes of militant nationalism and materialistic individualism, while secular humanists speak for those humane values which in recent decades have been identified with religious motivations.

At this perplexing point in the history of the United States the Anglican experience of relating religion to politics may have a helpful word to speak to Americans, both Christian and non-Christian. Let us examine some aspects of this potential witness under two headings: first, some of the characteristics of the established church in England which differentiate its experience from that of continental models. Second, a fundamental theological distinction between Anglicanism and those denominations which spring from the Protestant Reformation.

Perhaps the most important element in the make-up of the Church of England which is relevant to our discussion here is the designation of the Crown as its head. Such an arrangement has many infirmities which will immediately occur to those raised in a pluralistic culture. But on the positive side it asserted the union of religious and political authority in dramatic fashion.

Those continental churches which owe their primary allegiance to the papacy have always been suspected of a divided loyalty, and their positions on public policy are frequently regarded as parts of some papal diplomacy to which the nation's interest is at best secondary. This suspicion, often well-founded, has tended to engender in such established churches a kind of fortress or "we against them" mentality. Religious hierarchs become inordinately preoccupied with protecting their own turf on the one hand and on the other often lean over backward against any prophetic word in order to demonstrate the degree of their national commitment.

Whatever its vices the union of religious and political authority in the same sovereign, a tradition well grounded in Scripture, relates the spiritual elements of statecraft to its secular aspects in a quite natural and sustained fashion. The monarch can hardly be suspected of using religion to advance the interests of any foreign power, so that whatever the wisdom or lack thereof represented by such royal decisions, they are seen to fit into the total pattern of English life. Right or wrong, pious or impious, the influence of the crown upon ecclesiastical patterns affirms the inseparability of religious and political values.

Another blessing enjoyed by England, one which has encouraged a creative relationship between church and state, is the freedom of the British Isles from foreign invasions. This has obviated the kind of antagonism which inevitably arises when clerical authority is compelled to deal with politicians imposed upon society from without and has permitted a relatively uninterrupted development of the state-church dialogue.

A third element in the special character of establishment in England has been the use of the vernacular in public worship. When religion and politics speak quite literally the same language it becomes more difficult to separate them than when each has its own arcane vocabulary. Whatever may be said for the value of Latin as a universal medium of theologizing, its effect upon the general populace of specific countries was to underscore the "alien" aspects of the ecclesiastical establishment. And the folklore of all Europe is rich with the bitter humor by which lay men and women expressed their feeling in this matter.

Fourthly, one cannot overlook in such a discussion as this the historic, dogged concreteness of the English mind. As far back as the record runs Britons have tended to deal in particular ways with specific cases rather than involve themselves in grandly principled debates about abstractions. In diplomacy this habit has come to be generally admired as "muddling through," i.e. playing the game of foreign affairs by ear and from day to day rather than by rigid adherence to consistency and fixed objective. In religion this disposition makes up a foundational aspect of the "via media" and has helped the church of England avoid those endless doctrinal bickerings which engender unhealthy introversion in clerics and angry impatience in politicians.*

When people are called upon to relate their proposals or allegations to "instances" it becomes difficult to remain for long in the rarified atmospheres so beloved of continental theologians. And more to the point here, it inevitably necessitates quite specific reference to the daily events of the common life. English clerics have had little encouragement to indulge in the semantic game-playing which consumes a great deal of the energy of European religion. They have been required to "get to the point" in a way which necessitates the integration of theological considerations with all other areas of social interpretation, including politics.

Finally, although these brief paragraphs by no means exhaust the list of which they are but parts, it must be noted that the history of England during the period in which the established church was taking on its character was one of gradual movement, with notable lapses, toward constitutional monarchy and the democratization of the national ethos which this engendered. While much of Europe was commandeering every resource of society, including religion, to centralize political authority and achieve national unity at almost any cost, England, confident in her identity as a major power, was gradually dispersing power among increasingly numerous segments of its population. However inadequate those first faltering steps may appear today, they were in their own time radical affirmations of confidence in the ability of men and women to guide their own destinies. And they impinged upon the church in two important ways. They both influenced the development of internal governance procedures within the institution and allowed religious leaders increasing scope for asserting their legitimate concerns over-against the counsels of the primarily political mind.

The net result of these and many other influences at work in English life was a unique amalgamation of religion and politics. Both church and state were accepted as vehicles for the expression of God's will. It was taken for granted that religion would have important things to say about the national welfare in political terms. And it was equally taken for granted that public policy decisions would impinge directly upon the spiritual growth of individuals as well as upon the moral health of society at large. As

---

*Years of teaching in a theological seminary and entertaining both English and continental theologians give this point far greater weight than it may seem to the laity to deserve.

William Temple has pointed out, the method of expressing the concern would differ, but its substance would be the same. The tensions which inevitably arise in the relationship between church and state are more like the confrontation of Nathan and David over Bathsheba than a debate between Jerry Falwell and Bella Abzug about E.R.A.

The second basic characteristic of Anglicanism that played an important part in shaping its attitude toward the relationship of religion and politics is its emphasis upon reason and experience as means of knowing and obeying the will of God. In this respect it differs from Roman Catholicism and Reformation Protestantism in ways that need brief consideration for our purposes here.

The Roman Catholic Church has always given good standing to the life of the mind in the formulation of both doctrine and discipline. So much so that it was appalled by Protestantism's radical call for "faith alone." Unfortunately, however, its definition of reason tended to be rigidly scholastic and elitist. The rational process was dignified, but it was divorced from experience and regarded as the province of a select few theologians, from whose prudent ratiocinations the masses of the faithful would be handed all the truth needed for their salvation. The idea of unfolding revelation enshrined in experience was repugnant to Roman hierarchs until very recent decades, only slightly less repugnant than the idea that lay men and women ought to be encouraged to think through their own faith commitments.

The result of this in practical terms was to discourage general participation in even the discussion of political issues by the faithful and encourage docile acceptance of decisions handed down from above.

In radical reaction against what it regarded as Roman abuses of reason and authority the Protestant Reformation tended to discount the former almost completely and vest the latter in the Bible alone. The divine will reveals itself through grace, the Reformers announced. And the human intellect, hopelessly corrupted by the Fall, can do nothing to seek it out. The details of Christian obedience are spelled out in Scripture, to which one need only refer in order to understand what the Lord requires of him or her.

Here, again, was laid a somewhat different but equally debilitating basis for political irrelevance. If reason is hopelessly corrupt and all truth revealed in the Bible, those great debates in which issues of moment are lifted up for analyses, become pointless at best and sinful presumption at worst. The fact that such debates did, in fact, occur with some regularity in Protestant countries simply reveals how often the counsels of common sense neutralize or suspend the more outrageous allegations of theology!

For many reasons, some having to do with geography, others with cultural characteristics and only a few with doctrine, Anglicanism was able to develop a somewhat different understanding of the way in which reason and experience operate in human affairs. And, again, for various reasons, some of which have been mentioned here earlier, the right to reason responsibly about religion and its implications for all areas of life was at least tolerated among large numbers of nonclerical men and women.

One of the consequences of the Church of England's insulation against the more radical grace theology born in the Continental Reformation must also be noted here. When reason and experience are given a significant role in the means by which people relate to God human actions, i.e. works, take on an importance denied them in the theologizing of most of the major Reformation scholars. To say that ordinary men and women can do "good" things and avoid "bad" things by the exercise of their reason is to grant to individuals the ability to help shape their own spiritual quality. Thus, everything that they do takes on a profound significance. And those areas of activity, such as politics, in which the atmosphere of the common life is influenced become a special challenge to Christian conscience.

It would be grossly untrue to suggest that Anglican theology denies the centrality of divine grace as the means of salvation and puts its confidence in some supposed human capacity to discern and do the good by the sheer power of informed intelligence. Just as it would badly misstate the fact to credit the Church of England with a relentless enthusiasm for the education of the general populace.

The Anglican view of grace, however, while somewhat ambiguous, gives ample scope for human reason in its operation. It does not set out to denigrate the moral resourcefulness of the mind or demand that believers heap scorn upon their own intellectual capacity to know and obey the will of God. Divine grace operates to make faithful rationality possible, but unnecessary. And while the English clergy at one time shared the gentry's view that minimal education would do quite well for the lower orders, its proclamation of the gospel was not larded with anti-intellectualism as a religious virtue. The church was very early in the vanguard of those fighting for universal basic education.

This emphasis upon the role of reason in living the good life and the human potential for acts of spiritual quality did more for the relationship of religion to politics than merely encourage a sort of general thoughtfulness about the place of values in the formulation of public policy. It affirmed eloquently, rather, that there are manifestations of the divine will available in statecraft as well as in theology. The Church of England has never seen itself as *the* custodian of the divine will which sends missionaries forth to infiltrate the neutral political community and shape it surreptitiously by their zealous piety. It acknowledges a two-way flow of influence between religious and political institutions in which each speaks appropriately to the other about the nature and will of God in history. The faith which emerges from the disciplines of ecclesiastical inquiry helps to shape the legislation that guides human behavior. But that legislation, the proper labor of the state, helps to create an atmosphere in which that faith is honored and nourished—and at times judged and found wanting!

In Anglican theology God is not required to work through the channels of ecclesiastical institutions, but is expected to be active in even the most secular structures of the common life. In these secular structures elements of the divine will are available to human intelligence in ways which supplement, correct and even refute those revelations proclaimed by the church.

What one sees at work in Anglicanism, therefore, is not an historically inevitable antagonism between the "sacred" and "secular" arms of the community, a relationship in which each side assumes the worst about the other and struggles to protect the integrity of its special view of truth, but a kind of symbiotic interaction in which the right ordering of religion is as dependent upon the just administration of public affairs as the preservation of order in society is upon the inspiration and guidance of the church.

Now it is not difficult to discover serious weaknesses, even dangers, in such an arrangement. And many have been pointed out repeatedly by critics of establishment in England as well as by commentators abroad. The state is inevitably tempted to use its economic and appointive powers over the church to demand religious approval for whatever political expediency recommends.

It is an amazing fact of history, however, that the British Crown has so seldom undertaken to use that theoretical power, a fact obscured to many eyes by those instances of a dramatic nature in which it has done so. Just as the two major universities of England, Oxford and Cambridge, have been at times hotbeds of anti-establishment radicalism while drawing upon the establishment for their support, so the Church of England has been among the most outspokenly prophetic forces in that country. And some of its most vigorously dissenting voices have been raised to positions of honor and authority by the governments that they denounced. Indeed, many observers have noted with wonder that even grossly irresponsible political clerics have moved with relentless regularity up the latter of hierarchical preferment.

Many factors help to account for this anomaly. One of the more significant, surely, is the point just made, i.e. that Britons do not regard the church as having exclusive access to the will of God but understand that will to be manifest in all aspects of the nation's life. This confidence in their own ability to discern something of truth has made it unnecessary for English politicians to coerce theologians into convenient consent. When Church of England bishops speak for or against some specific political proposition they are listened to by political leaders as those with whom the latter have every right, even responsibility, to differ respectfully.

An American observer or one from a country in which there obtains a different relationship between church and state may, upon casting up the balances, conclude that the weaknesses of establishment greatly outweigh its advantages. That should not blind us, however, to the positive features of the English experience and the lessons about the role of religion in politics that it may teach us.

For the purposes of our consideration in this essay the chief asset of the pattern originating in England and transported in modified form to other parts of the world is a view of politics as a *truth discovering* rather than a *truth corrupting* process.

When the religious spirit of any society assumes that the church has *the* access to God's will and bears an obligation to conform the neutral or hostile state as fully as possible to that will politics becomes an arena, a battleground, rather than a forum in which it is assumed that truth will emerge to enlighten all participants. Every "victory" for faith is a defeat for unfaith, and every triumph of the secular arm means some degree of moral compromise by the church. Under such circumstances politics inevitably gets defined as a morally shabby business made necessary by the sinfulness of the race.

When, on the other hand, the church recognizes that God is at work revealing and effecting the divine will in the legitimate actions of government and the state acknowledges the dependence of sound public policy upon value judgments for which religion bears a primary responsibility, politics takes on a dignity of its own. It becomes not merely the process by which two aspects of revelation are *compromised*, but one in which those aspects are *synthesized* and new truth brought to light, truth neither explicit nor implicit in the positions of the two parties. One cannot read a history of English public life without becoming aware of the new moral ground broken in the interaction of church and state.

In spite of the conspicuous and notorious occasions upon which the Church of England and the British Crown have set themselves doggedly against one another upon some real or alleged issue of moment, the history of Anglicanism in its homeland provides a remarkable example of what might be called the organic relationship of religion to politics, one which has enriched both church and state.

Now it will be obvious that when Anglicanism moves out from under the shelter of the Church of England and its special historic position, when it is forced to develop a modus vivendi in nations that have rejected and outlawed the establishment of religion the methods by which it relates itself to the interaction of state and church and to the political process will change significantly. The broad range of socio-political contexts into which the Empire and its missionaries carried the faith demanded many modifications in the ecclesiology familiar to Britons. And the rapid, dramatic changes taking place today within former colonial cultures are demanding even further alterations in traditional institutional patterns, changes too varied for any brief discussion of their nature.

Removal from the land of its origin does not, however, render useless the insights which Anglicanism has acquired throughout its centuries of experience as the Church of England. To the United States of America standing at the challenging juncture described earlier it has important things to say.

First, the Anglican emphasis upon politics as a truth discovering process can help to moderate the intensity and balance the irrational ferocity of the current conflict between the Moral Majority and its secular humanist opponents. For the one thing that these two polarized groups have in common is their inability to discern a responsible middle ground between religious imperatives on the one hand and total personal autonomy on the other. Each sees the political mechanism of society as something to be captured and set to the service of its own passionate convictions.

The Moral Majority is disposed to define various modes of behavior as wrong, according to the precepts which it infers from the Bible. And what it deems to be *wrong* ought by the iron logic of its piety be outlawed. Engagement in political action by men and women who believe this consists largely of an effort to acquire sufficient power to dominate legislate bodies and executive decisions, as well as influence in time the will of the judiciary. These institutions are regarded as tools, mindless instruments, capable of being coerced but without any inherent wisdom to offer on the subjects over which they have jurisdiction. They must, say the New Conservatives, be compelled to support political programs clearly inferrable from Scripture.

Liberals have until recently tended to be somewhat less vocally dogmatic in taking this same purely instrumentalist view of politics, largely because the drift of the times has been in their direction. As long as legislative, executive and judicial authority articulated commitment to an absolute separation of church and state while at the same time advancing programs generally consistent with what might be called vaguely a "Judaeo-Christian" social philosophy, liberals had little need for militant action to keep America secular.

When, however, a number of complex moral issues, e.g. birth control, abortion, nuclear armaments, life prolongation ethics and so on, moved to the head of the public policy agenda the conservative clamor that these questions raised significant religious problems forced liberals to "fish or cut bait" on the matter of government's mandate to act in these areas. It was no longer possible to pretend that religious influences are not at work shaping public consensus at critical points.

So liberals, like their conservative neighbors, have begun to deal openly and militantly with the role of religion in public life. Not without considerable heartburn, remembering prayer vigils on the steps of Alabama courthouses during the civil rights struggles of the sixties, opponents of the Moral Majority have become increasingly militant in their demand that government make no obeisance to religion at all in its formulation of social policy and the conduct of foreign affairs.

In short, pietists and secularists alike treat the political process as the battleground upon which to struggle for ideological control of the state. Neither camp seems willing to grant a truth discerning potential to it.

The Anglican witness to both sides of this increasingly bitter struggle is quite clear. "The earth is the Lord's and the fullness thereof; the world and they that dwell therein." God cannot be made irrelevant to any aspect of human life, individual or social, and the divine will implies significant things for both church and state, as well as for economy, education, science and so on. It is an absurdity for non-religious people to demand that believers keep their religion out of any area of human experience.

It is equally absurd, however, for men and women of zealous faith to suppose that God must act only through *their* convictions or that they alone can know the divine will for particular historical situations. No aspect of human nature escaped the corruption of the Fall. The individual conscience and the commitments engendered by it are subject to the pride and selfishness which beset all other areas of personality. Those charged with the administration of Civilian Public Service Camps in World War II, projects in which conscientious objectors to military service spent time in non-military labor, will testify that the sincere pacifists who were gathered in those camps were as subject to prima donna complexes, uncooperative certainty and sheer meanness as an equal number of people gathered under any other auspices.

It is encumbent upon Christians, Anglicans would point out, to express their commitments in clear and concrete fashion in all social as well as personal contexts. But it is prideful of them to insist that they alone know what those spiritual commitments imply in specific public policy terms. The God who gives dignity to all human beings, believers and non-believers, does not disdain to reveal the divine will through the honest intelligence of either group. As they relate in responsible dialogue to one another men and women are acting out within history that freedom which was granted to the race at the dawn of time, the power to choose between good and evil. But the debates in which they engage are media by which good is discovered not simply verbal power struggles in which evil is routed by the innately superior logic of piety. God gives to the thoughtful humanist perspectives which are essential to intellectual wholeness and which other emphases, good and bad, often make unavailable to the spiritually devout.

Let us illustrate this general process in action: the illegal taking of a human life with malice and forethought is murder. Both the good Christian and Jew would say that such a thing must be prohibited and punished by law. And even the most radical humanist would agree. But what constitutes an "illegal taking of life?" And how does one define "malice" and "forethought?" Does the border guard who kills someone who is trying to enter the country illegally open himself to a charge of murder? How much ill-will is required to constitute malice? Are there time limits demanded in order to demonstrate forethought? There is not a religious answer to any of these questions.

The processes by which such issues are raised, explored and settled are forced to deal with aspects of human motivation and self-control and touch upon concepts such as "right" and "wrong." In the course of such deliberations the theological commitments of Christians and Jews merge, imperceptibly, into the psychological categories of their humanist neighbors. Out of the discussion of which we are speaking emerges some consensus about what kinds of acts done under what sorts of circumstances ought to be labelled "murder." And persons of widely diverse theological and philosophical views consent to adopt a given definition in order to make consistent, predictable judicial decisions possible.

Inevitably compromises are necessary along the way, and the final definition may not really satisfy anyone. But, the Anglican will argue, the willingness of God to act beyond the bounds of ecclesia means that these compromises can be interpreted as positive expressions of the divine will rather than corrupt concessions to human sinfulness. When God made human beings *free* that decision implied a kind of pluralism among them, through which pluralism the Creator has consented to act every day.

Thus, the political processes by which all segments of the community express their varying convictions and needs are hallowed precisely *because* of their diversity rather than in spite of it. The redemptive love of God in Jesus Christ, by which the human condition is made acceptable to the Almighty, transforms the babble of debate and dissent into a truth revealing medium of grace

All this does not mean, of course, that truth is finally determined by the counting of noses. In the last analysis each individual is called upon to decide the degree to which he or she can in good conscience go along with the consensus and obey the decrees of the state. What it does mean is that those decrees, in both their formulation and the human response to them, will be seen as part of the over-arching moral order implicit in the will of God. They need not always be obeyed, but, as Paul suggests, they must always be taken with utmost seriousness. And there will be, of necessity, a substantial measure of self-critical humility in those internal, personal deliberations that we honor as conscience.

The individual who feels called upon to resist some rule of law will realize that what is taking place within himself or herself is not *necessarily* a reflection of some cosmic conflict between good and evil, but may well be an honest but ambiguous effort to relate the God who speaks in the individual heart and mind to the God who speaks, no less authoritatively, through the community. Conscientious objection, a phrase used so carelessly of late, is identified in Anglicanism as a manifestation of the tragic in life, the effort of the finite to relate responsibly to the eternal. It can never become the self-righteous ego trip into which it often degenerated during the Viet Nam era.

Another way of saying this is that for Anglicans being "very members incorporate" in the Body of Christ has more than purely a metaphysical meaning. It describes not only their relationship to their Lord, but their responsibilities toward one another and the communities by which their lives are undergirded.

What this says to American life today is that the chronic dissenters at both ends of the religious spectrum need not fear to enter a legitimate two-way discussion with their opponents. A willingness on the part of the Moral Majority to open itself to the insights of secularism does not necessarily constitute a spiritual sell-out. And an admission by secular humanists that the basic values to which they subscribe have at least some of their roots in religious soil will enable them to understand and protect those values more effectively.

There is a second word of counsel which the Anglican experience can speak to the United States in our time as this nation struggles with the relationship between religion and politics. It flows so naturally from what has just been said as to need only a brief description here.

The willingness of God to act through the political process and in the apparently secular mandates of the state should make it clear that what happens in those spheres plays as much of a role in shaping human character as human character does in determining the moral tone of society.

It is commonly assumed by evangelical Protestantism, especially in the Western Hemisphere, that there is a one-way flow of influence between individual character and public policy, i.e. that the quality of human personality determines the degree of integrity exhibited by the state and is to no significant degree dependent upon the latter. The grace of God inspires "good" men and women to exert beneficent influences upon the organs of government, which is defined as being as best indifferent to spiritual concerns and at worst hostile to them. Former President and Born Again Baptist Jimmy Carter was both reflecting and pandering to this conviction in his successful first campaign for the presidency, when he made much of the fact that he was an "outsider" to the Washington scene and intended to deal with it in the indignant manner of a parent escorting Johnny to the woodshed! "We need," he would argue, "a government as decent as its people." In both attitude and word President Carter spoke for millions of his Protestant fellow-citizens.

Anglicans do not deny that individual moral commitment can and does play an important part in forming responsible public policy. But they will want to add that public policy in its turn can create an ethos in which the more creative elements in human nature are encouraged or discouraged. As Richard Hooker once said, "The state encourages what it honors." Laws which require people to act in responsible ways and rewards them with public approbation for doing so generate an atmosphere in which social responsibility is reinforced by external factors working with the admonitions of conscience. And in response to this conjunction of influences human personality can improve, just as it can deteriorate when public policy fosters degrading patterns of behavior.

It has been clearly demonstrated in recent decades that legislation which outlaws racial discrimination changes individual attitudes toward persons of other ethnic backgrounds. And testimony in the Nuremberg war crimes trials made it obvious that an official policy of brutality toward prisoners in concentration camps produced marked alterations in the values and personalities of their guards. Law has power to revise not simply outward actions but inner feelings as well. This will not surprise psychologists who understand the processes by which personality is fashioned. But it should present something of a theological problem for those evangelicals who view character as little more than the gift of divine grace.

Anglicanism needs to say to both Jimmy Carter and Ronald Reagan that while public policy is in large part the reflection of human character, it is also a significant influence in shaping that character. Humane government is as likely to produce humane citizens as humane citizens are to produce humane government.

The third and final comment which the Anglican tradition can make to those concerned with church-state relationships today springs from its historic confidence in the role of reason in the moral life. The radical grace theology which grew out of the Continental Reformation tended to generate in Protestantism a deep distrust of the human intellect as it bears upon the life of the spirit. The mind was conceived to be the most shrewdly corrupt of human faculties and therefore the most dangerous of them, especially in the lives of those not trained in theology.

This attitude was checked in various ways in its influence upon European culture. The deeply entrenched power of Catholic intellectualism inevitably neutralized to a considerable degree the suspicion which Protestant doctrine engendered toward humanity's rational faculties. But in the New World where legions of religious dissenters were free to act out their own values unhampered by well-established institutions a kind of populist distrust of reason was able to work itself into the patterns of the emerging society.

The result has been an almost religious hostility in the American mind to anything that smacks of careful analysis of complicated social problems. Americans are inclined to distrust leadership which invites them to think carefully and give rousing cheers for those who offer simple solutions to even the most complex dilemmas. Equivocations and qualifications in political utterance are almost invariably seen by masses of men and women as evidence of chicanery, an effort to conceal rather than expose the truth. (And often this suspicion is more than justified.)

Unwillingness to think carefully and analytically about politics, especially when that unwillingness is rooted in religious conviction, has always been a problem for the formulation of public policy in the United States. But as both domestic and foreign affairs become in fact more complex, as fewer and fewer issues of moment yield to the neat division of black and white, those moral axioms which once passed for legitimate comment on current questions serve the community even less helpfully than they were once supposed to. The slogans which used to separate the "good guys" from the "bad guys" are less and less able to make even such vague distinctions. And it is becoming painfully clear to a troubled public that the data, the facts, the dull statistics cannot be waved aside to make room for a parade of pious cliches.

It would be untrue and presumptuous to suggest that the Anglican experience offers solutions to the problems confronting modern society. What it does do, however, is affirm the religious rightness of approaching these problems with informed intelligence. It offers a theological antidote to the poisonous distrust of reason that has weakened the body politic in the United States. One cannot be aware of the great non-governmental schools organized and administered by Anglicanism throughout the English-speaking world without understanding the emphasis which the tradition places upon intellectual discipline as a tool of both individual and social development.

Unfortunately the Anglican communion in the United States has done very little to apply its insights effectively to the current political scene. Like most religious doctrine the Anglican confidence in reason will not infuse the mass mind by a kind of spiritual osmosis.

It needs to be both articulated and demonstrated in detailed fashion. Nor will it be sufficient to publish articles on the subject in diocesan journals. The life of every Anglican parish needs to make available to its people, and through them to all people, opportunities for informed study of the serious issues confronting humanity in this rapidly changing world. Classes, forums and special conferences led by specialists in the data, not simply spiritually sensitive theologians, will be an essential part of the witness that the Anglican experience can offer in our time. Without such things as these, the emphasis of the faith upon the religious uses of the mind will remain simply an eccentric view of a small part of the Christian community.

It is quite clear that when one speaks of the special insights or experiences of a particular church representatives of other parts of the Christian fellowship hasten to point out that their own traditions offer very much the same thing in slightly different language. Often a lecture or essay offered as the expression of a specific doctrinal viewpoint will be claimed by Lutherans, Baptists, Presbyterians, Methodists, Episcopalians and so on as an excellent statement of *their* position on the subject. That may well be the natural fate of this effort to suggest the ways in which Anglicanism can help lighten the present darkness of political discussion about church-state relations in the United States.

It has not been the purpose of this effort, however, to lay an *exclusive* claim for the Anglican experience in relating religion to politics. The intention has been, rather, to point out that the history of the Church of England and the churches that have grown out of it provides a useful basis upon which to think about the current debate on the subject and offers fewer theological barriers to such thought than many other Christian groups.

11

Anglican Attitudes and Behaviors Concerning War

by William W. Rankin

This chapter describes the development of Anglican thought and behaviors concerning war from the American Revolution to 1982. Its major conclusion is that strong elements of the just war, the crusade, and pacifism are to be found throughout Anglican history, with just war theory being used in many formal pronouncements, but a crusade type of attitude pervading many other statements and frequently being displayed in actual behaviors. (The crusading spirit seems as strongly evident in England's 1982 war in the Falkland Islands as in Elizabeth's battles with Philip II of Spain.) Pacifism appears in a relatively minor but continuous historical strand into the World War II era. More recently there is a growing recognition that the availability of nuclear weapons erodes the usefulness of the just war theory, and we find a resurgent pacifist mood in our own time.

I.

With the rise of anti-British sentiment in the American colonies, the Anglican Church in America found itself in an increasingly tenuous position. This difficulty was due to the loyalties felt by many Anglicans toward the English crown, but more especially by the "Oath of the King's Supremacy" which had been required of all ordained Anglican clergy, first upon ordination to the deaconate and then again upon ordination as priests.

At the outset of the American Revolution, there were probably 400 Anglican congregations meeting regularly in the colonies; these were served by approximately 300 clergy. Many of the clergy were missionaries of the Society for the Propagation of the Gospel in Foreign Parts, an organization of largely "high church" orientation and expecting a high moral commitment from its members. Slightly more than half the Anglican clergy (many from New England) seem to have demonstrated their loyalty to the British cause during the American Revolution, with a stronger majority of Anglican laity siding with the Americans. Twenty-two Anglican clergy, approximately twelve percent of the chaplain corps, served as clergy chaplains in the Revolutionary army.

The clergy "Oath" in particular seems to have been the major cause of Anglican clergy remaining loyal to the crown. The "Oath of the King's Supremacy" took its effective form for the English Prayer Book of 1775 in the earlier 1662 ordinal. The oath states, in part,

"I, A.B., . . . do declare, that no foreign Prince, Person, Prelate, State, or Potentate, hath, or ought to have jurisdiction, power, superiority, pre-eminence, or authority, Ecclesiastical or Spiritual, within this Realm. *So help me God.*"

The effect of the Oath, in the instance of the American Revolution, was to place Anglican clergy who supported the colonial cause in the position of perjurers. Within the just war context, the Oath disputed the justice of the colonial cause by disclaiming the legitimate authority of its leaders.

In addition to the Oath of Supremacy, the Anglican clergy were obligated by their vows to perform the daily offices without variation, which included prayers for the king and royal family. The litany also mentioned the king and royal family, and in the Holy Communion service at least one of two collects for the king had to be read after the Decalogue and before the collect for the day. To read such prayers after the July 4, 1776 Declaration of Independence was tantamount to showing public support of an enemy ruler, and this could not be done without inviting substantial trouble from the patriotic revolutionaries. Usually those Anglican clergy who decided to remain in areas controlled by the American patriots suspended services of public worship. This did not enable them entirely to escape their ordination obligations, but it did enable them to avoid making a public issue of them.

The record does not clearly show how theological or ethical views caused various clergy to align themselves on one side or the other in the revolutionary conflict, though it seems that some clergy felt that their loyalty in ministry to their constituents overrode their loyalty to the political ruler of England. As to whether, or how, or to what extent, loyalty to vows, King, local congregation, or God, were balanced with respect to each other, it is impossible to know. It is possible to say with some confidence only that those clergy who were seen as "loyalist" did not, by and large, with the admiration of many people. For this and other reasons, the American Revolution left Anglican parishes in a vastly weaker condition than they had been in prior to that struggle.

The Protestant Episcopal Church in the United States of America seems to have been better prepared for the War of 1812 than it had been for the 1776 war. Various antipathies and suspicions toward the Episcopal Church were still to be found, however, in early nineteenth–century America. This was owing primarily to the Church's historical ties to England and the still fresh memory of the Revolutionary War.

The bishops and priests of the Episcopal Church were of a more united outlook than in 1776 and generally supported the United States position against England in the 1812 war. This support was exhibited either by public statements or by the Church's refusal to question United States war aims. The Episcopal clergy in the South appeared to have been most strongly patriotic in a militaristic way, while a few clergy in Massachusetts and Philadelphia openly supported Britain, primarily because of their high regard for "British character." Bishops Dehon of South Carolina, Hobart of New York, and Clagett of Maryland were supportive of the United States cause in varying degrees, while Presiding Bishop William White tried to avoid political alignments within the Church by remaining silent on the war. The historical record, once again, does not reveal any clear and consistent applications to the 1812 situation of moral theologies concerning war.

The 1814 General Convention reinforced long-standing Church claims to lands granted to the Episcopal Church by the British monarch before the Revolution. This was done while asserting the Episcopal Church's independence from "the civil or . . . ecclesiastical authority of any foreign country." One historian of the 1812 war and the Episcopal Church's involvement in it concludes, "American Episcopacy . . . celebrated the war's end as it had endured the war's domestic strife: with prudence, loyalty, and a patriotic aversion to political involvement."

The American Civil War posed a number of challenges to the Episcopal Church in the United States, the chief perceived issue being that of avoiding a split between northern and southern church members. The major ethical concern of the Episcopal Church pertained not so much to the slavery controversy (which was the paramount issue for the Calvinist churches) as to the rightness or wrongness of rebellion. The 1861 General Convention recorded its hope that the Union would be preserved, though throughout the war the official statements of the Church remained guarded, out of a desire to avoid a North-South split in the denomination.

Despite the Church's general attitude of caution, there were a few Episcopal bishops who felt strongly that they had to align themselves with one side or the other. Thus, for example, Bishop Thomas Clark, in blessing the Union troops in 1861, displayed a crusading attitude when he reassured them that their cause was "holy and righteous" and that "the Lord of Hosts is on our side." His ethical warrant for asserting this was not that slaves were entitled to be liberated but that the nation needed to be saved from "the ravages of sedition, conspiracy and rebellion." In the South, Bishop Leonidas Polk resigned the Episcopacy to become a major general in the Confederate Army. By the end of the war, a General Convention was held in which great efforts were made, and successfully accomplished, to guarantee the unity of northern and southern Episcopal Church members. During this time of the bloodiest American war before or since, in terms of American casualties, there was no discernable new development or application by the Church of ethical theories concerning war.

The Church of England's views of the American Civil War are worth noting, since in general these views were different from those of the United States Episcopal Church, either in the North or South. The Anglican Church press understood the main issue in the Civil War to be slavery. As in Lincoln's Second Inaugural Address much Anglican Church commentary conceived the destruction caused by the Civil War as the just dessert of American accommodation to slavery at the founding of the republic. Another Anglican view was that the Civil War merely manifested the essential disunity of the United States, a disunity to be expected due to the absence of an established church. Other Anglican views were that the war was inevitable because of the supposedly significant social and ethnic differences between Northerners and Southerners, or due to the political error of building a system based upon too much democracy, including universal suffrage, which was viewed as an unwarranted excess. Apart from the slavery-social destruction connection made by some (who in making such a connection maintained a view consistent with that of the major Old Testament prophets), it is difficult to find many Anglican Church statements on the American Civil War bearing resemblance to recognizable Christian moral traditions.

Notwithstanding the moral sensibilities of many concerning the abomination of slavery, many in the Church of England openly sympathized with the South. Lincoln was portrayed frequently as an uncouth farmer, the North was accused of imperialistic aggression against a South that merely wanted its independence, and Confederate military and political leaders were portrayed from Church press and pulpit as noble aristocrats, patriots, learned gentlemen, and the like. *The Guardian* aptly conveyed the sense of Anglican opinion by stating in April 1863 that "we can sympathize with the South, without approving of slavery."

As the storm gathered in the United States leading finally to civil war, the European situation was clouded by commercial, political, and military maneuverings eventuating in the Crimean War. This conflict pitted the allied armies of England, France, Turkey and Sardinia against the armies of Russia. The Crimean War began in 1853 and was concluded in a Paris treaty on March 30, 1856, after Russian forces were pushed out of Turkish territory, back to the Crimean Peninsula.

British participation in the Crimean War began with a general fast, which was repeated once again after a number of costly battles, and never since repeated in British history. Anglican clergy preached two different views of the war: one, that God was requiring England's full commitment to the war; the other, that the war was God's retribution against England for its various sins. The predominant view of the war in its earlier years, however, seems to have been that of a holy crusade. As it drew to an end the war came to be portrayed as a valuable way in which God had "roused England from selfishness and complacency." But as before, there is in the experience of the Crimean War no discernable new theoretical development or innovative practical application of ethical thinking about war.

In New Zealand, the Treaty of Waitangi was signed in 1840 between Great Britain and the indigenous Maoris. This treaty gave England sovereignty over New Zealand, while guaranteeing British protection of Maori rights. By 1845, however, a Maori uprising occurred on the North Island, where the majority of the Maoris lived and where British settlers persistently sought to buy land from the reluctant natives. The uprising was quashed, but underlying racial antagonisms surfaced later. In 1860 another war broke out and continued sporadically until the defeat of Maori leader Te Kooti in 1872. The Anglican bishops and clergy who worked in missionaries among the Maori nearly unanimously opposed the British military actions in the Maori Wars. The British government, however, viewed the Wars as essential to establishing Britain's sovereignty. The Maoris and the Anglican missionaries saw the main issue instead as a land quarrel; hence, on this basis, they viewed the British cause as unjust. The missionaries were supported at home in their views by the Church Missionary Society, but their concerns had little positive effect upon the Maoris since the Maoris themselves tended to see all British as their adversaries, including the Anglican missionaries. Thus the good will of these church people was decisively undercut by the military actions carried out by their government. Insofar as Anglican Church opinion opposed government involvement in the Maori Wars, that opinion was demonstrably ineffectual.

Towards the end of the nineteenth century, the General Convention of the United States Episcopal Church began to express itself on various aspects of world peace. In 1892 the Convention called upon all Christian rulers to resolve international disputes by peaceful means. In 1898 the General Convention thanked the Russian czar for calling the first Hague Conference and registered its support for armaments reductions and a proposed world court. Subsequent Conventions expressed support for the International Peace Congress (1904) and the second Hague Conference (1910). In 1916, shortly before United States entry into the World War, the General Convention appointed a joint committee to work for peace and to participate in the work of the World Alliance for Promoting International Peace through the Churches.

Some of England's major theologians (Charles Kingsley, F. D. Maurice, J. B. Mozley, Bishop Westcott, and J. M. Wilson) consistently supported the traditional just war theory's concepts, from their earlier writings in the latter half of the nineteenth century into the pre-World War I period of the twentieth century. They tended to agree among themselves that war is not consistent with Christian ideals but that in the fallen world it seemed sometimes necessary. Westcott, for instance, saw earthly warfare as but a dim reflection of the warfare in heaven. Therefore war had a certain inevitability about it, but it should be fought only as a last resort. To take another example, in the widely publicized sermon "War," in 1871, Mozley held that wars are virtually inevitable and therefore both self defense and a forcible ordering by military means of conflict between *status quo* and newly emerging interests are necessary for human welfare in society. In other words, wars are inevitable and sometimes necessary.

During this period in South Africa, mounting disagreements and jealousies between the Dutch farmers and the British led to the First Boer War (1880–1881), in which the Boers defeated the British. A bit later gold discoveries in the Witwatersrand fields, in 1886, inflamed things again. In 1899 the Boer-controlled Orange Free State joined the South African Republic in a declaration of war against Great Britain. This conflict is known to history as the Boer War (1899–1902). By 1890 British forces under Lord Kitchener and Lord Roberts began to reverse the tide of early Boer victories, finally turning the situation to the advantage of the British. In 1900, with the surrender of General Botha's Boer army, and later the surrender of the Boer guerillas, the two vanquished republics were made British colonies.

The Anglican Church, though generally supportive of British participation in the Boer War, was nonetheless clearly divided. The socialist group in the Church of England had grown in strength, due largely to the leadership of Charles Gore and Henry Scott Holland. The socialist Anglicans opposed British involvement in South Africa, claiming it to be an expression only of imperialism against a people entitled to their independence. The socialists also particularly protested the conditions in the British concentration camps. Others, however, including the Christian Social Union's president, Bishop B. F. Westcott of Durham, thought imperialism to embody "the principles of brotherhood and service," by extending the nation's range of interest beyond its own borders, and so supported the war. Others agreed with Westcott, including H.E.J. Bevan, Gresham College Professor of Divinity, who preached to the 1900 Church Congress that war brings out the more noble aspects of human character. Bishop Winnington-Ingram preached in 1899 that the Church's appropriate role was to pray for Britain's success in South Africa. In South Africa itself many clergy and laity joined or supported the British forces.

Meanwhile the Lambeth Conference's 1897 encyclical urging the diplomatic resolution of international disputes—a view reaffirmed by Lambeth in 1908—seemed to have had no recognizable effect upon the majority (pro-war) feelings of Anglican Church people. The 1897 encyclical had stated, "Without denying that there are just wars and that we cannot prevent their recurrence entirely, yet we are convinced that there are other and better ways of settling the quarrels of nations than by fighting." Here in the Boer War the gap between formal statement and actual practice is clearly evident. The minority "pro-Boer" Anglican group later, in October 1910, became the founding nucleus of the Church of England Peace League. Withal, it might fairly be said that the respected minority of Anglican opinion found Britain's involvement in the Boer War unjust because imperialism itself was unjust; in taking this view the minority group were probably closer to the 1897 Lambeth position than were the majority group who favored Britain's participation in the war. Those who bothered to justify Britain's actions in the Boer War by appeal to just war criteria have provided history with no compelling new insights or, indeed, a persuasive application of those criteria to the South African situation.

II.

The peace sentiments arising largely from controversies surrounding the Boer War gained much strength during the years immediately preceding the outbreak of the First World War. Statements by leading Anglican Church leaders, theologians, and various ecumenical organizations reflected an apparently strong and widespread view that wars should not be fought, particularly by Christian nations and persons. Even as late as the 1913 Church Congress, less than a year before England's August 4, 1914 declaration of war against Germany, pronouncements were made concerning the importance of peaceful means to resolve international conflicts. When war was declared the Anglican Church immediately and with little dissent supported the government. The bishops and clergy, many taking it for granted that one's Christian duty as an Anglican included service in wartime to the state, energetically recruited men for service in the armed forces. The clergy variously described the conflict in terms of a holy crusade or a just war. The British commitment to treaty obligations, the just defense of a small nation (Belgium) against a large aggressor (Germany), the just defense of civilization against German militarism, and the duty of British patriots simply to fight for the right, were all offered and taken as self-evident justification for going to war. In general the war seems to have overwhelmed the Church suddenly and effectively, sundering its newly militaristic behavior from the full breadth of its own theological and ethical heritage.

The Church of England's peace movement went quickly over to support of the war, as did that of nearly every denomination.

Bishop Hicks, who as president of the Church of England Peace League had denounced the Boer War, perceived Germany to be "our bitterest enemy." In Hick's case this turned out to be true since his son was soon killed in military action against the Germans. Hick's colleague in the peace movement, Bishop Percival, also subsequently lost a son in combat. Percival came to the conclusion that duty required British warfare against Germany as the only means to establish "the law of Christ . . . as the paramount authority in all national and international affairs." Henry Scott Holland also supported the war effort, despite his earlier misgivings, as did the Christian Social Union of which he was the head. The Church Socialist League, however, remained divided.

Early in the war the official views of the Church were that England's cause was justifiable by the criteria of just war theory. Thus, for example, did Archbishop Randall Davidson of Canterbury, Archbishop Cosmo Lang of York, and Bishop Charles Gore of Oxford—all greatly respected Church leaders—declare the war against Germany to be just. But as the carnage intensified, the actual feelings conveyed in and aroused by public Church statements came to be increasingly a crusade sort. By the war's end the cycle of both official and general opinion had moved from a just war emphasis through a crusade psychology to a final disillusionment concerning the entire event. The final confusion, sadness, and bitterness included a lively memory of the Church's zeal to support the war. This memory did not leave the Church in a good position to minister credibly to a war-sickened nation at the conflict's end.

The principal events contributing to a rise in English crusading fervor were the German use of poison gas at Ypres on April 22, 1915, the German sinking of the passenger liner *Lusitania* off the Irish coast on May 7, 1915, the Bryce Commission's *Report on Alleged German Atrocities*, also published in May 1915, the Turkish massacre of the Armenians, and the German execution of Nurse Edith Cavell in late 1915. (Cavell was the daughter of an Anglican priest and had assisted the flight of Allied soldiers from Belgium.) Bishop Winnington-Ingram of London articulated as well as any the deepest outrage felt in England concerning the events of 1915. This "Bishop of the Battlefields" called upon the nation to mobilize for what he called a "Holy War."

Against a tide of increasing pro-war sentiment, the Anglican pacifist position seemed both insignificant and hopeless. The record shows only 16,500 military age objectors to war in all of Britain; this number represents about .33 percent of all those who entered military service. The Friends Service Committee estimated at the time that the Anglican representation in the objector group comprised only 7.5 percent of their total. Albert Marrin's meticulous study of the Church of England in the First World War concludes that there was not a "single man in Anglican Orders who denounced war for the reasons traditionally advanced by Christian pacifists, whatever their orientation." (Marrin finds Episcopal Bishop Paul Jones of Utah, in the United States, to be unique in his pacifist opposition to the war.) H.R.L. "Dick" Sheppard and Canon Charles Raven, both of whom were known later as strong pacifists did not state their opposition to the war at the time. Sheppard served as a noncombatant in France as long as his health permitted and Raven served also in France, as a chaplain.

In January 1916 the first conscription act was passed by Parliament. Unmarried men between the ages of 18 and 41 were required to serve in the military unless a special board excused them from such service due to hardships of a major economic or personal sort. Those who took an "absolute" conscientious position opposing their participation in any military service were subjected to severe oppression in prison. This caused some Anglican Church leaders, especially Archbishop of Canterbury Randall Davidson, to intercede for them. This was done in several cases, though with mixed results. The Church's concern for objectors was based upon the principles of the supremacy of law and the inviolability of individual conscience.

The Anglican Church's position regarding military service was that a person could be as legitimately called to the duties of soldiering as to the duties of a theologian, as F. D. Maurice had put it. The moral distinctions between ordinary murder and licit killing in war lay, for Maurice, in the following circumstances: in the authority given the soldier by the state; in the broader ends served in warfare between states (rather than those of individual conflicts as between persons); in the relatively equal risks taken between combatants on either side of a battle; and in the willing submission by the professional soldier to the disciplines and transcendent aims of his country's cause. Undergirding these moral statements was the characteristic Anglican presupposition that Church and State in England shared a common history and destiny. In wartime the practical duties of all citizens, whether Church members or not, were the same: fight if necessary for the nation. The extent of Church acceptance of this view was widespread. It is estimated that 30 percent of British army officers were sons of English clergy. The

(Anglican) Church Lads' Brigade supplied 120,000 men to Great Britain's armed forces.

Some restraints were proposed by Anglican Church leaders, however, concerning the conduct of war. Archbishop Davidson came out strongly against reprisals in kind for German use of poison gas. On this issue he was not successful. The Canterbury Convocation in February 1916 unanimously opposed British reprisals in kind because of German attacks upon civilian populations. The Convocation said that, "The principles of morality forbid a policy of reprisal which has, as a deliberate object, the killing and wounding of noncombatants." To adopt such a policy "even for barbarous outrages, would permanently lower the standard of honourable conduct between nation and nation."

The moderation found in Davidson's and Canterbury Convocation's statements was quickly overwhelmed by crusade hysteria. Impulses toward humanitarian concern for innocent noncombatants were largely ignored by clergy in pulpit and press, with Bishop Winnington-Ingram of London among the more strident advocates of victory at any price. The more persuasive arguments (at the time) supporting reprisals were that reprisals are just retribution against a ruthless enemy, they would shorten the war, and they would thereby "save civilization." On August 2, 1918, the Anglican *Church Times* urged even the use of dum-dum bullets on the Western Front.

At the war's outbreak, 400 of 1,274 Anglican seminary students dropped their studies and joined the armed forces. Concerning ordained clergy, Archbishop Davidson articulated the traditional Anglican Church view that clergy could serve the military in wartime only as noncombatants. On the whole there was surprisingly little encouragement from most of the Church's bishops for clergy to serve the military in any capacity; this, coupled with the 1916 exemption of clergy from military service altogether, caused resentment throughout much of Great Britain.

Things changed in the spring of 1918, however. The Germans launched their last major offensive on the Western Front. British losses were staggering, so that by April 9 clergy exemptions from military service were abolished. Archbishop Davidson reacted enthusiastically, preparing to open the way to clergy service in the armed forces, but Parliament then reversed itself immediately out of fear of another Irish uprising if Roman Catholic clergy were conscripted. Soon thereafter, on April 22, Davidson authorized diocesan bishops to release their clergy for volunteer service on the same basis as if they had not previously been exempted. A significant number of clergy then went off to Europe. When the Armistice was finally signed, 1,937 Anglican clergy were serving as military chaplains, 3,030 having served altogether during the war's four years, with 88 of the total killed in combat or dead of wounds or disease.

The frightful events of the war made its ending extremely difficult. Driven by what had become a crusade type of mood, a mood of mixed bitterness and sadness, the people and leaders of Church and State found it impossible to gather a requisite sense of moderation or fairness to end the struggle. Both religious and secular spokesmen and press spoke their outrage against Pope Benedict XV's, President Wilson's, and later Lord Lansdowne's, suggestions for bringing about peace. These various peace proposals were regarded as shockingly ignorant of the villainy of Germany and of the enormous suffering of Great Britain. Nothing less than total victory was deemed an appropriate conclusion to such a destructive conflict. The prevailing view in Church and society was that Germany must be humiliated, her war criminals prosecuted, her military apparatus dismantled forever, part of her territory taken away from her, and heavy reparations payments had to be levied against her. Church leaders in England who proposed, or might have proposed, a more lenient and far-sighted peace strategy apparently found it prudent to remain silent. Thus, as is known from hindsight, were the seeds of World War II planted in the vengeful soil of World War I's aftermath. Perhaps more interesting from a history-of-ideas point of view, the values of restraint, proportionality, the restoration of rights, and the like, which pervade just war thinking, along with the just war theory itself, collapsed swiftly before the massive emotionalism of the War's crusade psychology.

As fighting raged in Europe, in the United States the General Convention of the Episcopal Church stated in 1916 that "Present conditions call for clear recognition of the Christian principles of the brotherhood of men; the practice of righteousness and good will between nations and individuals; the substitution of judicial processes for war in the settlement of international disputes; and the embodiment of these principles in national policies and laws, not merely as an abstract ideal, but as a practical conviction for whose development the Christian churches have special responsibility." The same Convention had heard from the House of Bishops, via its Pastoral Letter, that concerning the European conflict "No self-isolation on our part is possible." The primary author of this letter, Bishop Brent, was apparently speaking more in opposition to a spirit of isolationism than to a principled pacifism.

The Episcopal Church, perhaps owing primarily to its historical and cultural ties to England, was quite sympathetic with the British cause in the war against Germany. Thus, once the United States declared war on Germany in 1917, a special meeting of the Church's House of Bishops in Chicago in that year issued a Pastoral Letter proclaiming the Bishops' "patriotic support of the [United States] government" and "pledging ourselves to cooperate in every possible way to aid, sustain, and protect the brave soldiers and sailors of this great Christian nation" in their wartime endeavors.

In August, 1917, Presiding Bishop Tuttle appointed a War Commission, with Bishop Lawrence from Massachusetts as its head. This commission supported Episcopalian chaplains in their various ministries to servicemen. The work of the Joint Commission on Army and Navy Chaplains was also supported. In all, the Episcopal Church supplied 187 army chaplains and 25 navy chaplains during the Great War.

The 1919 General Convention of the Church, convened three months after the Versailles Treaty was concluded, dissolved the War Commission and replaced it with a permanent Army and Navy Commission. This Convention also approved the Churchwomen's League for Patriotic Service and encouraged the establishment of a bureau of Christian Americanization within the Church's Board of Missions. An authorization was made to establish a Church of the Holy Trinity in Paris as "America's War Memorial Church in Europe for her Hero Dead." The establishment of an American Field of Honor in France was also approved. The Convention supported United States participation in the League of Nations and the House of Bishops expressed its support for pardoning wartime prisoners. The House of Deputies did not endorse the Bishop's position regarding prisoners.

As in England, the initial view of the Episcopal Church concerning the First World War was that to fight was justified by the principles of just war theory. Later the psychology of crusade predominated. Against this emotional background the role and plight of religious pacifists seemed bleak, as it was in England. The record shows seven pacifist Episcopal clergy during the 1917–18 period, five of these holding pulpits. Of the five, three held their jobs and two were forced to leave their jobs. The most prominent of the pacifist clergy were Bishop Paul Jones of Utah, Irwin St. John Tucker, A. L. Byron-Curtiss, and John Nevin Sayre, all socialists and members of the Church Socialist League.

The pacifist views of Bishop Jones caused him to be charged by some in his Utah missionary district with disloyalty to his country. A petition was drawn against him asking his resignation, and the House of Bishops appointed a commission to investigate the allegations. The commission on December 12, 1917 disagreed with Jones' view that war was un-Christian. It said, in part, "This church in the United States is practically a unity in holding that it [the war] is not an unchristian thing. In the face of this unanimity it is neither right nor wise for a trusted bishop to declare and maintain that it is an unchristian thing." The bishops continued, "If the compelling force of conscientious conviction requires such utterances, fairness demands that it not be made by a bishop of this church."

By April 1918 the House of Bishops, meeting as a whole, reviewed the Jones affair and adopted three resolutions: first, that war could indeed be both righteous and inevitable; second, that a bishop is entitled to speak his mind but that prudence suggests "a deep sense of the responsibility which rests upon one who occupies a representative position"; and third, that the bishops would not accept the resignation of a bishop "in deference to an excited state of opinion"—though they did accept Bishop Jones' resignation when he immediately offered it without providing a reason.

The United States Episcopal Church did not in the end make any notable contribution to the theory or practice of ethics with respect to war. More, it seems that little effort was made to analyze United States involvement in the First World War by a sincere and rigorous study of just war criteria. Rather, as with wars before and since, the operative criteria for governing Church positions have had to do largely with measuring official statements in light of prevailing public opinions, as is shown explicitly in the Bishops' second resolution in the Jones case.

III.

The focus of Church attention following the end of the First World War was upon the League of Nations. In 1918 the Upper House of Canterbury and the Lower House of York Convocations encouraged England's participation in the League. By early 1919 the Upper House of York also supported the League. The Lower House of Canterbury finally approved it in November 1920. The

1920 Lambeth Conference also supported the League, including the admission of the former enemy nations into its body. The Lambeth Encyclical Letter spoke optimistically of a family of nations, held together in the League by "the one Spirit of fellowship, which is the Spirit of God."

In the United States, the Episcopal Church supported the League of Nations quite energetically. The 1919 General Convention supported the League, as did the Episcopal Church Congress in the same year. The *Living Church* and *Southern Churchman* also supported the League, and went so far as to upbraid those in the United States Senate who refused to vote for United States participation in the League. The peace spirit in the Episcopal Church was manifested subsequently in a 1922 General Convention statement recognizing that "the high development of scientific skill has produced . . . devices that render possible the wholesale destruction of human life." The Convention resolved therefore to place the Church on record as supporting peaceful resolutions to international disagreements and in particular supporting the 1922 Washington nine-nation conference limiting naval forces.

The 1925 General Convention continued in a peace vein, resolving that "unless civilization can destroy war, war will destroy civilization." The Convention stated too that "a warless world is a possibility." It added that work by all persons in the spirit of Christ is both "the individual duty of every Christian citizen" and "the only practical method of security for the future." In this convention, and in the subsequent 1928 Convention, the Church endorsed the Permanent Court for International Justice. The 1928 Convention also praised the 1928 Pact of Paris (the Kellogg-Briand Pact), which renounced war as an instrument of national policy. Said the Convention, "We . . . heartily sympathize with the efforts looking to disarmament and security treaties. We commend with unqualified approval the effort of our own Government to achieve the outlawing of war. . . ."

There was a concern in the Church of England to bring into better focus social analysis and Christian ethical commentary, which combination was popular in the post World War I years. This concern led to the Conference on Christian Politics, Economics and Citizenship (C.O.P.E.C.), held in Birmingham in April 1924. Though ecumenical in scope, C.O.P.E.C. was largely in Anglican endeavor, inspired and led by Gore, Raven, Tawney and William Temple. The conference was attended by 1500 delegates, and its eighth report, entitled *Christianity and War*, stated that war is "contrary to the spirit and teaching of Jesus Christ," and that "the Christian faith is fundamentally opposed to the spirit of imperialism as expressed in the desire of conquest, the maintenance of prestige, or the pursuit, in other forms, of the selfish interests of one nation at the expense of another." Resolution No. 7 of the same report recognized the difficulty, yet the urgency, of holding to the Christian anti-war stance "when war is imminent, . . . even if the Press and public opinion" make adherence to it personally costly.

The C.O.P.E.C. sentiment concerning war was reflected later in a significant statement in Anglican Church history: "The Conference affirms that war as a method of settling international disputes is incompatible with the teaching and example of Our Lord Jesus Christ." So spoke the 1930 Lambeth Conference in setting forth a view which has been restated in many times and places since. Lambeth asserted further that "the moral judgment of humanity needs to be enlisted on the side of peace" and that "the Christian Church in every nation should refuse to countenance any war in regard to which the government of its own country has not declared its willingness to submit the matter in dispute to arbitration and conciliation." More, "the Conference believes that the existence of armaments on the present scale amongst the nations of the world endangers the maintenance of peace, and appeals for a determined effort to secure further reduction by international agreement." Here can be found a recognition similar to that of the 1922 United States Episcopal Convention—namely that efforts for peace in the modern period require efforts at arms control.

The 1930 Lambeth Conference was influenced by and reflective of the prevailing general optimism toward the League of Nations. Moreover the Kellogg-Briand Pact of 1928 had been signed by fifty-eight diplomats, in which war was renounced as an instrument of national policy. Fifty-two of the fifty-eight Kellogg signatories went further in signing the "Optional Clause," pledging to submit to the Court of International Justice any dispute holding potential for rupturing international relations. In a sanguine mood concerning the peaceable resolution of international disputes, the Lambeth Encyclical Letter called upon Christians to condemn war "not merely because it is wasteful and ruinous, a cause of untold misery, but far more because it is contrary to the will of God." The Letter went on to say that peace is "something greater than a mere refusal to fight." Peace "depends on truth and justice" and all Christians were "summoned to make war on injustice, falsehood and covetousness within ourselves and in the world around us."

The 1930 Lambeth resolutions on peace and war specifically reaffirmed the Conference's support in the League of Nations, the Kellogg-Briand Pact's principles and the World Alliance for Promoting International Friendship Through the Churches. The more extended report of the Lambeth subcommittee on Peace and War describes the dangers of "the inflamed and aggressive Nationalism that ignores the rights of other nations in the determination to assert its own." The rights of minorities and fear and distrust between nations were all seen as factors having particular significance for the prospects of war or peace. Concerning disarmament, the Lambeth subcommittee said, "Unquestionably, the nations of the world are spending on armaments a sum far in excess of the minimum that we recognize to be necessary for the effective policing of the world." The Christian Church therefore "is bound to work for an increasing process of disarmament, as the nations grow accustomed to the settlement of disputes by other means than war." In 1930, then, the leadership of the Anglican Communion seemed to recognize the need to resist war and its primary causes. Here can be seen a major emphasis upon addressing the incipient problems that lead toward war as a means to prevent war in the first place. A shift is discernible, away from a consideration of war in light of just war criteria and toward an active determination to cut wars off at their political, economic and social roots.

But alas, the decade of the 1930s saw the rise of National Socialism in Germany, the erosion of effective peace efforts in the League of Nations, and finally the outbreak of the Second World War. In the early part of the decade the Geneva Disarmament Conference was in session from 1932 to 1934, with Anglican Church leaders taking a strong interest in it. William Temple in particular hoped that the Geneva Conference would produce an international police force, and he openly criticized the Versailles treaty's placing of sole blame for World War I upon the Central Powers.

Thus the clouds of another World War gathered in the 1930s, during which time political and religious forces seemed equally incapable of bringing about peace. The invasion of Manchuria by the Japanese in 1931, the Italian incursion into Abyssinia in 1935, the German entrance into the Rhineland in 1936, and the outbreak of the Spanish Civil War in the same year, all demonstrated the League's ultimate ineffectiveness. The "appeasement" strategy of Great Britain during this time was supported by Cosmo Lang, the Archbishop of Canterbury, who recorded his support for the mollification of Hitler in a 1936 address to his convocation. Near the end of the decade, opinion in the Church of England became increasingly divided on issues of militarism. The Church Assembly's 1937 debate on Peace and National Defense, for example, heard a motion reaffirming the 1930 Lambeth Report but asserting the need to maintain a minimum amount of armaments for defense. In this debate, pacifism was both strongly attacked and strongly defended. The matter was ended by Temple's theological assertion that Christian peacemaking is an imperative, but each situation has to be understood in its proper context. The earlier clarity of theological and ethical pronouncement began to break down under the pressure of world events.

The 1937 Oxford Conference, an ecumenical affair to which the Church of England was a party, denounced war and nationalistic feelings. The Munich Conference in 1938, at which Prime Minister Chamberlain "appeased" Hitler, was supported at the time by Archbishop Lang, Archbishop Temple, the *Church Times* and the *Guardian*. It was criticized, however, by *Christendom* and *The Socialist Christian*. In England, among Church and non-Church people alike, growing reaction against Munich began to set in, and by the time of the September 3, 1939 declaration of war against Germany, England and those in her national Church were ready to fight.

During the 1930s the affairs of the Episcopal Church in the United States generally followed a course parallel to that of the Church of England. The 1931 General Convention adopted as its own statement a House of Bishops Pastoral Letter which said, in part, "The Christian conscience . . . is now called to condemn war as an outrage on the Fatherhood of God and the brotherhood of all mankind." The statement found the origins of war in "a narrow and aggressive Nationalism," the distrust between nations, economic competition, and "excessive armaments, which arouse fears and suspicions and can never insure safety. . . ." The statement concluded, "If you wish peace, prepare for peace."

A 1933 Pastoral Letter from the House of Bishops notes the ominous signs of enmity between nations, and warns against mutual suspicions and excess feelings of nationalistic emotion, and asserts, "Love of country must be qualified by love of all mankind; patriotism is subordinate to religion. The cross is above the flag." In the following year the 1934 General Convention accorded formal recognition of conscientious objectors to war who were willing to "risk their lives in noncombatant service," and provided for a national register of Episcopal Church members conscientiously opposed to participation as combatants in war. The Convention also urged the United States Government to withhold "sales of munitions and loans of money to any belligerent government which has not exhausted all possibilities of peaceful settlement before having recourse to arms. . . ." Support of the World Court was advocated, a commission was established to work with other denominational groups to prevent war, and an endorsement was made of a world conference dealing with problems of war and peace.

In 1934 about half of the Episcopal clergy interviewed in a Kirby Page poll said that they could not support or participate in a future war. The Page poll's question was later presented to 878 Episcopal clergy. This time 346 stated they could not "sanction any future war or participate as an armed combatant." One hundred five clergy were undecided. As the decade grew to a close the Episcopal Church tended to become increasingly convinced that military force would have to be used to counter the military force of an aggressor. In 1936 the deterioration of the European situation became evident, and the House of Bishops called for all signatories to the Kellogg-Briand Pact to convene for the purpose of avoiding possible war. By Armistice Day 1939 the Episcopal Pacifist Fellowship was created and as Europe went to war, the United States, and in some degree the Episcopal Church, tried to decide whether to fight against fascism or to remain neutral.

The Episcopal Church House of Bishops in 1940, recognizing the "instability and insecurity of World Peace," urgently warned against the "mad race for supremacy in armament . . . that must inevitably issue in a conflict more terrible than the world has ever known." After the Japanese attack on Pearl Harbor the Episcopal Church, with only a few pacifist exceptions resignedly regarded war against Japan and her Axis allies as a necessary endeavor. What seemed more clear than ever is that Church pronouncements, and non-Church pronouncements as well, could be more or less valid as to fact and morally commendable as to intent, but the actions and sacrifices essential to preventing war still lay beyond human will or capability.

IV.

World War II's impact upon England was different from that of the 1914–1918 War in the primary respects that several British cities were heavily bombed, children and young mothers had to be evacuated to the countryside (both in 1939 and 1944), and weapons of unprecedented destruction were used by all sides. Air raids on civilian population centers in several instances indiscriminately killed civilians and combatants alike. In England those cities especially devastated were London, Coventry, Portsmouth, and Canterbury itself. Allied bombing of the Germany cities of Hamburg and Dresden caused vast firestorms, due to the lavish use of both incendiary and high explosive bombs. In Hamburg, 43,000 persons died, including 5,000 children, Dresden lost 135,000 persons in 36 hours of "obliteration" bombing.

Britain's mood upon entering the Second World War seems to have been more subdued than at the beginning of the earlier World War. Rather than a crusading type of spirit, there seemed instead to be an attitude of wariness. Early on, Church leaders spoke in measured terms of the need for restraint. The October 4, 1940 *Church Times* said, "The reason why, even to win the war or win it quickly, this country cannot adopt methods of the jungle is simply that it does not wish the world to be a jungle when the war is finished. . . ." The paper continued, "The allied nations are dedicated to the cause of Christian civilization. . . . There are some steps they cannot take without abandoning the standards for which they are fighting."

Earlier in that year, on June 11, an Anglican Pacifist Fellowship "deputation," led by Archdeacon Percy Hartill, the Reverend R. H. LeMessurier, and Canon Charles Raven, and representing 2,571 communicant members, including 371 clergy of the Church of England, met with the Archbishops at Lambeth Palace. The pacifists questioned the Church's support of Britain's war aims as if the "things which belong to God" could essentially be "defended by force of arms." The Archbishops replied that a Nazi victory would create a condition within which the practice of the Christian religion in worship or in public life would be most difficult. The Archbishops subsequently went on to say that, "Protest should certainly be made by the Church against reprisals, involving deliberate attacks upon civilians, but the moral issue involved in the victory of the allies is of greater importance than the harsh fact of fighting by methods that one deplores." Later, in a February 9, 1944 debate in the House of Lords, Bishop George Bell of Winchester spoke in opposition to obliteration bombing reprisals against German population centers. Bell, who was by no means a pacifist, argued that by undertaking such bombing raids, Great Britain was only creating the occasion for future bitterness in Germany. He insisted that "there must be a fair balance between the means employed and the purpose achieved. To obliterate a whole town because certain portions contain military and industrial establishments is to reject the balance. . . ." Bell's speech was answered by Viscount Cranborne, the Secretary of State for Dominion Affairs, who said that the basic idea was to end the war as quickly as possible and that therefore the prevailing bombing policy was not likely to be changed.

Undoubtedly the paramount theological figure in England during the early War years was William Temple. Temple supported England's involvement in the Second World War as necessary and justifiable according to just war criteria. He especially understood England to be acting defensively rather than aggressively, though he recognized that in any conflict no party is entirely innocent. Temple's position was therefore different from that of the pacifists, whose sincerity he respected and whose witness he saw as valuable, if not entirely appropriate to the requirements of the moment. Temple thus worked hard to ensure the fullest protections of the law for persons conscientiously objecting to participation in the war—this in spite of his own view that force was sometimes essential to hold evil in check. Though he respected the sincerity of pacifists he easily became impatient with them. At one moment he said: "The British pacifist at this moment is not merely taking no part; he is weakening the British capacity to fight and so far is increasing Hitler's chance of victory. He may be right to do this; but let us—and let him—face the fact that he is doing this."

Like Reinhold Niebuhr, Temple thought that nations could not be expected to exhibit the kinds of virtues expected from individuals. Justice is a moral quality more to be demanded of a nation than is love, which is more appropriately to be required of individuals. Like Abraham Lincoln and the biblical prophets, Temple understood war as the whirlwind reaped from sowing the wind with seeds of injustice.

Temple died on October 26, 1944, by which time he had gleaned a certain knowledge of Hitler's destruction of large numbers of Jews. With dogged persistence he sought Britain's help for the Jewish victims of the Nazis. Temple also actively sought a negotiated peace with Germany; in this he opposed those holding rigidly to the "unconditional surrender" position. He was a diligent visitor to England's military installations and industrial plants, and he frequently preached by radio to British forces in Africa, Europe and at sea. He visited the parishes of several communities enduring heavy bombing attacks. Through all this Temple remained one of

England's most impressive theologians and ethicists, applying with precision and rigor the criteria of the just war to England's struggle, and finding England's cause to be consistently just.

In the United States the first conscription act was passed in 1940. Bishop Henry Knox Sherrill's Army and Navy Commission assisted the United States Government in recruiting military chaplains and in supporting them administratively in their work. When the United States entered the war, the Episcopal Church was one of the first churches to meet its quota of military chaplains; by the war's end 557 clergy had served in the chaplaincy. The mood of the Episcopal Church seemed to be similar to that of the Church of England: no exuberant crusading spirit, but rather a general sense that the war simply had to be fought. The Pearl Harbor attack made clear to the satisfaction of most that neither pacifism nor isolationism seemed to be fully adequate to the exigencies of the world situation. To fight seemed justifiable by the criteria of the just war.

By the time of the 1943 General Convention, the Episcopal Church expressed its wish that there be established a joint lay-presbyter-bishop commission to assure Episcopal Church conscientious objectors "of the continuing fellowship of the Church with them and care for them" and otherwise be an advocate for the rights and welfare of conscientious objectors. At the same Convention the Church advocated the creation of "an International Authority based on law, and provided with power to enforce that law." This hope was subsequently realized, at least partially, by the formation in 1945 of the United Nations.

At the war's end the United States atomic bombing of the Japanese city of Hiroshima signalled the beginning of a new era in the history of warfare. The ability of an atomic weapon, later of thermonuclear weapons, to kill combatants and noncombatants indiscriminately meant that at least two of the "just war" criteria (that the war's means should be proportionate to its end and that all possible moderation should be used in its conduct) could never justify the use of such weapons. The recognition of this fact by a growing number of men and women in the Church of England, the United States Episcopal Church, and elsewhere in the Anglican Communion, shaped in a new way the thinking of growing numbers of Church people since 1945.

The Anglican Church's recognition of the moral challenge presented by the atomic bomb is evidenced in the work of the "Selwyn Commission," meeting in 1948, and, somewhat more ecumenically, in the work of the British Council of Church's "Oldham Commission." The Selwyn Commission, appointed by the Archbishops of Canterbury and York, condemned obliteration bombing of any sort and stated, "The atomic bomb is inadmissible as a means of attack upon objectives in inhabited cities." Yet the Commission did not go so far as to propose the destruction of atomic weapons since, in the Commission's view, those weapons still had legitimate purpose as deterrents to aggression. Thus "The Commission believes . . . that in certain circumstances defensive 'necessity' might justify their use against an unscrupulous aggressor."

The 1946 "Oldham Commission" of the British Council of Churches contained a minority categorically opposing the use of, or intention to use, atomic weapons for any reason. The majority held, however, that "the mainstream of Christian tradition has recognized the legitimacy of war for a just cause" and that the responsibility to fight a just war cannot be "diminished or altered by technical advances and the introduction of new weapons, even though the resulting problems may be more acute."

Three years after the Hiroshima and Nagasaki bombings, the 1948 Lambeth Conference Encyclical Letter asserted that "Marxian Communism" was a danger to much that democratic societies held dear, but also that Communism is itself an indication of the injustices which oppress the world's "depressed and downtrodden." The Letter went on to locate the chief causes of war less in Communism's threats and more in "national selfishness" and "suspicion, fear, and hatred." The Letter asserted, "New and terrible weapons of destruction have been forged which may bring ruin upon the earth" and concluded, "We call upon all nations . . . to pledge themselves never to use [atomic power] for the purposes of war." In its resolutions the Conference also affirmed that "it is the duty of governments to work for the general reduction and control of armaments of every kind and for their final elimination, except those which may be necessary for international police protection. . . ." In the meantime, however, the Conference recognized that "there are occasions when both nations and individuals are obliged to resort to war as the lesser of two evils."

Ten years later the Lambeth Encyclical Letter of 1958 called upon Christians to "work positively for peace" since the "hideous weapons of destruction" in the world's nuclear arsenals made peace-making more urgent than ever. Going further, the Conference said, "The use of nuclear weapons is repugnant to the Christian conscience," though the Letter stated, as ten years earlier, that while some found their use "in any circumstances . . . morally indefensible," others could consider their use preferable to "political enslavement." In the end, the Letter advocated the abolition of all nuclear weapons as an imperative, and urged all Christians to work through their governments "for the banning of such weapons" and to enable adequate "inspection and control so that no government may make them." Finally, "we urge governments to devote their utmost efforts toward comprehensive international disarmament."

The Anglican Church of Canada in 1964 published a pamphlet at the request of its House of Bishops, putting forth the official statements of the Church on arms and warfare. This document draws upon discussions and actions of various Church groups, including the General Synod and Executive Council, for more than a fifteen-year period, and establishes six major points about which there has been general agreement in the Canadian Church: that war as a means of settling disputes is incompatible with the teaching of Christ; that all governments should work for arms control and reduction; that weapons of mass destruction should be banned everywhere; that the United Nations should be supported fully; that Christians should continually work and pray for peace; and that world conditions of economic and political injustice giving rise to conflicts should be effectively ameliorated.

The 1968 Lambeth Conference continued to proclaim its alarm over war and over nuclear weapons in particular. The Conference reiterated the words of Lambeth 1930 that "war as a method of settling international disputes is incompatible with the teaching and example of our Lord Jesus Christ." More, the Conference "states emphatically that it condemns the use of nuclear and bacteriological weapons." It stated further that the Church should support the right of conscientious objection, that the Church should "oppose persistently the claim that total war or the use of weapons however ruthless or indiscriminate can be justified by results" and that Christians should work diligently for peace in the world.

Ten years after that, Resolution No. 5 of the 1978 Lambeth Conference once again expressed the Church's concern over nuclear weapons, which were taken to be "the most striking example of corporate sin and the prostitution of God's gifts." The Conference deplored and condemned the various forms of violence manifest in the world, and called upon Christians to study their own "attitudes toward, and their complicity with, violence in its many forms." Christians were exhorted to work diligently for peace and especially "to protest in whatever way possible at the escalation of the sale of armaments by the producing nations to the developing and dependent nations, and to support with every effort all international proposals and conferences designed to place limitations on, or ar-range reductions in, the armaments of war of the nations of the world."

Alarm over nuclear weapons continued to grow. In May 1981 the Scottish Episcopal Church's Representative Church Council expressed its opposition to the British Government's intention to permit deployment in England of nuclear-tipped Cruise and Trident Missiles. The Scottish Church called upon its members to "consider their own position as peacemakers" and instructed the Church's Social Service Board to "promote a study of the Arms Race and the use of nuclear weapons on as wide a base throughout Scotland as possible." In their action the Scottish Church seemed mindful of Archbishop Runcie of Canterbury's April 1981 statement that "It may be that the most hopeful way at present would be some attempt to negotiate a ban on tactical nuclear weapons which contribute to the dangerous illusion that limited nuclear war is possible." Runcie suggested that "We might also try to gain a pledge from each of the nuclear powers that they would not be the first to use nuclear weapons." Runcie's views were echoed at the same time (April 1981) in a Washington statement by the Primates of the Anglican Communion, who said, "We pledge ourselves to work for multilateral disarmament and to support those who seek, by education and other appropriate means, to influence those people and agencies who shape nuclear policy."

The relative ease with which peace pronouncements are made, however, stands in sharp contrast to the difficulty with which conflicts are avoided. By early spring of 1982 the British were fighting Argentine forces in the Falkland Islands. Archbishop Runcie declared that Britain's use of military force in this endeavor was justified as a proportionate use of force to resist Argentina's aggression. Runcie was supported by a number of Anglican Church leaders, including the Bishop of London. An opposing view of the Falklands conflict came from both the Anglican Pacifist Fellowship, which asserted that the use of military force was contrary to the requirements of the Gospel, and from Bishop John A. T. Robinson, who quoted the 1930 Lambeth statement that "war as a method of settling international disputes is incompatible with the teaching and example of our Lord Jesus Christ."

In the late fall of 1982 a report was released by a working group of the Church of England's Board of Social Responsibility. Entitled *The Church and the Bomb: Nuclear Weapons and Christian Conscience*, this controversial document applied just war criteria to the prospect of war waged with nuclear weapons. With particular attention to the expectations of success in war and the proportionate relationship of the war's foreseeable social costs to its social benefits, the report concluded that, "the use of nuclear weapons cannot be justified. Such weapons cannot be used without harming noncombatants and could never be proportionate to the just cause and aim of a just war."

Britain was exhorted to renounce unilaterally its own nuclear weapons, while otherwise honoring its membership obligations to the North Atlantic Treaty Organization: "We do not rule out the use of nuclear weapons in all circumstances, but we do think it better for the world that as few states as possible should possess them. We are therefore renouncing our own. We have no objection if some other power interposes a threat of nuclear retaliation to warn off someone who plans to attack us, but we do not have this capability ourselves. . . . We accept whatever loss of security this involves, in order to lessen the risk of nuclear war."

Though presently lacking the standing of official General Synod policy—it will be debated in General Synod in 1983—*The Church and the Bomb* constitutes a notable and perhaps landmark development in Anglican thinking about war in the nuclear age.

In the United States the Episcopal Church early recognized the moral implications of the new atomic, later thermonuclear, weapons. The Bishops' Pastoral Letter of 1946 noted in the aftermath of Hiroshima and Nagasaki that "we face the specter of mankind's obliteration," and called upon all persons to work and pray for peace. In the same year the General Convention created a three million dollar program for reconstruction of war-torn areas. Resolutions were passed in support of a strong United Nations and in support of amnesty for conscientious objectors then imprisoned. The Bishops resolved that the idea of war with Russia should not be entertained, but the House of Deputies failed to support the Bishops' position concerning the Soviets.

Against the background of a frustrating war in Korea, the 1952 Bishops' Pastoral Letter, finding that "the conception of absolute national sovereignty is an anachronism," expressed its hope in the "collective security" promised by the United Nations organization or some similar kind of world federation. Mindful of the nuclear capability of the United States, the 1952 General Convention stated its opposition to "preventive war," since to conduct such a war would place the United States in "an indefensible moral position before the world."

Ten years later, in 1962, the House of Bishops declared that "because of the nature of the Christian faith, we have an imperative obligation to pray and work for peace among men and nations."

The Bishops' Pastoral Letter on "War and Peace" observed that the notion of "total war" in the nuclear era has created a need to re-evaluate the just war theory. The new situation, "at once more difficult and more deeply critical for the Christian conscience," is one in which "at all levels of its life, the Church must charge its people with the insistent duty of working with all their strength for the prevention and elimination of war." The Bishops said further, "All-out modern war cannot protect the world's peoples" and that "an atomic holocaust cannot serve the purpose that war may once have served" and that "total war under modern conditions is self-defeating and that it will utterly fail to secure peace with the enemy or even peace within the borders of the countries waging it." Therefore "Christians are called to be peace-makers."

In the midst of a growing polarization within the United States over the Indochina War, the 1967 General Convention recognized the right of conscientious objectors to serve alternate duty either as noncombatants or in entirely civilian service. The Convention encouraged Congress to confer the same rights upon non-religious conscientious objectors as were available to religious objectors, and urged further that draft exemptions of seminarians be discontinued. In the following year the House of Bishops declared that a person could properly be opposed to a particular war ("selective conscientious objection") without having to be opposed to war in principle or all wars in general.

The General Conventions of 1973 and 1976 expressed the desire that programs of peace education be developed by and disseminated throughout the Episcopal Church. The 1976 Convention also took note of the manufacture and sale of armaments to nations with "repressive governments," and concluded that such arms trade "threatens world peace." Therefore the United States Congress was asked to "adopt suitable legislation" restricting arms sales abroad by United States firms. The 1976 Convention also spoke its alarm concerning nuclear arms proliferation throughout the world and supported United States government attempts to control such proliferation. The Strategy Arms Limitation Talks (SALT) were also commended, and the Convention expressed its "hope for a time when we may end our dependence on the use of nuclear weapons as a deterrent to war. . . ."

The 1979 General Convention encouraged young Episcopalians who regarded themselves as conscientious objectors to war to register in the Church's Executive Council office. The Convention also requested continued provision of counseling for persons facing the draft, expressed opposition to peacetime conscription, adopted "as its own" the 1978 Lambeth Resolution on "War and Violence," and established a Joint Commission on Peace to prepare an action plan to implement the 1962 Bishops' Pastoral Letter concerning war and peace.

By 1980 the House of Bishops in a Pastoral Letter stated, "Since nuclear armaments here and in the Soviet Union have created a world in which the whole can nowhere be protected against its parts, our own national security has reached the zero point. The issue is no longer the survival of one nation against another. We stand now in mortal danger of global human incineration." This was followed by another Pastoral Letter in 1981, which stated, "Never before has it been so clear that reason forbids the use of force, or the threat of it, as a means of securing one society against another. . . . The real unit of security is the totality of the human family." The Bishops pledged "repeated challenge to the leaders of the United States and other nations of the world that they repudiate reliance on military threats in favor of the more demanding discipline of military restraint and negotiation for arms control."

By September 1982 the General Convention of the Episcopal Church, owing largely to the untiring efforts of the Reverend George F. Regas, had committed itself on a wide range of issues related to the threat of nuclear war. Noting the "unlimited and indiscriminating" nature of modern weaponry, the Convention stated its belief that "nonviolent refusal to participate in or prepare for war can be a faithful response" by an Episcopal Church member to war and preparations for war.

The Convention voted to continue the General Convention Joint Commission on Peace for another triennial, and recognized peace-making as "of the highest priority" by authorizing $150,000 annually and a peace coordinator position to carry out the Commission's work through cooperative efforts with the various dioceses. Going further, the Convention recognized that "increased military spending is inseparably linked with greater impoverishment of the poor and oppressed" and called for "a reordering of Federal budget priorities from continuing increases in military spending to maintaining, restoring, and expanding human services."

Perhaps the most widely publicized actions of the 1982 Convention were its actions endorsing a verifiable U.S.-Soviet freeze on the "testing, production and further deployment of all nuclear weapons, missiles and delivery systems," and calling for a negotiating endeavor with the Soviety Union "for an immediate verifiable across-the-board reduction by fifty percent of the nuclear arsenals" of both nations. Equally widely publicized was the Convention's call for both the United States and the Soviet Union to "adopt a policy of no first use of nuclear weapons."

Taking the various anti-nuclear war resolutions together, one can conclude that the 1982 Convention has come a considerable way toward developing a coherent platform for addressing the nuclear weapons issues in the coming years. More, the mechanism for carrying out the educational and advocacy programs of such a platform at diocesan levels promises to add force and effectiveness to the Convention's pronouncements. In having come to a relatively clear and coherent position on the major aspects of today's nuclear arms race, the Episcopal Church in the United States takes its place alongside all the other major U.S. Christian denominations, which expressed identical or similar concerns during 1982.

V.

When one takes an overall view of Anglican statements, attitudes, and behaviors concerning war, it seems apparent that at their best Anglicans have recognized and appropriately warned against the horrors of war. There have been moments of remarkable insight and undoubtedly of courageous and sacrificial actions to expose and struggle against the things that make for war.

Yet it is equally apparent that at times of growing fear, suspicion, and nationalistic fervor, the causes of wars have been permitted to grow, and wars themselves have been supported and fought without widespread criticism by either the Church of England or the Episcopal Church in the United States.

For better or worse Anglican responses to wars and their causes therefore seem not recognizably more or less virtuous, more or less restrained, more or less reflective of Christian sentiment, than the response of many other groups in the Western world, whether religious or non-religious.

From a rigorously intellectual point of view, the pronouncements of major Church bodies seem somewhat lacking in strong moral argumentation. In general, claims are asserted without much elaboration as to why a given position is warranted explicitly by the Christian ethical heritage in general or in any of its parts. It is uncertain whether or not a fuller and more explicit ethical support for Church pronouncements would add force and effectiveness to Church statements on war. One notes that the Church has tended to assume that the force of its pronouncements comes from the pronouncements themselves and from the authority of the body making them; lesser importance seems to have been given to the ethical rationale supporting the various positions taken.

Though the major structure of ethical thinking about war has been provided over the years by the just war theory—with pacifism and crusading attitudes being evident as well, as indicated throughout this chapter—the recent appearance of nuclear weaponry has begun to shock Church people into a profound soul-searching concerning the urgent requirements of peacemaking. Mindful of their magnitude of destruction and the speed with which nuclear weapons can be delivered, various Anglican Church bodies have concluded that nuclear war is an overwhelming evil to be resisted with the greatest possible energy.

For the future, Anglican women and men are recognizing that the destruction potentials of nuclear weapons make most urgent a greater depth and extent of Christian commitment to effective peacemaking—this because of the traditional principle that the destruction wrought in warfare should be justified by the greater benefits attending peace at its conclusion. It is now recognized that there is no end for which a nuclear war is an appropriate means.

The nuclear annihilation of hundreds of thousands, perhaps hundreds of millions of human beings, or perhaps the extinction of the human species, is a prospect of unprecedented magnitude now facing the Church and all humankind. The former ways of thinking about war, either as a crusade or as justifiable according to traditional criteria, are overwhelmed by the capabilities of the weapons themselves. With respect to attitudes and behaviors concerning war, Albert Einstein was absolutely correct: the weapons have changed everything except our way of thinking, and thus we drift toward a disaster of unprecedented proportions.

For Christians the essential moral issue will be whether in the end God's incarnation will have been but a prelude to human immolation by thermonuclear weaponry, or instead a prelude to the establishment of justice, generosity, beauty and peace. The responsibility for either end lies largely in human hands; the vision of a peaceable world is in the keeping of the Church.

Notes

Introduction

[1]Martin Thornton, *Feed My Lambs* (Greenwich, Conn., 1961), p. 44

[2]Karl Barth, *Protestant Theology in the Nineteenth Century* (London, 1972), p. 317.

[3]Jürgen Habermas, *Knowledge and Human Interest*, tr. Jeremy Shepro (Boston, 1971), pp. 301 ff.

[4]H. G. Gadamer, *Wahrheit und Methode* (Mohr, 1960), pp. 290–324.

Chapter 1. The English Reformation: A Lively Faith and Sacramental Confession

[1]Jewel, *Works*, PS (Cambridge, 1845–50), 1:120.

[2]William Maskell, *Monumental Ritualia Ecclesiae Anglicanae*, 2nd ed. (Oxford, 1882), 3:296–297.

[3]Thomas Tentler, *Sin and Confession on the Eve of the Reformation* (Princeton: Princeton University Press, 1977), pp. 348–349.

[4]Ibid., pp. 364–365.

[5]*Certaine Sermons or Homilies* (London: Printed by John Bill, 1623), facsimile ed. (Gainesville, Fla.: Scholar's Facsimiles and Reprints, 1968), p. 22.

[6]Tyndale, *Works*, PS (Cambridge, 1848–1850), 1:57, cited in Philip Edgcumbe Hughes, *Theology of the English Reformers* (London: Hodder and Stoughton, 1965), p. 79. Professor Hughes' presentation of the English Reformers' understanding of sanctification is invaluable.

[7]Becon, *Early Works*, PS (Cambridge, 1843), p. 80.

[8]*The Book of Common Prayer 1559*, ed. John Booty (Charlottesville, Va.: The University Press of Virginia for the Folger Shakespeare Library, 1976), pp. 283–287. Hereafter *BCP 1559*.

[9]*Lawes*, V.18.3; The Folger Library Edition of *The Works of Richard Hooker*, vol. 2, W. Speed Hill ed. (Cambridge, Mass.: The Belknap Press of Harvard University Press, 1977), p. 66. Hereafter, Folger *Works*.

[10]*Certaine Sermons and Homilies*, pp. 40–41.

[11]Ibid., p. 39.

[12]Loc. cit.

[13]See Cranmer, *Works*, PS (Cambridge, 1844–46), 1:66, 70–71, 91, 127, 271, 283, etc.

[14]Ibid., pp. 42–43.

[15]Hooker, *Lawes*, VI.3.4; Folger *Works*, vol. 3, P. G. Stanwood, ed. (Cambridge, Mass., 1981), p. 11.

[16]*BCP 1559*, pp. 259–260.

[17]Ibid., p. 265.

[18]For instance, in his visitation of the diocese of Lichfield and Coventry in 1565 Bishop Bentham ordered that the Ten Commandments should be located "in the

place where the sacrament did hang" (W.P.M. Kennedy, *Elizabethan Episcopal Administration*, Alcuin Club. Coll. XV, London: Mowbray, 1924, 1:lxvii). On education, see the Royal Injunctions (1536), Art. 5 (Henry Gee and W. J. Hardy, *Documents Illustrative of English Church History*, London: Macmillan, 1914, p. 272).

[19]See Ralph Houlbrooke, *Church Courts and the People During the English Reformation, 1520–1570* (Oxford: Oxford University Press, 1979) and F. G. Emmison, *Elizabethan Life: Disorder* (Chelmsford: Essex County Council, 1970), dealing with Essex Sessions Records in the sixteenth century, and Emmison, *Elizabethan Life: Morals and the Church Courts* (Chelmsford: Essex County Council, 1973).

[20]A. J. Willis, *Church Life in Kent, being Church Court Records of the Canterbury Diocese, 1559–1565* (London and Chichester, Phillimore, 1975), pp. 44, 51.

[21]Latimer, *Works*, PS (Cambridge, 1844–45), 1:200, cited in Hughes, *Theology*, p. 130.

[22]Jewel, *Apology of the Church of England*, John Booty, ed. (Ithaca, N.Y.: Cornell University Press for the Folger Shakespeare Library, 1963), pp. 26–27. And see Hughes, *Theology*, p. 185.

[23]*The Sermons of John Donne*, G. R. Potter and E. M. Simpson, eds. (Berkeley and Los Angeles: University of California Press, 1953–1962), 2:166–167.

[24]See Colet's sermon in C. H. Williams, ed., *English Historical Documents, 1485–1558* (New York: Oxford University Press, 1967), p. 654; for Latimer, see his *Works*, PS, 1:239f, where he means by covetousness an inordinate desire for riches, grasping, avarice, as in the Grk. Πλεογεξίας; on the Commonwealth Men, see *The Godly Kingdom of Tudor England*, John Booty, ed. (Wilton, Conn.: Morehouse-Barlow Co., Inc., 1981), pp. 32–38; and on Jewel, see John Booty, "The Bishop Confronts the Queen: John Jewel and the Failure of the English Reformation," *Continuity and Discontinuity in Church History*, F. F. Church and T. George, eds. (Leiden: E. J. Brill, 1979), pp. 215–231.

[25]See Whitney R. D. Jones, *The Tudor Commonwealth, 1529–1559* (London: The Athlone Press, 1970), Ch. 9.

[26]*A Discourse of the Commonweal of This Realm of England*, Mary Dewar, ed. (Charlottesville, Va.: The University Press of Virginia for the Folger Shakespeare Library, 1969), p. 16.

[27]*Certaine Sermons preached before the Queenes Maiestie, and at Paules crosse* (London: Christopher Barker, 1583), sig. U.iii[r].

[28]Ibid., sig. U.vij[r].

[29]Ibid., sigs. U.vij[r]–U.viij[r].

[30]Ibid., sigs. X.j[v]–X.ij[v].

[31]*BCP 1559*, p. 323.

[32]Ibid., p. 303.

[33]Ibid., p. 257.

[34]*Lawes*, VI.6.14; Folger, *Works*, 3:96.

[35]*The Works of William Perkins*, Ian Breward, ed., The Courenay Library of Reformation Classics 3 (Appleford, Abingdon, Berkshire, England: The Sutton Courtenay Press, 1970), p. 67.

[36]Hooker, *Discourse of Justification*, sec. 19 (see also, sec. 13); *Works*, 7th Keble ed. (Oxford, 1888), 3:505.

[37]I am here much influenced by the excellent analysis made by Lee W. Gibbs, "Richard Hooker's *Via Media* Doctrine of Justification," *Harvard Theological Review*, 74:2 (April 1981), pp. 211–220.

[38]*Discourse of Justification*, sec. 6; *Works* (1888), 3:490.

[39]Ibid., sec. 21; *Works* (1888), 3:507.

[40]I am indebted to Egil Grislis' discussion in a draft of his Introduction to the Sermons and Tractates of Hooker included in vol. 5 of the Folger Library Edition of the *Works of Richard Hooker,* yet to be published by the Harvard University Press.

[41]See Booty, "Richard Hooker," *The Spirit of Anglicanism,* W. J. Wolf, ed. (Wilton, Conn.: Morehouse-Barlow Co., Inc., 1979), pp. 17–20.

[42]*Lawes,* V.56.1; Folger, *Works,* 2:234.

[43]Ibid., V.56.7; Folger, *Works,* 2:239.

[44]Ibid., V.56.11; Folger, *Works,* 2:243.

[45]Ibid., V.56.12; Folger, *Works,* 2:244.

[46]Hooker, Dublin Fragments, 16; The Folger Library Edition of the *Works of Richard Hooker,* Vol. 4, J. E. Booty, ed. (Cambridge, Mass.: The Belknap Press of Harvard University Press, 1982), p. 117.

[47]Loc. cit.

[48]Ibid., 17; Folger, *Works,* 4:119.

[49]*Lawes,* V.60.2; Folger, *Works,* 2:255.

[50]Ibid., V.67.1: Folger, *Works,* 2:331.

[51]Ibid., VI.3.5; Folger, *Works,* 3:12; and see John Booty, "Contrition in Anglican Spirituality: Hooker, Donne, and Herbert," *Anglican Spirituality,* W. J. Wolf, ed. (Wilton, Conn.: Morehouse-Barlow Co., Inc., 1982), pp.

[52]*Lawes,* I.12.3; Folger, *Works,* 1:121–122.

[53]Ibid., I.7.2; Folger, *Works,* 1:77–78.

[54]Ibid., I.7.2; Folger, *Works,* 1:77.

[55]Ibid., I.7.6; Folger, *Works,* 1:79.

[56]*A Christian Letter,* 5; Folger, *Works,* 4:17–19.

[57]See Egil Grislis, "The Role of *Consensus* in Richard Hooker's Method of Theology Inquiry," *Heritage of Christian Thought,* R. E. Cushman and E. Grislis, eds. (New York: Harper and Row, 1965), pp. 74–75.

[58]Hooker, Dublin Fragments, sec. 9; Folger, *Works,* 4:109. See intro., ibid., pp. xxix–xl.

[59]Ibid., sec. 13; Folger, *Works,* 4:113.

[60]*Lawes,* I.11.2; Folger, *Works,* 1:112.

[61]*Lawes,* I.11.6; Folger, *Works,* 1:118.

[62]See Robert K. Faulkner, *Richard Hooker and the Politics of a Christian England* (Berkeley, Los Angeles, London: University of California Press, 1981), p. 94. Faulkner is helpful but misleading. When he speaks of "actions done by the will" he must mean the *rational* will with all that that implies for Hooker.

[63]See note No. 5, above.

Chapter 2. Anglican Moral Theology in the Seventeenth Century

[1]e.g. Bernard Häring, *The Law of Christ* (1959); *Medical Ethics* (1972); Gerard Gilleman, *The Primacy of Charity in Moral Theology* (1959); Josef Fuchs, *Human Values and Christian Morality* (1970); *Natural Law* (1965); Enda McDonagh, *Invitation and Response* (1972); *Doing the Truth* (1979).

[2]*The Documents of Vatican II* (1966), W. M. Abbott, ed., pp. 451–2, *The Decree on Priestly Formation.*

[3]*Co-responsibility in the Church* (1968), pp. 148–150.

[4]John Michael Sailer, *Handbuch der Christlichen Moral* (1817).

[5]Some of the material incorporated in this essay was delivered, but not published,

in the Scott Holland lectures for 1973. For the inventory of the elements of modern moral theology, cp. H. R. McAdoo, "Christianity and Secularism," *The Furrow* (Jan. 1974).

[6]The Tyndale Press (London, 1948).

[7]Ibid., p. 3.

[8]*The Law of Christ*, I, 23–4. One has only to compare this with the picture of moral theology as seen, for example, by T. Slater (*Cases of Conscience* [1925] I, 36): The object of moral theology, he writes, "is not to place high ideals of virtue before the people and train them in Christian perfection ... its primary object is to teach the priest how to distinguish what is sinful from what is lawful ... it is not intended for edification nor for the building up in character." Ten years later, H. Davis could take much the same line: "It is precisely about law that moral theology is concerned. It is not a mirror of perfection, showing man the way of perfection. It shows him the way of salvation, which will be attained by the observance of the commandments of God and of the Church. It must, at the same time, be admitted that a man who aims only at keeping within the four corners of the law, will find himself in a very perilous situation ... not because moral theology offers him the broad road and lax principles, but because man himself does not act up to the principles offered" (*Moral and Pastoral Theology,* [1935], I, 4).

[9]Ibid., p. 35.

[10]Ibid., p. vii.

[11]Ibid., p. 61.

[12]*Human Values and Christian Morality* (1970), p. 3.

[13]*Invitation and Response* (1972), p. vii.

[14]*A New Introduction to Moral Theology* (1964), p. 28.

[15]cp. "It follows that a moral theology founded in Christ is, by its most intimate exigency, an imitation of Christ. He inspires us interiorly to express in our virtuous activity His own attitudes adapted to the circumstances in which we live; at the same time He teaches us and shows us exteriorly, in the Gospel revelation, the living doctrinal rule of morality" (Gerard Gilleman, *The Primacy of Charity in Moral Theology,* p. 197).

[16]*The Law of Christ*, I, 317.

[17]Ibid., I, 52.

[18]*Loving on Principle*, p. 137.

[19]*Human Values and Christian Morality* (1970), p. 34. Note the comments on the distinction between mortal and venial sin.

[20]*The Law of Christ*, I, 261.

[21]*Medical Ethics* (1972), p. 7.

[22]*Human Values and Christian Morality* (1970), p. vii.

[23]H. R. McAdoo, *The Structure of Caroline Moral Theology: An Investigation of Principles* (London, 1949).

[24]Kevin Kelly, *Conscience: Dictator or Guide? A Study in Seventeenth-century English Protestant Moral Theology* (London, 1967).

[25]Ibid., p. 162.

[26]Loc. cit.

[27]John K. Ryan, *The Reputation of St. Thomas Aquinas among English Protestant Thinkers of the Seventeenth Century* (Washington, 1948).

[28]See the shorter of the two exhortations in the Book of Common Prayer when notice is given of the celebration of the eucharist. "... if there be any of you, who by this means cannot quiet his own conscience herein, but requireth further comfort or counsel, let him come to me, or to some other discreet and learned Minister of God's

Word, and open his grief; that by the ministry of God's holy Word, *he may receive the benefit of absolution, together with spiritual counsel and advice, to the quieting of his conscience, and avoiding of all scruple and doubtfulness.*"

[29]cp. the description of the elements constitutive of the Church in Acts 2: 41-2; ". . . that they . . . were baptized . . . continued stedfastly in the apostles' doctrine and fellowship, and in breaking of bread, and in prayers."

[30](1587–1663); author of *De Obligatione Conscientiae* (1660) and *Cases of Conscience* (posthumous) and his *Sermons* are full of "practick divinity."

[31]*Conscience: Dictator or Guide?*, p. 67.

[32]Sermon III Ad Clerum, n.34; Vol. II, p. 105, and cp. Sermon IX ad Aulam, n.28, Vol. I, p. 242 (Oxford, 1884).

[33]For John Wilkins, Cromwell's brother-in-law and later Bishop of Chester, an exponent of the new scientific interests, see H. R. McAdoo *The Spirit of Anglicanism* (London and New York, 1965), pp. 203–41. Wilkins, who played a rôle in Latitudinarian theology, was influenced in his practical divinity by Aquinas and the Wisdom literature.

[34](1613–1667): Editions, R. Heber (1828), C. P. Eden (1850). *Holy Living* (1650), *Holy Dying* (1651), *Unum Necessarium* (1655) and *Ductor Dubitantium* (1660) are the main works on the subject.

[35]*Unum Necessarium*, Preface and C.III, 1.

[36]Ibid., p. 68.

[37]*Three Issues in Ethics* (1970), pp. 74–5.

[38]In the *Primacy of Charity in Moral Theology* (1959), Gilleman asks what alterations are urgently required in the structure (a word he frequently uses) if moral theology is to be rescued from its fundamental defect (cp. the Caroline reappraisal) which is that the manuals "do not formulate morality with sufficient reference to the interior life, which is left to a special branch of theology called spirituality" (loc. cit, p. xxxiii). His method is to construct a reappraisal in accordance with "authentic Thomistic theology" by way of showing charity—love to be formative, the soul of moral life, "the nourishing substance of all virtues," and the New Testament reference is constantly there as he formulates his principles. The effect of this on moral theology is to set it on a course which is "Christian, ontological and sacramental." Just because love is personalizing, it will be a personalist and *positive moral theology* taking into account the whole range of the individual Christian's experience and his membership in the Family of Christ: "Our purpose is to establish a method of formulating moral teaching and of molding it faithfully on Revelation and true Christian life. In this way, moral theology would find in each moral act the innermost and universal presence of charity" (ibid., p. xxxii).

[39]Introduction to *Ductor Dubitantium*.

[40]*English Spirituality* (1963), p. 239.

[41]Ibid., p. 248.

[42]*English Casuistical Divinity during the Seventeenth Century* (London, 1952), p. 65.

[43]*Works* (1829), I, 191. John Sharp (1645–1714) was Archbishop of York from 1691 and preached at the coronation of Queen Anne.

[44]2 Cor. 5:17: "So that if anyone be in Christ there is a new creation."

[45]*Unum Necessarium*, Chapter II, Section II.

[46]cf. *The Law of Christ*, I, 72–3, 257, 261.

[47]See his *Plain and Full Exposition of the Catechism* (1655).

[48]*Unum Necessarium*, Ch. I, Sect. IV.

[49]*A Practical Discourse of Repentance*, end of book and cf. Ch. I, Sect. III, by

William Payne (1650–1696).

[50]Edward Stillingfleet (1635–1699), *Works* (1710), V, 69, VI, 574. Roger Boyle, *Summa Theologiae Christianae* (1681), Pt. V, Sect. XIV. See the article by John E. Booty, "Contrition in Anglican Spirituality: Hooker, Donne and Herbert," in *Anglican Spirituality*, William J. Wolf, ed. (Wilton, Conn.: Morehouse-Barlow Co., Inc., 1982), pp. 25–48.

[51]*Unum Necessarium*, Ch. II.

[52]William Wake (1657–1737), Archbishop of Canterbury and ecumenist: see *Sermons and Discourses* (1716), Sermon VII.

[53]Robert South (1634–1716), cf. *Works* (1828 ed.), Vol. I., Sermon X; Vol. V., Sermon VI; Vol. VI, Sermon XXXVI.

[54]Sharp, *Works* (1829 ed.), Vol. II, Sermon VIII.

[55]*Works* (1710 ed.), Vol. VI, p. 574.

[56]Sanderson, *XXXV Sermons*, II, Ad Populum; Taylor, *Unum Necessarium*, Ch. II, Sect. 1.

[57]Francis White (1564?–1638), *Orthodox Faith and Way of the Church Explained*, Ch. II, Art. 13.

[58]*Unum Necessarium*, Ch. III, Sect. 4.

[59]*A New Introduction to Moral Theology* (1964), pp. 100–1.

[60]K. E. Kirk, *Some Principles of Moral Theology* (1920), p. 247.

[61]*XXI Sermons*, IV, Ad Aulam; *XXXV Sermons*, IV, Ad Populum.

[62]cf. Sanderson's *De Juramenti Obligatione*, Prae. III, Sect. XV.

[63]*Darwell Stone* (1943) by F. R. Cross, p. 225.

[64]*Unum Necessarium*, Ch. III.

[65]*Works*, Vol. I, Sermon X.

[66]*English Spirituality* (1963), p. 251.

[67]Ibid., p. 249.

[68]See the first book of Richard Hooker's *Ecclesiastical Polity* (1592, 1594?).

[69]Preface to *Ductor Dubitantium*.

[70]See his second discourse on conscience (Works, Vol. II).

[71]*Conscience: Dictator or Guide?*, pp. 175–176.

[72]Ibid., pp. 171–172.

[73]Richard Hooker, *Of the Laws of Ecclesiastical Polity*, Bk. I, Ch. I–IX.

[74]Kelly, *Conscience: Dictator or Guide?*, pp. 161–162.

[75]Preface to *Ductor Dubitantium*.

[76]*Works* (1823 ed.), Vol. II, Sermon XXIII.

[77]Joseph Hall (1574–1656), bishop of Norwich and ejected by the Puritans: Preface to *Resolutions and Decisions of Divers Practicall Cases of Conscience* (1649).

[78]cf. *Ductor Dubitantium*, Bk. I, Ch. I, Rule IX.

[79]For references to Wilkins, see his *Sermons* (1682) e.g. VI, VII.

[80]*Conscience: Dictator or Guide?*, p. 168.

[81]*Works*, Vol. II, second discourse on conscience.

[82]*Works* (1823 ed.), Vol. II, Sermon XXIII.

[83]Ibid., p. 61, and cf. pp. 173–174.

[84]*Ductor Dubitantium*, "Of a Doubtful Conscience," Rule VII.

[85]Preface to *Ductor Dubitantium*.

[86]*XXXV Sermons*, II, Ad Clerum, and cf. *XXXI Sermons*, XI, Ad Aulam, and *De Conscientiae Obligatione*, VI, Sect. xvii.

[87]*Ductor Dubitantium*, Bk. I, Ch. V, Rule V.

[88]Ibid., Ch. IV, Rule V.

[89]All references are from the second discourse on conscience (*Works*, II, 1829).

[90]Sharp amplifies that by safer side is meant "that which is freest from all dangers and inconveniences of all kinds whatsoever so as that shall always be the safer side of a doubtful case, which, after all things considered, doth appear to be the most agreeable to the man's duty in the circumstances he is in, or which is attended with the fewest absurdities and evil consequences of all sorts, and doth best serve all the interests, spiritual and temporal taking both together, that a wise and good man can purpose to himself." (loc. cit.).

[91]*The Law of Christ*, I, 182, 189.

[92]See *De Conscientiae Obligatione*, VI, sect. xvii; *XXXV Sermons*, II, Ad Clerum; *XXXI Sermons*, XI, Ad Aulam.

[93]Edward Reynolds, *The Life of Christ* (*Works*, 1826 ed., I, 320).

[94]*Episcopal Charge*, 1661.

[95]For an evaluation of these books, see H. R. McAdoo, *The Structure of Caroline Moral Theology* (1949), Ch. VI.

[96]P. H. Osmond, *Isaac Barrow, His Life and Times* (1944), p. 1.

[97]*Twenty-two Sermons selected from the Works of the Rev. Isaac Barrow* (1801 ed., second selection, Vol. II, Sermon XV, pp. 358–9).

[98]*A Priest to the Temple, or, The Country Parson* (1652), Ch. XXI.

[99]*The Life of Christ* (*Works*, 1826 ed., I, 368).

[100]*Twenty-Two Sermons* (1801 ed., Vol. II, Sermon XXII, p. 532).

[101]*The Divine Life*, Pt. I, Ch. V.

[102]*Holy Living* (*Works*, ed. Herber, III, I).

[103]*The Life of God in the Soul of Man* (1677).

[104]Ibid., Pt. I., Ch. I.

[105]*Liberal and Mystical Writings of W. Law*, p. 123.

[106]*The Life of God in the Soul of Man* (1677).

[107]Preface to the book.

[108]*A Companion to the Temple.*

[109]*The Great Exemplar* (1649), Sect. V, Discourse III, Of Meditation.

[110]William Beveridge, Dedication to *The Church Catechism Explained.*

[111]*Explanation of the 110th Psalm* (*Works*, II, 67).

[112]Foreword to *The Law of Christ*, I, vii.

Chapter 3. Politics and the Kingdom: The Legacy of the Anglican Left

[1]See F. D. Maurice, *Tracts on Christian Socialism, No. 1: Dialogue between Somebody (A Person of Respectability) and Nobody (The Author).* (London, 1850), p. 1.

[2]But of course they had to, because of the dearth of references to the Christian Socialist tradition in contemporary Anglican writing.

[3]E. R. Norman's claim that the Anglican radicals were merely aping secular intellectuals is mistaken. See his *Church and Society in England, 1770–1970* (Oxford, 1976).

[4]Studies which have emphasized Maurice's caution, such as Charles E. Raven's *Christian Socialism, 1848–1854* (London, 1920), and Torben Christensen's *Origin and*

History of Christian Socialism tr. Bjerglund Andersen (Aarhus, 1962), have obscured this point. Christensen's argument that Maurice had no influence on later thinkers will be shown by this article to be mistaken. See Christensen's *The Divine Order: A Study of F. D. Maurice's Theology* (Leiden, 1973), p. 300.

[5]Maurice, *Tracts on Christian Socialism*, p. 10.

[6]In his recent apology for political quietism, E. R. Norman treats the Incarnation as just such a brief incursion. See his *Christianity and the World Order* (Oxford, 1978), p. 77. A perceptive criticism of his view is E. L. Mascall, "Christianity Reinterpreted and Politicized," in *Christianity Reinterpreted*, Kenneth Leech, ed. (Penarth, 1979), pp. 7–12.

[7]See F. D. Maurice, *The Kingdom of Christ* (2 vols., London, 1903), II, 321; and idem., *On the Reformation of Society* (Southhampton, 1851), p. 23.

[8]The only published biography of Headlam is F. G. Bettany, "Stewart Headlam, A Biography" (London, 1926). A more recent study is Kenneth Leech, "Stewart Headlam and the Guild of St. Matthew" in *For Christ and the People*, ed. Maurice B. Reckitt (London, 1968). The most comprehensive summary of Headlam's life and work is my own doctoral dissertation *The Mass, the Masses, and the Music Hall: A Study of Stewart Headlam's Radical Anglicanism* (Columbia University, 1976).

[9]Bettany, *Stewart Headlam*, p. 22.

[10]See Stewart Headlam, *Priestcraft and Progress* (London, 1878), p. 64; and idem., *The Church Catechism and the Emancipation of Labour* (London, 1875), p. 3.

[11]Some of the Tractarians, most notably Dr. Pusey and W. G. Ward, called upon the Church to champion the cause of the poor. But for all their zeal, neither Pusey nor Ward advocated anything more radical than modest factory legislation and increased almsgiving.

[12]Stewart D. Headlam, *The Laws of Eternal Life* (London, 1888), p. 24.

[13]Ibid., p. 52.

[14]Stewart D. Headlam, *Theatres and Music Halls*, 2nd ed. (London, 1878).

[15]Some of the more notable members of the Guild were Percy Dearmer, Charles Marson (the author of a savage indictment of preordination training in England entitled *Huppim, Muppin, and Ard*), Thomas Hancock (a brilliant but neglected theologian), Frank Weston (later Bishop of Zanzibar), Conrad Noel, and Percy Widdington. The last two will be discussed in this chapter.

[16]My account of Headlam's theology draws heavily upin his commentary on the Prayer Book catechism, The Laws of Eternal Life.

[17]Stewart D. Headlam, *Muinicipal Puritanism* (London, 1905), p. 9.

[18]See Maurice B. Reckitt, *P.E.T. Widdrington* (London, 1961), pp. 31–32.

[19]Headlam was one of the few clergymen to stand by Charles Parnell after the latter's affair with Kitty O'Shea was revealed. He opposed efforts to drive prostitutes out of London music halls. He helped bail Oscar Wilde out of prison. But Headlam was no advocate of a new morality. He merely despised Pharisaism, and was indignant at the common prejudice that sexual sins were more loathsome than economic or political sins.

[20]Bettany, *Stewart Headlam*, p. 90.

[21]This was C. W. Stubbs, who became Bishop of Truro. After the Guild disbanded, Frank Weston became Bishop of Zanzibar.

[22]See Peter d'A. Jones, *The Christian Socialist Revival, 1877–1914* (Princeton, 1968), pp. 183–186. It is worth noting that many members of the Union were partly responsible for some of its accomplishments.

[23]Ibid., p. 177. But see also Headlam's and Thomas Hancock's criticism of the Union's statement of principles in the *Church Reformer* Nov., 1889), p. 246, and December 1889, p. 274.

²⁴See e.g. Francis Paget's argument that the natural order is sacramental (p. 353), Gore's observation that all nature is consecrated by the Holy Spirit (p. 273), and Scott Holland's view of human nature (p. 17). Interestingly enough, W.J.H. Campion's essay on Christianity and Politics is one of the most cautious contributions (Charles Gore, *Lux Mundi* [11th ed., New York, n.d.]).

²⁵Both Holland and Gore could be bitterly outspoken. "I hate the Church of England," the usually restrained Gore once exploded. He said the Anglican Establishment was "an ingeniously devised instrumentality for defeating the object which it is supposed to promote" (cited Maurice B. Reckitt, *Maurice to Temple* [London, 1946] p. 147).

²⁶For Huntington's early views see his *Human Society: Its Providential Structure, Relations, and Office* (New York, 1860). On his later radicalism see Arria S. Huntington, *Memoirs and Letters of Frederic Dan Huntington* (Boston and New York, 1906), pp. 353–55.

²⁷See James O. S. Huntington, "Philanthropy: Its Success and Failure," and "Philanthropy and Morality," in Jane Addams, et al., *Philanthropy and Social Progress* (New York, 1893), pp. 89–204.

²⁸See Richard B. Dressner, "William Dwight Porter Bliss's Christian Socialism," *Church History*, 47 (March, 1978), 66–82. See also Henry F. May, *Protestant Churches and Industrial America* (New York, 1949), pp. 186, 247; and D. G. Paz, "The Anglican Response to Urban Social Dislocation in Omaha," *Historical Magazine of the Protestant Episcopal Church*, 51 (June, 1982), 131–46.

²⁹When the 1908 Pan-Anglican Congress's committee on the Church and Human Society held its meeting, the Rev. Lord William Cecil confessed to feeling uncomfortable because he seemed to be the only speaker who did not believe in socialism. Pan-Anglican Congress, *Official Proceedings*, vol. 2: *The Church and Human Society* (London, 1908), p. 102. See also Conference of Bishops of the Anglican Communion, *Encyclical Letter from the Bishops with the Resolutions and Reports* (London, 1907), pp. 56–57, pp. 155–60.

³⁰Joseph Fletcher, *William Temple, Twentieth-Century Christian* (New York, 1963), p. 180.

³¹See, e.g., the report of the Archbishop's Fifth Committee of Inquiry, *Christianity and Industrial Problems* (1918), summarized in John Oliver, *The Church and Social Order* (London, 1968), pp. 48–56. See also Spencer Miller, Jr. and Joseph F. Fletcher, *The Church and Industry* (New York, 1930), pp. 232–50.

³²A striking example of this change was the fate of the Navvy Mission. Originally intended to evangelize and civilize dock workers, the mission merged with the Christian Social Union after the War to form the Industrial Christian Fellowship.

³³William Temple, *Essays on Christian Politics and Kindred Subjects* (London, 1927), p. 65.

³⁴The only biography of Widdrington is by Maurice B. Reckitt (see note 18 above).

³⁵Hence the interest in guild socialism, syndicalism, and G. K. Chesterton's distributivism: all of them efforts to pursue the goal of social justice without the necessity of the bureaucratic State.

³⁶P.E.T. Widdrington et al., *The Return of Christendom* (New York, 1922). Charles Gore wrote the introduction to the book but did not identify himself with its views. The epilogue was written by G. K. Chesterton, one of the last pieces he wrote as an Anglican.

³⁷See especially Lionel Thornton's essay, "The Necessity of Catholic Dogma," and Henry Slesser's "The Return of Dogma."

³⁸See Maurice B. Reckitt's essay, "The Idea of Christendom in Relation to Modern Society," and A. J. Carlyle, "The Mediaeval Theory of Social Order."

³⁹Thornton, p. 65.

[40]P.E.T. Widdrington, "The Return of 'The Kingdom of God,' " pp. 106–107, 102.

[41]Among the most interesting works of the Christendom Group are V. A. Demant, *God, Man, and Society* (London, 1932); and Maurice B. Reckitt, ed., *Prospect for Christendom* (London, 1946). The group also published a quarterly review, *Christendom: A Journal of Christian Sociology.*

[42]Reckitt, *Faith and Society,* pp. 252–257.

[43]Christopher Lasch makes this point forcefully in *The Culture of Narcissism* (New York, 1978), pp. xvi–xvii.

[44]Eric Mascall, "The Social Implications of Worship," in *Worship: Its Social Significance*, P.T.R. Kirk, ed. (London, 1939), p. 78.

[45]This is not to say that Widdrington and the others were indifferent to the problems faced by the parish priest. See, e.g., Reckitt, *Widdrington*, pp. 57–58.

[46]A fine admiring biography of Noel is Reg Groves, *Conrad Noel and the Thaxted Movement* (London, 1967). An excellent introduction to Noel's theology is Robert Woodifield, "Conrad Noel, Catholic Crusader," in *For Christ and the People*, pp. 135–175. Also valuable, though poorly edited, is Conrad Noel, *An Autobiography*, ed. Sidney Dark (London, 1945).

[47]The tourists are still coming. Thaxted is the only Christian Socialist shrine recommended in *English on Fifteen Dollars A Day.*

[48]Groves, *Conrad Noel*, pp. 221, 331.

[49]Reckitt, *Widdrington*, p. 91.

[50]Reg Groves, ed., *The Catholic Crusade, 1918–1936* (London, 1970), pp. 9, 13. This is a text of the Crusade manifesto.

[51]See Conrad Noel, *Life of Jesus* (London, 1937). For his understanding of patristic and medieval social thought see his *Socialism in Church History* (London, 1910).

[52]Woodifield, "Conrad Noel," pp. 155–158; Conrad Noel, *Jesus the Heretic* (London, 1939), pp. 219–220.

[53]Woodifield, "Conrad Noel," p. 152; Groves, *Catholic Crusade*, p. 16; Noel, *Jesus the Heretic*, p. 222.

[54]The best introduction to Temple's views is his *Christianity and Social Order* (London, 1942; reprint ed., London, 1976). Ronald Preston's introductory essay is very helpful in unravelling Temple's elusive politics. See also Temple's *Essays* cited earlier, and his *Hope of a New World* (New York, 1942), pp. 17, 52. The most thorough examination of the development of Temple's political ideas is Robert Craig, *Social Concern in the Thought of William Temple* (London, 1963). Those who think that Temple's conservatism was merely the caution of a conscientious bishop should ponder the remarkable exchange of letters between Temple and a vociferous Right-wing critic in William Temple, *Some Lambeth Letters* (London, 1963), pp. 93–95.

[55]See Stewart D. Headlam, *The Socialist's Church* (London, 1907), pp. 12–13, 29.

[56]"The Hymn of the Universal Social Revolution" is the title of a sermon by Thomas Hancock, the text of which is printed in the *Church Reformer*, November 1886, pp. 244–46.

[57]Thomas Merton, Daniel Berrigan, and the Sojourners Group have all made this very point in recent years. One of the most forceful advocates of this bond between prayer and action among Anglicans is Kenneth Leech. See, e.g. the treatment of prayer and politics in his *True Prayer* (London, 1980), pp. 69–83. Leech has played an important part in the establishment of Jubilee Groups in Britain and the United States. These groups are autonomous and informal gatherings of Anglicans dedicated to reviving the Christian Socialist tradition in the Anglican communion.

Chapter 4. Early Evangelical Ethics: Preparing for Today

[1]For details of the Clapham Sect see E. M. Howse, *Saints in Politics: the 'Clapham Sect' and the growth of freedom* (London and Toronto, 1971). Members included

Henry Thornton M. P. and banker; John Venn, rector of Clapham; Charles Grant of the East India Company; William Wilberforce M. P.; Isaac Milner, Provost of Queen's College, Cambridge; Zachary Macaulay, founder of the colony of Sierre Leone and editor of *The Christian Observer*, together with others. *The Christian Observer*, financed by the Sect, began to appear in January 1802 and was an important publication for over half the century.

[2]*C.O.* (1803), pp. 349–50.

[3]*C.O.* (1805), p. 696.

[4]A. Pollard & M. Hennell, *Charles Simeon (1759–1836)* (London, 1959), pp. 84, 115–8, 126–7 & 139.

[5]*C.O.* (1802), p. 789.

[6]*C.O.* (1803), preface, p. vii.

[7]J. Bateman, *The Life of Daniel Wilson* (London, 1860), Vol. 1, pp. 205–6. See also C. Simeon, *Horae Homileticae* (London, 1846), Vol. XVI, Discourse 1933.

[8]See Pollard & Hennell, *op.cit.*, pp. 29ff.

[9]C. E. Raven, *Christian Socialism* (London, 1920).

[10]Howse, *op.cit.*, pp. 134–5.

[11]Cf. the comments of R. Anstey, *The Atlantic Slave Trade and British Abolition* (London, 1975), pp. 158–162. Anstey has some useful insights into the mind of Evangelicals.

[12]For Scott see the *Dictionary of National Biography* and A. C. Downer, *Thomas Scott, the Commentator* (London, 1909). See also the perceptive comments on Sir James Stephen, *Ecclesiastical Biography* (London, 1849), Vol. 2, p. 99.

[13]Cited by Howse, *op.cit.*, p. 119. A modern biography of Wilberforce is by John Pollock, *Wilberforce* (London, 1977).

[14]See P. Toon, *Evangelical Theology 1833–1856* (London and Atlanta, 1979) and the various sources there listed and cited.

[15]This is found in many sources, most particularly in the general acceptance of *The Lausanne Covenant* (1974) and in the documents produced at the Keele (1967) and Nottingham (1977) Evangelical Congresses. There are now (late 1982) the signs of change towards a holistic view.

[16]For Gisborne see the *D.N.B.* and note the comments of Sir James Stephen, *op.cit.* Vol. 2, p. 199 on his powerful oratory.

[17]The 5th edition appeared in 1798. Other books by him on moral philosophy which had wide readership were *An Enquiry into the Duties of Men in the higher and middle classes of society in Great Britain* (1794) and *An Enquiry into the duties of the Female Sex* (1792).

[18]*Principles* (5th ed), pp. 21–22.

[19]Ibid., pp. 101–2.

[20]Ibid., pp. 198–9.

[21]Ibid., p. 201–2.

[22]See e.g. Ian Bradley, *The Call to Seriousness: The Evangelical Impact on the Victorians* (London, 1976).

[23]See e.g. G.B.A.M. Finlayson, *The Seventh Earl of Shaftesbury* (London, 1981).

[24]W. J. Conybeare, *Essays Ecclesiastical and Social* (London, 1855), Essay 2.

[25]I wish to thank the Rev. G. S. Forster, Rector of Northenden, Manchester, for help in providing the material in this section.

Chapter 5. Thoughts After Lambeth

[1]George Malcolm Thomson, *The Lambeth Conference*, Criterion Miscellany.

[2]Some time ago, during the consulship of Lord Brentford, I suggested that if we

were to have a Censorship at all, it ought to be at Lambeth Palace; but I suppose that the few persons who read my words thought that I was trying to be witty.

[3]i.e., in 1931.

[4]Under the heading *Nature of Space: Professor Einstein's Change of Mind*, I read in The Times of 6th February 1931, the following news from New York: "At the close of a 90-minute talk on his unified field theory to a group of physicists and astronomers in the Carnegie Institution at Pasadena yesterday, Professor Einstein startled his hearers by smilingly declaring, 'Space can never be anything similar to the old symmetrical spherical space theory.'

"That theory, he said, was not possible under the new equations. Thus he swept aside both his own former hypothesis that the universe and the space it occupied were both static and uniform, and the concept of his friend the Dutch astronomer, De Sitter, that though the universe was static it was non-uniform, which De Sitter had based upon the hypothesis that instead of matter determining space it was space that determined matter, and hence also the size of the universe.

"Astronomers who heard Professor Einstein make his declaration said it was an indication that he had accepted the work of two American scientists, Dr. Edwin P. Hubble, an astronomer in the Mount Wilson Observatory, and Dr. Richard C. Hace Tollman, a physicist of the California Institute of Technology, who hold that the universe is non-static, although uniformly distributed in space. In the belief of Dr. Hubble and Dr. Tollman the universe is constantly expanding and matter is constantly being converted into energy."

Our next revelation about the attitude of Science to Religion will issue, I trust, from Dr. Hubble and Dr. Tollman.

[5]See *Theology*, December, 1930, p. 307. It has been pointed out to me that here *dissimulatio* should perhaps be translated as "tactfulness" rather than "dissimulation"; but a tactfulness which consists primarily in not asking awkward questions seems to me to be pretty close to simulation and dissimulation.

Chapter 6. Revising Anglican Moral Theology

[1]Robert M. Cooper and W. Taylor Stevenson, *Anglican Theological Review* 61 (1979) 1:5.

[2]Bernard Lonergan, "The Transition from a Classicist World-View to Historical Mindedness," *Law For Liberty*, ed. James Biechler (Baltimore: Helicon Press, 1967), pp. 126–133.

[3]See Henry Davis, *Moral and Pastoral Theology*, 4 vols. (New York: Sheed & Ward, 1935); Arthur Preuss, *A Handbook of Moral Theology Based on the "Lehrbuch der Moraltheologie" of the late Anthony Kock;* 5 vols. (St. Louis: B. Herder, 1925); and Thomas Slater, *A Manual of Moral Theology for English-Speaking Countries* (New York: Benzinger Bros., 1908).

[4]James Skinner, *Synopsis of Moral and Ascetical Theology* (London: Kegan Paul, Trench & Co., 1882).

[5]Gordon R. Dunstan, Foreword to *The Vision of God*, by Kenneth E. Kirk, abridged ed. (Greenwood, S.C.: Attic Press, 1977).

[6]Kenneth E. Kirk, *Some Principles of Moral Theology* (London: Longmans, 1920), p. viii. Hereafter cited as *Principles*.

[7]John J. Elmendorf, *Elements of Moral Theology Based on the Summa Theologiae of St. Thomas Aquinas* (New York: James Pott, 1892); and William Walter Webb, *The Cure of Souls, A Manual for the Clergy* (New York: James Pott, 1892).

[8]Edward B. Pusey, *The Abbé Gaume's Manual for Confessors* (London: James Parker & Co., 1878).

[9]Francis J. Hall and Frank H. Hallock, *Moral Theology* (New York: Longmans, 1924).

[10]Skinner, *Synopsis*, p. viii.

[11]Kirk, *Principles*, p. 10; see also Kenneth E. Kirk, "Moral Theology," in *The Study of Theology*, ed. Kirk (London: Hodder & Stoughton, 1939), pp. 363–405.

[12]James M. Gustafson, "Theology and Ethics," *Christian Ethics and the Community* (Philadelphia: Pilgrim Press, 1971), pp. 83–100; and idem, *Christ and the Moral Life* (New York: Harper & Row, 1968), pp. 1–10.

[13]Kirk, *Principles*, pp. 14, 15.

[14]Ibid., p. 9.

[15]Ibid.

[16]Ibid.

[17]Frederick Olafson, *Principles and Persons* (Baltimore: Johns Hopkins Press, 1967), pp. 1–104.

[18]Kirk, *Principles*, p. 38.

[19]Olafson, *Principles and Persons*, p. 4.

[20]Kirk, *Principles*, p. 181.

[21]Ibid., p. ix.

[22]Ibid., p. 185.

[23]Kirk, "Moral Theology," p. 363.

[24]Kirk, *Principles*, p. 10; see Kenneth E. Kirk, *The Vision of God* (London: Longmans, 1931); and Kirk, "Moral Theology."

[25]Ibid., p. 183.

[26]Kenneth E. Kirk, *Ignorance, Faith and Conformity* (London: Longmans, 1920), p. 1.

[27]Kenneth E. Kirk, *Conscience and its Problems* (London: Longmans, 1927), p. xix.

[28]R. C. Mortimer, *The Elements of Moral Theology* (London: Adams & Charles Black, 1947), p. v.

[29]Herbert Waddams, *A New Introduction to Moral Theology* (London: SCM Press, 1964; revised ed., 1972); and Lindsay Dewar, *An Outline of Anglican Moral Theology* (London: A. R. Mowbray, 1968).

[30]See H. R. McAdoo, *The Structure of Caroline Moral Theology* (London: Longmans, 1949); Thomas Wood, *English Casuistical Divinity During the Seventeenth Century* (London: S.P.C.K., 1952); and Kevin T. Kelly, *Conscience: Dictator or Guide? A Study in Seventeenth Century English Protestant Moral Theology* (London: Geoffrey Chapman, 1967).

[31]See Kirk, *Conscience and Its Problems*, pp. xi–xxiii; Dewar, *Anglican Moral Theology*, pp. 1–20 and Waddams, *Introduction to Moral Theology*, p. 34.

[32]On this diversity see C. F. Allison, *The Rise of Moralism* (London: S.P.C.K., 1966).

[33]McAdoo, *Caroline Moral Theology*, p. 4.

[34]H. R. McAdoo, *The Spirit of Anglicanism, A Survey of Anglican Moral Method in the Seventeenth Century* (New York: Charles Scribner's Sons, 1965), p. v.

[35]Ibid., pp. v, vi.

[36]McAdoo, *Caroline Moral Theology*, p. 6.

[37]Stephen W. Sykes, *The Integrity of Anglicanism* (New York: Seabury Press, 1978), p. 87.

[38]Charles Curran, "Natural Law," *Themes in Fundamental Moral Theology* (Notre Dame: University of Notre Dame Press, 1977), pp. 27–80; and David Little, "Calvin and the Prospect for a Christian Theory of Natural Law," in *Norm and Context in Christian Ethics*, ed. Gene H. Outka and Paul Ramsey (New York:

Charles Scribner's Sons, 1968), pp. 175–198.

[39]McAdoo, *Caroline Moral Theology*, p. 23; and see Richard Hooker, *Of the Laws of Ecclesiastical Polity*, ed. Georges Edelen (Cambridge, Mass.: Belknap Press, 1977), I: 11, 12.

[40]Robert Sanderson, *De Obligations Conscientiae*, ed. William Whewell (London: Cambridge University Press, 1831), I: 2; Kelly, *Conscience: Dictator or Guide?*, p. 54; see also McAdoo, *Caroline Moral Theology*, p. 27.

[41]McAdoo, *Caroline Moral Theology*, pp. 37, 38.

[42]Jeremy Taylor, *Ductor Dubitantium, or, The Rule of Conscience*, ed. Alexander Taylor (London: Longman, Brown, Green, & Longmans, 1851), bk. II, chap. 1, rule 1, par. 8, 31.

[43]Ibid., par. 59.

[44]Ibid., par. 36.

[45]See James M. Gustafson, *Protestant and Roman Catholic Ethics* (Chicago: University of Chicago Press, 1978), esp. pp. 1–29; and Outka and Ramsey, *Norm and Context in Christian Ethics*, pp. 168–322.

[46]See Sykes, *Integrity of Anglicanism*, p. 68.

[47]William J. Wolf, "Frederick Denison Maurice," in *The Spirit of Anglicanism*, ed. William J. Wolf (Wilton, Conn.: Morehouse-Barlow Co., Inc., 1979), pp. 49–98; see also H. Richard Niebuhr, *Christ and Culture* (New York: Harper & Row, 1951), pp. 218–229; and David Tracy, *Blessed Rage for Order* (New York: Seabury Press, 1975), p. 37, n. 24.

[48]McAdoo, *Caroline Moral Theology*, p. 15.

[49]See notes 11 and 12 above.

[50]Lonergan, "Transition"; also see Curran, "Natural Law," pp. 46–49.

[51]H. Richard Niebuhr, "The Center of Value," *Radical Monotheism and Western Culture* (New York: Harper & Row, 1960), pp. 100–113.

[52]Lonergan, "Transition," p. 127.

[53]Ibid., pp. 127, 128.

[54]Ibid., p. 130.

[55]Alfred Schutz, *Collected Papers I* (The Hague: Martinus Nijhoff, 1971), pp. 218–222.

[56]Lonergan, "Transition," p. 128.

[57]Ibid., p. 129.

[58]Gustafson, *Ethics*, pp. 153–156.

[59]See John Horgan, comp., *Humanae Vitae and the Bishops* (Shannon, Ireland: Irish University Press, 1972).

[60]Mortimer, *Moral Theology*, p. 178.

[61]Kirk, *Conscience and Its Problems*, pp. 290–294.

[62]Waddams, *Introduction to Moral Theology*, pp. 148–153; Dewar, *Anglican Moral Theology*, pp. 74–79.

[63]Dewar, *Anglican Moral Theology*, p. 78.

[64]Waddams, *Introduction to Moral Theology*, pp. 144, 145.

[65]See Anthony Kosnik et al., *Human Sexuality: New Directions in American Catholic Thought* (New York: Paulist Press, 1977), pp. 65, 66, 219–229; see also Philip S. Keane, *Sexual Morality: A Catholic Perspective* (New York: Paulist Press, 1977), pp. 59, 60.

[66]Curran, "Sin and Sensuality," *Fundamental Moral Theology*, pp. 165–190.

[67]Curran, "Conscience," *Fundamental Moral Theology*, pp. 191–231.

[68]Dewar, *Anglican Moral Theology*, pp. 43–64; and Waddams, *Introduction to*

Moral Theology, pp. 63–92.

[69]H. Richard Niebuhr, *The Responsible Self* (New York: Harper & Row, 1963), p. 65.

[70]See Curran, "Conscience"; and Bernard Häring, *Free and Faithful in Christ* (New York: Seabury Press, 1973), pp. 223–301.

[71]See also Kirk, *Principles,* p. 10.

[72]Kirk, "Moral Theology," p. 363; see also Waddams, *Introduction to Moral Theology,* pp. 24–30.

[73]Bernard Häring, *The Law of Christ,* 3 vols. (Westminster, Md.: Newman Press, 1961–66; first published in German in 1954); on this change see Charles Curran, "Catholic Moral Theology Today," *New Perspectives in Moral Theology* (Notre Dame: Fides Publishers, 1974), pp. 1–46, reprinted from *Theological Studies* 34 (1973) 3: 446–467; Gustafson, *Ethics;* Albert Jonsen, *Responsibility in Modern Religious Ethics* (Washington: Corpus, 1968); Richard McCormick, "Notes on Moral Theology," *Theological Studies,* 1965–present; and Timothy E. O'Connell, *Principles for a Catholic Morality* (New York: Seabury Press, 1978).

[74]Häring, *Free and Faithful in Christ,* p. 59.

[75]See Curran, "Conscience"; and Gustafson, *Christ and the Moral Life.*

[76]See Gustafson, *Ethics,* esp. pp. 126–137.

[77]See Walter M. Abbott, ed., *"Gaudium et Spes,* Pastoral Constitution on the Church in the Modern World," *"Lumen Gentium,* Dogmatic Constitution on the Church," *The Documents of Vatican II* (Racine, Wisconsin: American Press, 1966); and David Hollenbach, "A Prophetic Church and the Catholic Sacramental Imagination," in *The Faith that Does Justice,* ed. John C. Haughey (New York: Paulist Press, 1977), pp. 234–263.

Chapter 7. The *Via Media* as Theological Method

[1]John K. Yost, "Hugh Latimer's Reform Program, 1529–1536, and the Intellectual Origins of the Anglican *Via Media,*" *Anglican Theological Review,* 1971.

[2]Henry R. McAdoo, *The Spirit of Anglicanism* (New York: Scribners, 1965), p. 1.

[3]Richard Hooker, *Of the Laws of Ecclesiastical Polity,* The Folger Library Edition of the Works of Richard Hooker (Cambridge, Mass.: Harvard University Press, 1977), I.7.2.

[4]See: *The Spirit of Anglicanism,* ed. William J. Wolf (Wilton, Conn.: Morehouse-Barlow Co., Inc., 1979), ch. 1.

[5]Richard Hooker, *Of the Laws of Ecclesiastical Polity,* I.8.2.

[6]Ibid., I.8.3.

[7]Ibid., I.5.1.

[8]Jeremy Taylor, *Ductor Dubitantium,* Part I. vol. IX of *The Whole Works* (London: Longman, Brown, Green & Longmans, 1855), p. 55.

[9]Ibid., p. 319.

[10]Taylor, *Ductor Dubitantium,* Part II, p. 617.

[11]Taylor, *The Whole Works,* vol. IX, p. 356.

[12]Joseph Butler, *Five Sermons Preached at the Rolls Chapel* (Indianapolis: Bobbs-Merrill, The Library of Liberal Arts, 1950 ed.), p. 21.

[13]Ibid., p. 31.

[14]John Henry Newman, *The Via Media of the Anglican Church,* Volume I (Westminster, MD: Christian Classics, 1978), p. 16.

[15]Ibid., p. 23.

[16]Ibid., p. 25.

[17]Ibid., p. 129.

[18]Ibid., p. 133.

[19]Owen Chadwick, *The Victorian Church*, Part I, third edition (London: A. & C. Black, 1979), p. 169.

[20]Frederick Denison Maurice, *The Kingdom of Christ*, Volume 2 (London: SCM Press, 1958), p. 331.

[21]A key passage in this regard is found in Volume 1 of *The Kingdom:* "All these notions, it seems to me, assume that the words 'system' and 'method' are synonymous, and that if the first is wanting in the Scriptures the last must be wanting also. Now to me these words seem not only synonymous, but the greatest contraries imaginable: the one indicating that which is most opposed to life, freedom, variety; and the other that without which they cannot exist." (Maurice, *The Kingdom of Christ*, Volume 1, London: SCM Press, 1958 edition, p. 236.)

[22]F. D. Maurice, *Social Morality* (London: Macmillan, 1869), p. 434.

[23]Ian T. Ramsey, *On Being Sure in Religion* (London: The Athlone Press, 1963), p. 75.

[24]William Temple, *Nature, Man and God* (1964 ed., London: Macmillan, 1934), pp. 58–59.

[25]William Temple, *Men's Creatrix* (1961 ed., London: Macmillan, 1917), p. 179.

[26]William Temple, *Christus Veritas* (1962 ed., London: Macmillan, 1924), p. 29; p. 30.

[27]Ibid., p. 33.

[28]Temple, *Nature, Man and God*, p. 208.

[29]William Temple, *Christianity in Thought and Practice* (New York: Morehouse Publishing Co., 1936), pp. 83–84.

[30]Temple, *Nature, Man and God*, p. 520.

[31]William Temple, *Christianity and the Social Order* (1977 ed., New York: Seabury Press, 1942), p. 82.

[32]See Temple, *Nature, Man and God*, pp. 410–11.

[33]Temple, *Nature, Man and God*, p. 405.

[34]Herbert Hensley Henson, *Christian Morality* (Oxford: Oxford University Press), pp. 29–30.

[35]Kenneth E. Kirk, *Some Principles of Moral Theology* (London: Longmans, Green & Co., 1920), p. 183.

[36]Ibid., p. 184.

[37]Austin Farrer, *Finite and Infinite* (Westminster, Dacre Press, 1943), p. 145.

[38]Ibid., p. 156.

[39]For a complete bibliography of Ian Ramsey's published works see Jerry Gill, *Ian Ramsey: To Speak Responsibly of God* (London: George Allen & Unwin, Ltd., 1976). His most noted books were: *Religious Language* (1957), *On Being Sure in Religion* (1963), *Models and Mystery* (1964) and *Christian Discourse* (1965).

[40]See Ian T. Ramsey, ed., *Christian Ethics and Contemporary Philosophy* (New York: Macmillan, 1966), "Moral Judgments and God's Commands" and "Towards a Rehabilitation of Natural Law."

[41]Ian T. Ramsey, ed., *Christian Ethics and Contemporary Philosophy* (New York: Macmillan, 1966), p. 166.

[42]Ibid., p. 171.

[43]John A. T. Robinson, *Honest to God* (Philadelphia: Westminster Press, 1963), p. 114.

[44]Ibid., p. 118.

⁴⁵Joseph Fletcher, *Situation Ethics* (Philadelphia: Westminster Press, 1966), p. 30.

⁴⁶Fletcher's theological foundation, "we only serve God by serving our neighbors" (*Situation Ethics*, p. 158) at best involves a radically limited concept of God. It is better understood as a pantheistic viewpoint or a disguised atheism.

⁴⁷James A. Pike, *Doing the Truth* (New York: Macmillan, 1965), p. 169.

⁴⁸Herbert Waddams, *A New Introduction to Moral Theology*, rev. ed. (London: SCM Press, 1964 and 1972), see especially p. 56 ff.

⁴⁹Londsay Dewar, *Moral Theology in the Modern World* (London, A. R. Mowbray Co., Ltd., 1964), p. 113.

⁵⁰John Macquarrie, *Three Issues in Ethics* (New York: Harper and Row, 1970), pp. 114–115.

⁵¹John Macquarrie, *Principles of Christian Theology*, 2nd ed. (New York: Charles Scribners, 1977), pp. 85–86; see also pp. 57–86. Particular attention should be given to concepts such as "unveiling" and "concealed" which are so prominent a part of Heidegger's apparatus.

⁵²Ibid., pp. 504–507.

⁵³Aristotle, *Nicomachean Ethics*, Book II, 1105 b: 9–12.

⁵⁴Paul L. Lehmann, *Ethics in A Christian Context* (New York City: Harper and Row, 1963), see especially p. 315 ff.

⁵⁵Lehmann indicates that he has not read and studied the primary texts of Hooker, Taylor and Sanderson but has relied upon secondary sources for his opinions about them. Such a shoddy procedure is not worthy of serious attention.

⁵⁶James M. Gustafson, *Ethics from a Theocentric Perspective* (Chicago: University of Chicago Press, 1981), pp. 62–68.

⁵⁷John Macquarrie, *Principles of Christian Theology*, 2nd ed. (New York: Charles Scribner's Sons, 1977), p. 34.

Chapter 8. Anglicans and the New Morality

¹Joseph Fletcher, *Situation Ethics: The New Morality* (Philadelphia: The Westminster Press, 1966), p. 26.

²Representative samples of the writings of these defenders of situation ethics would include James Pike, *You and the New Morality—74 Cases* (New York: Harper & Row, 1964); W. Norman Pittenger, *Loving Says It All* (New York: The Pilgrim Press, 1978); O. Sydney Barr, *The Christian New Morality: A Biblical Study of Situation Ethics* (New York: Oxford University Press, 1969); John A. T. Robinson, *Christian Freedom in a Permissive Society* (Philadelphia: The Westminster Press, 1970); Douglas Rhymes, *No New Morality* (Indianapolis: Bobbs-Merrill, 1964); Harry A. Williams, "Theology and Self-Awareness," in A. R. Vidler, ed.; *Soundings: Essays in Christian Understanding* (Cambridge: The Cambridge University Press, 1963).

³William A. Spurrier, *Natural Law and the Ethics of Love: A New Synthesis* (Philadelphia: Westminster Press, 1974).

⁴The most systematic delineation of the failure of Christian social ethics in the modern era is found in R. H. Tawney, *Religion and the Rise of Capitalism* (New York: Harcourt, Brace & World, Inc., 1926).

⁵Kenneth Kirk, *Some Principles of Moral Theology* (London: Longmans, Green and Co., Ltd., 1926), pp. 5 and 6.

⁶Kirk, op. cit., pp. 7 and 8.

⁷See Robert C. Mortimer, *The Elements of Moral Theology* (London: A. and C. Black, 1947).

⁸See Herbert Waddems, *A New Introduction to Moral Theology* (New York:

Seabury Press, 1965).

[9]Fletcher, op. cit., p. 69.

[10]See Mark 12:28–34, also Matt. 22:34–40 and Luke 10:25–28.

[11]James A. Pike, *A Time for Christian Candor* (New York: Harper & Row, 1964), pp. 8 and 9.

[12]Pike, op. cit., p. 24.

[13]J.A.T. Robinson, *Honest to God* (Philadelphia: Westminster Press, 1963).

[14]Robinson, *Honest to God*, pp. 39 and 40, admits that this conception of God was never actually held by informed orthodox theologians but was instead a popular misunderstanding.

[15]*Honest to God*, p. 105. Robinson emphasized the inseparability of theology and ethics by stating that "assertions about God are in the last analysis assertions about Love—about the ground and meaning of personal relationships."

[16]*No New Morality*, pp. 40 and 91.

[17]Five years before the publication of *Honest to God*, William Nichols delineated the failure of Anglican theology to speak to contemporary questions in any depth: "On Living in the Twentieth Century" in D. M. Paton, ed., *Essays in Anglican Self-Criticism* (London: SCM Press, 1958).

[18]*Situation Ethics*, pp. 12 and 13.

[19]See especially *Situation Ethics*, pp. 36 and 37. Wilford O. Cross, "The Moral Revolution: An Analysis, Critique, and Appreciation," in Harvey Cox, ed., *The Situation Ethics Debate* (Philadelphia: The Westminster Press, 1968), p. 169, offers this useful comment upon the contribution of Joseph Fletcher: "Situationism merely . . . substitutes another method of casuistry to help us in our doubtful and perplexed states of indecision. Professor Fletcher states this when he insists that his ethic is not a system, but a methodology; Situationism is a new method of casuistry to be put alongside of tutiorism, probabiliorism, and probabilism. It gives us the guiding maxim Do the most loving thing because upon this hang all the Law and the Prophets. This maxim is the test of the rightness of our conscience and of the authenticity of the moral law. The primacy of charity has been reaffirmed as the spring of morality."

[20]Douglas A. Rhymes, *Prayer in the Secular City* (London: Lutterworth Press, 1967).

[21]Thomas Luckmann, *The Invisible Religion: The Problem of Religion in Modern Society* (London: Macmillan Co., 1967).

[22]Ibid., p. 105.

[23]Ibid., p. 109.

[24]*Situation Ethics*, p. 158.

[25]*Some Principles of Moral Theology*, p. 131.

[26]Eph. 2:206–21.

Chapter 9. Contraception and Natural Law: A Half-Century of Anglican Moral Reflection

[1]I acknowledge with deep appreciation and thanks the research assistance for this paper by the Reverend Mark David Haverland.

[2]For details, see H. R. McAdoo, *The Structure of Caroline Moral Theology* (London, 1949).

[3]Cited in Ian T. Ramsey, *Christian Ethics and Contemporary Philosophy* (London, 1966), pp. 12–13.

[4]Joseph Fletcher, *Moral Responsibility* (Philadelphia, 1967), pp. 59, 60, 61, 72. This chapter was originally titled "Anglican Theology and the Ethics of Natural

Law" and appeared in *Christian Social Ethics in a Changing World*, ed. John C. Bennett (New York, 1966).

[5]For present purposes, I will define contraception as a directly willed prevention (a) of conception or (b) of the possibility of conception or (c) of the necessary precondition(s) for conception, a prevention which modifies or is meant to modify an act of sexual intercourse in its circumstance(s) or result(s). This definition will take account of contraception whether practiced by fertile or infertile persons by locating the meaning of the action in both intention and practice. I should underscore that contraception is *not* "birth control" and that abortifacients and abortion are beyond the scope of this paper. I will also prescind from contraception via sterilization.

[6]Richard Hooker, *The Laws of Ecclesiastical Polity* (London, 1594), I.ii.1.

[7]*The First and Second Prayerbooks of Edward VI*, intro. Douglas Harrison (London, 1968), p. 252. This formulation remained unchanged in subsequent English Prayerbooks until the twentieth century. The 1979 revision of the American *Book of Common Prayer* stands in somewhat (if not stark) contrast: "The union of husband and wife in heart, body, and mind is intended by God for their mutual joy; for the help and comfort given one another in prosperity and adversity; and, *when it is God's will*, for the procreation of children and their nurture in the knowledge and love of the Lord. Therefore marriage is not to be entered into unadvisedly or lightly, but reverently, deliberately, and in accordance with the purposes for which it was instituted by God." Cf. The *Book of Common Prayer* (New York, 1979), p. 423. Underscoring mine. There is not only a reordering of the priorities but qualification of them as well, further indicated by the *optional* prayer: "Bestow on them, *if it is your will*, the gift and heritage of children, and the grace to bring them up to know you, to love you, and to serve you. Amen." Ibid., p. 429. Underscoring mine.

[8]I am aware that some imprecision currently attaches to this term and its cognates, and that it remains a matter of debate among scientists and philosophers alike whether conception occurs at fertilization or nidation. But since I have excluded both abortifacients and abortion, whether induced or spontaneous, from the scope of this paper, I will forbear this discussion as well. Consistent with my earlier definition of contraception, I will for present purposes regard conception as synonymous with fertilization and impregnation.

[9]K. E. Kirk, *Conscience and Its Problems* (London, 1949), pp. 291–293.

[10]*The Lambeth Conference 1930: Encyclical Letter from the Bishops with Resolutions and Reports* (London, 1930), p. 43. The text of the two resolutions is as follows: "13. The Conference emphasises the truth that the sexual instinct is a holy thing implanted by God in human nature. It acknowledges that intercourse between husband and wife as the consummation of marriage has a value of its own within that sacrament, and that thereby married love is enhanced and its character strengthened. Further, seeing that the primary purpose for which marriage exists is the procreation of children, it believes that this purpose as well as the paramount importance in married life of deliberate and thoughtful self-control should be the governing considerations in that intercourse" (p. 43).

"15. Where there is a clearly felt moral obligation to limit or avoid parenthood, the method must be decided on Christian principles. The primary and obvious method is complete abstinence from intercourse (as far as may be necessary) in a life of discipline and self-control lived in the power of the Holy Spirit. Nevertheless in those cases where there is such a clearly-felt moral obligation to limit or avoid parenthood, and where there is a morally sound reason for avoiding complete abstinence, the Conference agrees that other methods may be used, provided that this is done in the light of the same Christian principles. The Conference records its strong condemnation of the use of any methods of conception-control from motives of selfishness, luxury, or mere convenience" (pp. 43–44).

[11]*The Lambeth Conference 1958: The Encyclical Letter from the Bishops Together With the Resolutions and Reports* (London, 1958), p. 1.57. The reference is to

Resolution 115: "The Conference believes that the responsibility for deciding upon the number and frequency of children has been laid by God upon the consciences of parents everywhere: that this planning, in such ways as are mutually acceptable to husband and wife in Christian conscience, is a right and important factor in Christian family life and should be the result of positive choice before God. . . ."

¹²"The Family in Contemporary Society," in Ramsey, op. cit., pp. 340–381.

¹³Ibid., p. 366.

¹⁴Ibid., pp. 356–6. One wonders whether a certain irony is not intended in the last clause of this statement inasmuch as the report clearly favors, at times, separating the latter from the former.

¹⁵*The Lambeth Conference 1968: Resolutions and Reports* (London, 1968), p. 36.

¹⁶Cf. R. C. Mortimer, *The Elements of Moral Theology* (New York, 1960), pp. 8–14.

¹⁷Ibid., p. 14.

¹⁸Ibid., p. 74. Mortimer's example is "to kill a baby in the womb to save the mother's life."

¹⁹First is the moral intuition: "we cannot contemplate the possibility that it might ever be in accordance with the will of God that a child should be punished by torture. . . . We may attempt to justify our convictions of (such) points by argument, but the argument is obviously *post factum* . . . nothing in the argument adds to the strength of the conviction. . . ." Second are utilitarian considerations as to the incompatibility of an action with social welfare or some other ideal, whose value is intuited. Third is revelation which establishes, for example, duties of prayer, fasting, and almsgiving. And finally is history, or "the progress of Christian civilisation" which "has established certain moral positions from which it seems impossible that it should ever recede," (e.g., that slavery is wrong). Kirk, ibid., pp. 72–74.

²⁰Ibid., pp. 75–76.

²¹Ibid., p. 76.

²²Ibid., p. 77.

²³Ibid., p. 79.

²⁴Ibid., p. 78.

²⁵Ibid., p. 79.

²⁶Cf. Ibid., p. 77.

²⁷Ibid., p. 336.

²⁸Ibid., p. 295.

²⁹Ibid., pp. 295–8.

³⁰Ibid., pp. 299–300.

³¹Ibid., p. 300ff. Kirk does not comment on whether (2) or (3) presents the stronger case.

³²Mortimer, *Elements*, pp. 98–99. Mortimer's appeal here is to "probabilism," a notion based on the principle that "a doubtful law does not oblige." An action is thus deemed lawful is there is any doubt, however slight, about its *un*lawfulness. In its extreme form, probabilism holds that it is lawful to follow a probable opinion that an action is lawful even though it is more (or even much more) probable that the action is unlawful. From the nineteenth century onwards, this has become the predominant system of moral theology in Roman Catholicism.

³³Fletcher, *Moral Responsibility*, pp. 72–3.

³⁴Fletcher cites, for example, Jeremy Taylor's *Ductor Dubitantium* (published in 4 volumes in 1660, and probably the greatest treatise on moral theology by an English Churchman) as evidence of the acknowledgement that "all men talk of the law of nature" but differ as to its precepts and how they are discovered, "whereas if the law

of nature were such a thing as is supposed generally, these differences would be as strange and impossible as that men should disagree about what is black, or what is yellow." Ibid., p. 60.

[35]Ibid., p. 76.

[36]Loc. cit.

[37]Ibid., "On Fertility Control," pp. 112, 117, 119, 121.

[38]Ibid., pp. 123–4.

[39]I have offered a fuller and more systematic treatment of this judgment in "When Love Becomes Excarnate," with John Bennett, et al., *Storm Over Ethics* (Philadelphia, 1967), pp. 88–111.

[40]John Macquarrie, *Three Issues in Ethics* (New York, 1970), pp. 82–110.

[41]Ibid., p. 85.

[42]Ibid., pp. 85–6.

[43]Ibid., pp. 98–103.

[44]Ibid., pp. 103–5. Macquarrie's entire essay, but this section in particular, contains interesting similarities with Karl Rahner's critical natural law theory; but that is an analysis *beyond* the scope of this paper.

[45]Ibid., pp. 106–7.

[46]Ibid., p. 89.

[47]Ibid., p. 109.

[48]Ibid., p. 47.

[49]Ibid., p. 107.

[50]Ibid., pp. 48–9. This treatment of contraception, incidentally, is similar to that in Macquarrie's *Principles of Christian Theology* (New York, 1966).

[51]Ibid., p. 145.

[52]Herbert M. Waddams, *A New Introduction to Moral Theology* (London, 1972). pp. 44–9.

[53]Ibid., pp. 49–53.

[54]Ibid., pp. 53–6.

[55]Ibid., pp. 56–62.

[56]Ibid., p. 149.

[57]Ibid., p. 152.

[58]The Greek antonym for "orthodoxy" is "heresy," but that is probably an inappropriate label in Anglican circles unless interpreted strictly as "an opinion or doctrine at variance with established religious beliefs."

[59]Fletcher, op. cit., p. 63.

The Authors

Paul Elmen is Professor Emeritus of Moral Theology at Seabury-Western Theological Seminary. He is a graduate of Northwestern University (B.A., M.A.) and Harvard University (PhD) and was ordained as an Episcopal Priest in the Diocese of Chicago. He is a past president of the American Society of Christian Ethics, the Chicago Theological Institute, and vice-president of the Swedish Pioneer Historical Society. His published books include *The Restoration of Meaning to Contemporary Life, William Golding,* and *Wheat Flour Messiah: Eric Jansson of Bishop Hill.*

John E. Booty is dean of The School of Theology, The University of the South, Sewanee, Tennessee. He is a graduate of Wayne State University, Virginia Theological Seminary and Princeton University (M.A., PhD). Dean Booty has been professor of Church History at Virginia Theological Seminary and Episcopal Divinity School and is the author of numerous books including *The Godly Kingdom of Tudor England, The Servant Church, What Makes Us Episcopalians* and *John Jewel.*

Henry R. McAdoo is Archbishop of Dublin, Primate of Ireland and Metropolitan. He was Dean of Cork Cathedral and subsequently Bishop of Ossory, Ferns and Leigh prior to being made archbishop. His published works include *The Structure of Caroline Moral Theology, The Spirit of Anglicanism* and *The Unity of Anglicanism.*

John Richard Orens received his doctorate in history from Columbia University in 1976. He has taught at Boston University and elsewhere, and is currently affiliated with the Rhode Island School for Deacons. He is the author of several articles on the Anglican Left, a coauthor of *F. D. Maurice: A Study,* and one of the contributors to *Essays Catholic and Radical.*

Peter Toon, a priest in the Church of England, is Director of Post-Ordination Training for the Diocese of St. Edmundsbury and Ipswich and Rector of Boxford, England. He was formerly on the faculty of Oak Hill College and is the author of several books including *Evangelical Theology, Jesus Christ is Lord, God's Church for Today* and the forthcoming volume, *The Anglican Way: Evangelical and Catholic.*

Thomas Sterns Eliot. The late T. S. Eliot was a noted poet and writer whose works have appeared in many editions. His essay on Lambeth is reprinted with the permission of his publisher.

Timothy F. Sedgwick is Assistant Professor of Ethics and Moral Theology at Seabury-Western Theological Seminary.

Theodore Alan McConnell is a priest of the Episcopal Church, a graduate of Grinnell College, Yale University (M.Div., S.T.M.) and the Episcopal Theological School. He has been editor-in-chief and editorial director of several publishing houses and is the author of *The Shattered Self.*

Edwin G. Wappler is rector of St. Wilfrid's Church, Marion, Alabama. He was formerly dean of Bloy House and assistant professor of Ethics and Religion, The School of Theology, Claremont. He is a graduate of Northwestern University, Seabury-Western Theological Seminary and Duke University (PhD).

Harmon L. Smith is professor of Moral Theology and Community Health Science, Duke University. He is a graduate of Millsaps College and Duke University (B.D., PhD) and is a priest of the Episcopal Church. His previously published books include *Ethics and the New Medicine, Decision-Making in Personal Life,* and *The Christian and His Decisions.*

William Muehl is a graduate of the University of Michigan and the University of Michigan Law School. Formerly a practicing attorney in Michigan, he has been a member of the faculty of Yale Divinity School since 1944, and is now Clement Professor of Christian Methods. His previously published books include *The Road To Persuasion, Politics in Action, Mixing Religion and Politics* and *All The Damned Angels.*

William W. Rankin is rector of St. Stephen's Church, Belvedere, California. He is a graduate of Duke University (A.B., M.A., PhD) and the Episcopal Theological School (B.D.), was formerly associate rector of All Saint's Church, Pasadena, and is the author of *The Nuclear Arms Race: A Study in Christian Ethics.*